SOCIAL ASPECTS OF PLANNING IN NEW TOWNS

To Sheila

2000

Social aspects of planning in new towns

H.M. WIRZ M.A., Ph.D
*Department of Social
Administration,
Edinburgh University*

SAXON HOUSE LEXINGTON BOOKS

Published by

SAXON HOUSE, D. C. Heath Ltd.
Westmead, Farnborough, Hants., England.

Jointly with

LEXINGTON BOOKS, D. C. Heath & Co.
Lexington, Mass. USA.

ISBN 0 347 01094 6
Library of Congress Catalog Card Number 75-28607
Printed in Great Britain by Butler & Tanner Ltd., Frome and London

Contents

List of tables

List of figures

Acknowledgements

My first thanks are due to Professor Spencer for his generous contribution of the foreword, and indeed for his advice and support throughout the period of the research which underlies this book.

I further wish to express my thanks for the assistance given to me in the completion of this work by the following: Dr R. Jones, M.A., Ph.D. and Dr A.J. Crosbie, M.A., Ph.D., for their help and advice in the geographical aspects of this study; Mr A. Fielding, B.Sc., M.Sc. for his help with the statistical evaluation of the data, and Mr J. Nimmo and his staff, Social Science Research Centre, Edinburgh University for processing so much of it.

Without the active co-operation of the respective development corporations much of the work would not have been possible. I am therefore grateful for their help; in particular to: Miss E. Farquhar, M.A., Dip.T.P., then research officer with Glenrothes Development Corporation; Mr G. Millar, M.A., Dip.T.P., then research officer, Livingston Development Corporation; Mr F. Richardson, B.A., Dip.T.P., AMTPI, Senior Planning Officer, East Kilbride Development Corporation; and (the then) Provost W. Niven, C.A., J.P., East Kilbride Town Council.

Above all, I am grateful to the secretaries of the social organisations in these three towns, who took the time and trouble to see me for discussions and to fill in the questionnaires; to Mr R. Harris, cartographer, who did much of the technical work on the maps; and to Mrs N. Hamilton for typing the manuscript.

Much of the material in this book was included in a thesis which was approved for the Ph.D. degree of the University of Edinburgh. Excerpts from chapter 4 have also been published in the journals *Policy and Politics*, and *Centro Sociale*.

H.M.W.
Edinburgh, 1975

Foreword

The new town movement and the new towns themselves owe much to the inspiration and the persistence of those early visionaries and pioneers who built the foundations for future policy. Letchworth and Welwyn Garden City were the first practical results of their labours. But almost forty years have now elapsed since the first new town, under the New Towns Act of 1946, was designated at Stevenage. New towns have long since moved out of the pioneering stage. During this period however, the literature which has grown up has suffered from the lack of a book which sets out to examine the social consequences of the thirty-five new towns (including six in Scotland) which now exist in Britain.

In this study of three Scottish new towns at Glenrothes, East Kilbride and Livingston Dr Hans Wirz set himself the challenging research task of analysing their social development. The book which he has written is, in the best sense of the word, an essay in social policy, for it provides a model of how to examine its consequences. Policy formation indeed requires visionaries, but it also needs analysts. The analysts are still in short supply but their studies are essential if we are to test the outcome and evaluate the results of a particular policy.

In the case of the policy for new towns the task is particularly hard. The major difficulties arise from the fact that the criteria for success in new towns policy are open to widely differing interpretations. As the sociological literature makes clear, there are few words which have acquired such a misleading accretion of ideas as that of 'community'. The new towns themselves have often been labelled as 'communities', but by doing so we incur the danger both of enlarging and of confusing the range of criteria.

Dr Wirz is clear about the measuring rod which he has adopted. Since his research is in the field of social policy he has taken as his starting point the legislative 'foundation stone' for the building of new towns in Britain, the report of the New Towns Committee under the chairmanship of Lord Reith which reported in 1946. If he were a sociologist he might well have gone about his research task differently. For as he points out in his first chapter, he has used as his yardstick the assumptions of the Reith Committee rather than the views of the inhabitants themselves on the extent to which they feel that their social needs have been met.

The Reith Committee has certainly been criticised, as have many other committee reports in the field of social policy, for its lack of a research base. But it was clear about its own policy assumptions of which Dr Wirz identifies the nine most important ones in his first chapter. Nor would it be right to conclude that he ignores the inhabitants. In fact the very reverse is the case, since he made use of the answers to his questions from over 180 organisations in addition to information from key inhabitants and to the advice of planners and officials.

The key chapter in his book, chapter 4, deals with the important subject of the occupational status of membership and leadership. His findings are later related, in summary form at the end of chapter 4 and in his concluding chapter, to the assumptions about social cohesion in the Reith report. By means of his very careful analysis he has been able to relate the facts about occupational status to a discussion about social goals which have not only given rise to controversy, but which have tended to remain vague and imprecise. It is the merit of this chapter that it enables the reader to assess for himself the viability of the goal of social cohesion. In part his research supports the observations of those sociologists, such as Bottomore, who have carried out research into social stratification in social organisations. At the same time Dr Wirz helps us to appreciate better some of the differences not only between organisations of different kinds but also between leadership and members.

Turning from his discussion of the social characteristics of the organisations to the problems of bricks and mortar and the siting of social facilities he shows the absolute necessity for planners to take account of the different needs and preferences of different categories of organisation. It is much too easy to suppose that there is a single set of criteria for siting, to meet all the requirements of social organisations. This was implicit in some of the early theories of neighbourhood development. His findings enable us to appreciate the importance of differentiation between kinds of organisations and their own particular patterns of use.

A further important focus of this book concerns the process of social development and the role of the social development officer. Here Dr Wirz examines the contrast between the model standards for the post of social development officer and the actual practice of the three Scottish new towns. As he explains there is a marked contrast between English and Scottish practice in the role of social development officer. Whereas English policy has generally been to follow the recommendations of the Government circular of 1963 by the appointment of social development officers of chief officer rank and by the delineation of his functions in terms of social planning, relationships with other organisations, community development, public relations and research, the Scottish practice has been to link the social development role with that of other functions such as that of housing manager at Livingston.

Dr Wirz is rightly critical of the Scottish new towns' failure to appreciate the importance of a chief officer responsible for social development or to avoid the difficulties arising from a conflict of roles. Yet the reader may well ask whether, given the growth and vigour of the social organisations themselves, this failure has in fact handicapped their social development. As he says, it is impossible to give a precise answer to this question without a controlled study of comparisons between new towns in England and Scotland. Nevertheless, the point must be emphasised that not only are there many different contributions to social development from within the development corporation itself, but there is also the work of a wide range of individuals and of voluntary associations, in particular the churches, which is devoted to this end.

It only remains to draw attention to one other factor which must be considered in the study of new communities of whatever kind, but which has frequently been overlooked: this is the significance of *time* as a factor in their development. Here Dr Wirz has been careful to emphasise the significance of time, when making comparisons between East Kilbride, Glenrothes and Livingston. He points out, for example, that over time organisations in all categories become more representative of the town's population and that increased levels of satisfaction in the older towns are largely a function of time and maturity of the town. On the other hand the frustrations of newness in the early years were exacerbated by inadequate provision of facilities. Yet the policy implications of this point of contrast are all too frequently ignored.

John Spencer
University of Edinburgh

1 The Reith Report - Ideas of Social Development in New Towns

The legislative 'foundation stone' for the building of new towns in Britain, was laid on 19 October 1945, when the so-called New Towns Committee was appointed under the chairmanship of Lord Reith, with the following terms of reference:

> To consider the general questions of the establishment, development, organization and administration that will arise in the promotion of New Towns in furtherance of a policy of planned decentralisation from congested urban areas; and in accordance therewith to suggest guiding principles on which such towns should be established and developed as self-contained and balanced communities for work and living.[1]

The fact that these new towns should be developed as 'self-contained and balanced communities for work and living' was particularly emphasised since they were intended to become the antithesis of the 'dormitory suburb;[2] of which the inter-war housing estates had become examples, and which now, at all costs, were to be avoided.

Apart from considerations as to the physical layout and the economic life of the new towns to be built, the final report,[3] which the Minister of Town and Country Planning and the Secretary of State for Scotland presented to Parliament in July 1946, incorporated a number of suggestions, as to the kind of social life and recreational opportunities which should be available to the people living in the new towns.

These suggestions were based on a number of assumptions, some of which were intended to serve as desirable policy goals to the bodies responsible for the development of the new towns. For instance, in para. 185, p. 42, the committee observed:

> Of the groups and societies to which men and women are attached, perhaps the most important, next to the family, is the local or geographical community. In great cities and towns the sense of

community membership is weak and this is one of the most serious of modern urban ills. In a true community, everybody feels, directly or through some group, that he has a place and a part, belonging and counting. He cannot put down roots in, nor become conscious of responsibility for a place that does not give him that feeling.

Underlying the statement of this particular paragraph is the assumption that people need a sense of belonging and an opportunity for participation. If this assumption is accepted, it follows that social policy in a new town should be directed towards encouraging a sense of participation amongst individuals and groups. The next paragraph in the committee's report therefore deals with the social life in the new towns, and particularly the function of the voluntary association as a strong binding force, and the creation of clubs and societies. Thus para. 186 states:

Social life in a new town has to be built up, and while this has disadvantages, it also has advantages. Where so many people are strangers to each other, there cannot for some time be the social cohesion of a long-established community, with its known and tested public personalities and its habits and traditions of collective life. All the institutions have to be created, and errors of popular judgment in choosing leaders, officers and representatives are likely. On the other hand, the small size of the initial community, and its necessary dependence for a time on voluntary associations for many purposes are strong binding forces. The building of the town itself is a common interest of a novel and compelling character. And, though strangers to each other, the inhabitants will have much in common. They will quickly select associates, sharing their diverse interests in religion, politics, social welfare, sports and games, study, gardening, and the arts and hobbies; and the creation from the void of societies and clubs for all these things is an absorbing interest in itself. Men and women coming from districts in large towns where community life is weak may indeed appreciate its meaning and value for the first time.

Here the committee presented its vision of what it thought ought to happen regarding social life in new towns. The assumptions on which this 'vision' was based can best be summarised as follows: (a) that social cohesion is a desirable goal of social policy; and (b) that societies and clubs have a role to play in bringing about participation, and through it, social cohesion.

Following on from these assumptions, the committee then

recommended that certain facilities should be made available, as early as possible, by the development corporations. Thus para. 187 states:

> It is not possible, and even if it were, it would not be wise, to prescribe the social and cultural pattern of a new town. The interests, groupings and cultural activities of citizens must grow of themselves and may differ between one new town and another as widely as between one old town and another. It is this variety that gives character to towns, and any thought of standardizing the equipment must be dismissed. There are however, certain facilities that are found in any fair-sized town in Britain, and that have come to be regarded as indispensable for a fully developed urban life. Obviously the quantity and quality of these facilities depends on the size of the population.

The committee's assumptions about buildings and facilities, which are contained in the above paragraph can be summarised as follows: (a) that certain facilities are to be regarded as essential; and (b) that a diversity of buildings is desirable.

The subsequent paragraph, 188, takes the point about the desirability of diversity a step further, and relates it not only to buildings and facilities, but also to the type of activities and organisations, which would use them, and the different people they would be expected to cater for. Thus para. 188 states:

> As the majority of inhabitants will have come from urban environments and many of them from the inner parts of large cities, they will wish to have available, at the earliest possible date, facilities equivalent to those to which they have been accustomed, though not necessarily of the same range or in the same proportions. In a town where houses and gardens prevail, where space for outdoor recreation is available, and where the country is within easy reach, there will not be the same uses of leisure. Experience in the new towns built already, confirms however, that many of the same facilities will be wanted.

The above paragraph contains the assumption that incomers into the new towns will come from diverse cultural backgrounds, and that the provision of facilities should take due account of the culture that people brought with them.

Paragraph 189 once again returns to the discussion about buildings, and particularly related to the characteristics of the buildings which in the view of the committee are required:

3

At the very beginning it is essential to provide a building containing several rooms, capable of being used for a variety of purposes. This should include at least one large room for social gatherings, dances, concerts, plays, church services, temporary schools, lectures, political meetings, and possibly for cinema shows. There should also be several smaller rooms for meetings of committees and societies. The building should be so placed and constructed that it would remain useful for a number of years; indeed if the right situation can be found for it at the beginning it might be permanent though its multiple use would be temporary.

Once again, the assumptions relating to the buildings as described in the above paragraph were quite specific; they can be summarised as follows: (a) buildings should be multi-purpose in nature, initially, but adaptable to single purpose use later; furthermore, they should contain a number of smaller rooms; (b) the siting of the building is of considerable importance.

The report[4] goes on to suggest that permanent buildings should be provided in advance of full demand (para. 190); suggestions are made for buildings for theatre, music, the arts and dance halls (paras. 191–6); there should be an adequate library service (paras. 197–9); arrangements should be made for preserving local archives and archaeological remains (para. 200); special attention should be paid to places of refreshment, including hotels and a variety of restaurants as well as tea-shops and cafés (paras. 201–4); licensed premises should vary in character and size, and restaurants serving substantial meals should be able to obtain licences, etc. A further five paragraphs are devoted to the question of licensing laws in new towns.

In para. 219 however, the committee returned to a discussion on facilities for young people:

Though schools' playing facilities are the concern of the local education authority, the provision of playgrounds and of premises suitable for boys' and girls' clubs and for other activities of young people may be largely a matter for the agency (i.e. development corporation) itself. The need must be assessed and the means for meeting it planned at the outset.

The committee, in making this specific recommendation, was assuming that young people have special needs, which require special consideration. However, in para. 221, which is complementary to the above one, it was made clear that young people are not its only concern:

For those who are older, provision must be made for voluntary activities, complementary to their daily work in school or factory, and no less important in moulding character. Their needs are by no means uniform. To one it is for physical recreation; to another for a quiet place to read or study; a third demands a workshop in which to pursue some hobby; to a fourth the team activities of scouts, guides, brigades and cadet corps have a strong appeal. It is essential to ensure the provision of suitable ground and buildings for all these purposes, not merely for the established organisations, but for others that will emerge spontaneously as time goes on.

Once again the committee stresses the point about buildings, in the form of a further assumption, i.e. that there will be a need for a diversity of buildings in relation to a diversity of activities.

The committee then went on to emphasise that for certain groups the possession of quarters of their own is essential; thus in para. 222 it states:

We do not imply that it is good for boys and girls to find ready made and to hand buildings equipped for any and every enterprise that may take their fancy. There is virtue in improvisation, and we believe that the more they can be encouraged to equip, decorate and perhaps even help to build their own premises, the better. But we deprecate that variety of 'community building and social centre' to be found in some urban areas, in which the same scanty accommodation is made to serve a long programme of youth and adult services in turn. Apart from the fact that certain activities, notably an effective young people's club, need to be carried on every night of the week, including Sundays, such an arrangement is inimical to that pride in corporate ownership which begets in young people a sense of corporate responsibility.

The recommendations contained in this particular paragraph appear to have as their basis the assumption that certain groups will only flourish if they are able to have quarters of their own.

It is of interest to note that the Reith committee on the question of ownership of premises anticipated research findings of people such as Nicholson,[5] Willis,[6] Sykes and Woldman,[7] and Morely,[8] who all show, together with this present study, that uniformed organisations especially, because of the nature of their programme, prefer to have their own premises, and that where groups are required to pack up all their equipment after every meeting to make way for some entirely different activity, friction arises. Furthermore, although the Reith committee in the above paragraph stated that in its view 'there is virtue in improvisation', there is, as Nicholson[9] confirms, considerable opposition by some development corporations against the erection of huts and small club buildings, both on aesthetic grounds and on grounds of space.

Having already indicated in previous paragraphs, what kind of social life the committee envisaged for the new towns, it then returned to the theme of social development:

> Paragraph 223 states: But from what we have said, we must not be thought to oppose the principle of community centres, if established for what we conceive to be their proper purpose, namely the provision of certain important communal buildings to which all social groups, adults as well as juvenile have access at appointed times. Although we believe that each group should be encouraged to develop separately on its own lines, the additional provision of some common facilities at centres of this kind seems to us invaluable. Social activities in which all members of a family can share, help to strengthen the unity of family life by giving it a common loyalty.

This last line states a further assumption about the purpose and potential of social activities.

The above extracts from the Reith report have been deliberately quoted at some length, since these recommendations were closely observed in the New Towns Act which followed, and therefore became a kind of blueprint, not only for the physical and economic development, but also as a model for the social development of new towns.

Summary of assumptions

1   People need a sense of belonging and an opportunity for participation.
2.(a)   Social cohesion is a desirable goal of social policy;
   (b)   voluntary organisations have a role to play in bringing about opportunities for participation, and through it, social cohesion.
3 (a)   Certain minimum facilities are to be regarded as essential in a new town from the very outset;
   (b)   a diversity of buildings is desirable.
4 (a)   New town residents will come from diverse cultural backgrounds;
   (b)   facilities and activities should take due account of the culture that people brought with them.
5 (a)   Characteristics of buildings required at early stage: need to be both multi-purpose in nature, and contain a number of smaller rooms;

(b)   siting of buildings is important.

6   Young people have special needs, which need special consideration.

7   There is a need for a diversity of buildings in relation to diversity of activities.

8   Certain groups will flourish if they are able to have quarters of their own.

9   Social activities in which all members of a family can share, help to strengthen the unity of family life, by giving it a common loyalty.

These, then, are some of the assumptions underlying the Reith committee's recommendations regarding the social development of new towns. This study of three Scottish new towns attempted to test some of these assumptions in the light of almost twenty-five years of experience which have passed since the deliberations of the Reith committee. Nicholson[10] points out 'that it is possible to compare the achievements of the new towns with the proposals of the Reith committee, what matters more is the extent to which they meet the needs of those rehoused there'. This does not mean to say, however, that these proposals do not provide a useful yardstick, against which present day provision and policy can be measured and taken into account when future policies are decided.

The Reith committee has been criticised for the fact that its proposals were not based on sufficient research. This may be true, although one also has to accept that at the time the social sciences in this country were still in their infancy, and that therefore research facilities and methods were not as readily available as they are today. Furthermore, appendix 2 of the final report[11] lists the considerable number of government bodies, local authorities, learned societies and individuals with whom discussions were held or from whom written evidence was received, and this would suggest that the Reith committee did go to great lengths in an attempt to have its findings supported by a considerable body of opinion. Nevertheless, the criticism regarding lack of research must be allowed to stand, but should perhaps be levied at the Ministry of Housing and Local Government, whom Lloyd Rodwin[12] accused of being 'penny-wise and pound foolish' for not promoting socio-economic research. Apparently the ministry's attitude at the time was the one quoted in 'Town and Country Planning, 1943–1951',[13] i.e.: 'research contributing to thought and knowledge about town planning is primarily the responsibility of universities and non-governmental bodies. For the ministry and for local planning authorities, concerned as they must be to keep their staff demands to a minimum, the question must always be whether any particular study makes a direct and demonstrably useful contribution to their planning administration.' This attitude, in Rodwin's view, allowed a dangerous gap to develop. However, this has to be seen within the context of economic stringency prevailing at the time, when according to the ministry's instruction [14] every proposal for capital expenditure had to be judged by its contribution to the 'dollar earning and dollar saving projects'. The postwar economic crisis had indeed an influence in new towns policy, and on the degree to which it was put into practice. However, what seems to be more important, is not whether the committee based its proposals on a great deal of theoretical research, but whether these proposals have stood the test of time. Sir William Hart [15] for one seems to think so and suggests that the report will 'repay reading again'.

Apart from anything else, the speed with which the committee produced its reports was exceptional by any standard. On 19 October 1945 it was appointed. In March 1946 it presented the first Interim Report, [16] a month later, in April 1946 the second Interim Report [17] was put before Parliament and in July of the same year there followed the Final Report. [18]

According to one member of that committee, Sir Frederic Osborn, [19] the 'speed and efficiency with which information was collected and converted into practical recommendations, was largely due to the skill of Lord Reith's chairmanship'. But one also has to point out that he had the advice of two members who had had experience in developing the garden cities of Letchworth and Welwyn, [20] and another member [21] had been resident architect of Welwyn. However, this did not appear to prevent the committee from being objective. According to Osborn: [22]

> nothing that these members advised, was accepted on their evidence alone. Every element of policy and practice, of methods and standards, was studied *ab initio*, and examined in the light of the views of the bodies and persons concerned with the relevant aspect of urban affairs, from religion to finance, from family life to art, from drainage to landscaping, from work to leisure, from pubs to universities – in short, from A–Z.

Nevertheless, the almost 'idyllic' vision of the social life and character of a new town, which the committee would appear to have had, is closely reminiscent of Osborn's description of the social atmosphere which had prevailed in Letchworth, [23] and which he described as follows:

> Yet an extremely vigorous and enjoyable community life sprang into being from very early days. The absence of commercial entertainment threw people back on their own resources, and there was no

lack of spontaneous leadership in running a wide variety of societies and clubs — for music, drama, politics, religion, sports, rambling, dancing, gardening, natural history, arts and crafts and serious study.

This was a kind of social life, which clearly the committee had hoped would repeat itself over and over again, in each of the new towns. A good deal of its optimism and enthusiasm carried over into the debate of the New Towns Bill in the House of Commons, which took place on 8 May 1946. Once again, the Minister of Town and Country Planning, the Rt Hon. Lewis Silkin put the emphasis on providing a better life: [24]

> Many towns have built new housing estates on the outskirts. These have largely failed in their purpose of providing a better life for their people and have almost invariably become dormitories consisting of members of one income group, with no community life or civic sense ... I am most anxious that the planning should be such that the different income groups living in the new towns will not be segregated. ... when they leave to go home I do not want the better off people to go to the right, and the less well-off to go to the left. I want them to ask each other 'Are you going my way?' ... I want to see the new towns gay and bright, with plenty of theatres, concert halls and meeting places. The new towns should provide valuable experience in the *best use of leisure, a commodity which is, and should become, more and more plentiful.*

Another M.P., Mr Wilfred Roberts, [25] reiterated the Reith committee's concern for the needs of young people and children [26] when he said the following: 'I look forward to seeing good-looking towns in which it is possible to live a good life; towns which are well planned for children and young people. Appallingly little thought has been given in the past to the development of town life to meet the needs of children and young people'. In the House of Lords, which debated the bill on 11 July 1946, the same enthusiasm and good intentions for this new instrument of social policy were to be found. Thus the Earl of Listowel: [27]

> Finally, we want a community free from the occupational and income snobberies of town life to-day. There must be no West Ends and East Ends, no suburban villas for the professional and black-coated workers, and central tenements for the factory hands. Each of the neighbourhoods, into which the new towns will be divided, will be planned as a cross-section of every occupational and income group in the population.

A slightly more realistic note (or was it veiled scepticism?) was introduced by the Earl of Munster,[28] when he pointed out that the realisation of these plans will take a great deal of time:

> New towns, like new ports, take many years to mature, and it must be some considerable time before any new town contemplated under this bill will be provided with all the essential, modern requirements which will be agreeable to the taste of the multitudes for whom it is to be provided.

And yet, in spite of all the enthusiasm and good will, which launched the new towns programme, a good many problems, particularly in the field of social development, still have to be overcome. Lord Reith himself, in a later article[29] commented:

> The new towns were seen as 'an essay in civilization', and the reports set standards of living conditions appropriate to that aspiration. I am told that twenty-four new towns have already been started in Great Britain, and that as a result of British initiative, new towns are being built or are under consideration in many other countries; and that these British reports are being studied all over the world. This is something to the good, but one wonders if this country is moving fast enough, and the standards are high enough. I should be more pleased about my part in the initiation if I could be sure that the *original intentions and ideals were being regarded and preserved.*

The leader of the Liberal Party, Mr Jeremy Thorpe, in the same journal[30] pinpoints the issue thus: 'In spite of all that the Reith committee had said, the provision of community buildings was too little and too late to foster a rapid growth of social cohesion.'

In Mr Thorpe's terms, what did the Reith committee say? It stressed the importance to people of belonging to some group or other. It foresaw the necessity for many purposes, of voluntary associations, and the need for facilities to be ready at the very beginning. Furthermore, it emphasised the importance of the right situation of amenities. The needs of children and young people were particularly singled out. The committee showed a great deal of insight into these needs by underlining the importance of premises of their own to youth organisations. It also anticipated the inappropriateness of the youth service age range (fourteen to twenty years), as laid down by the Albemarle Report,[31] which has prevented youth organisations depending on grant-aid, from doing work with the whole family. The Youth Service Development Council in only 1969[32] 'repealed' this particular regulation.

But whatever the shortcomings, particularly relating to the Mark 1 new towns, they are not necessarily due to faults in the original concepts of the Reith report, or in their own master plans, but are partly due to stringent financial control by the government in the late forties and early fifties. This had been borne out by comments obtained from officials of the development corporations of the new towns of East Kilbride and Glenrothes which, together with Livingston, were the subject of this study. In a recent report by the Scottish Education Department, [33] this financial stringency was acknowledged as one of the main hindrances to the creation of more community facilities. Thus para. 30, referring to powers in respect of grants reads: 'For some years the prospects were good. However, as a result of economic difficulties and financial restrictions, which began in 1948 only little progress was possible'. Dame Evelyn Sharp in her foreword to Viet's bibliography on new towns[34] highlights the problem in this way:

> One of the most difficult problems in the new towns has arisen over the provision of recreation and entertainment. All concerned with new towns would like them to have the best in the way of playing fields, meeting places, dance halls, swimming baths and so on; but who is to pay for them? It is a responsibility of the local authorities to provide for recreation in so far as private enterprise cannot do so; but the local authorities of the new towns are faced with heavy expenditure on educational, health and welfare services, and while their revenue from rates is building up, they do not yet feel able to spend much money on amenities. They tend to think that the corporations should see to these; but the corporations are commercial undertakings, trying to pay their way, and while they will contribute to the provision of amenities, they will not undertake the whole cost. In the result, provision lags.

and Wyndham Thomas, then Mayor of Hemel Hempstead, wrote in an article in *The Times* in 1959: [35]

> It is in its social equipment that the town has lagged. The Development Corporation has never had the freedom of operation in this field many feel it should have had. It seems to be preferable that the authority providing the housing, should also provide the community buildings.

These highly relevant comments were made in 1959 and 1960 respectively. Since then, however, legislative measures have been passed which now make it possible for the development corporations and local authorities to get together and co-ordinate their priorities relative to community buildings. The extent to which development corporations choose to exercise their spending power is a kind of indicator of their social policy and of the priority they give to social development within that policy. Broady[36] illustrates this point:

> Perhaps more typical of present British practice, however, is the fact that so few schemes have been developed that take advantage of the £4 per head of population which since 1963 it has been possible to levy for social development projects in the new towns; and that this has mostly been because the development corporations, the public authorities and local organisations have been unable to find a formula for co-operation and finance.

A further, related aspect is the development and 'availability' of social organisations, although it is realised that not all social intercourse is necessarily organised in formal activity. As Professor Wilson put it: [37] 'A good community is not necessarily one which hums with universal activity' — but under the conditions which make for a good community he lists, *inter alia*: 'It should be as easy as possible for voluntary assocations to be formed for cultural, recreational and philanthropic purposes. Local authorities should appoint community development officers ... their function should be to ease into life any promising efforts, even if only temporary, that private citizens may be making for mutual benefit.' This applies equally to development corporations of new towns — and again one could consider it to be an indicator of their priorities whether or not they have appointed a social development, or social relations officer, such as was suggested to them in Circular XT/290/5/2, issued by the Ministry of Housing and Local Government in August 1963. Again Broady [38] comments on this:

> The ambiguity of the idea of social development in British Town Planning is indicated by the fact that by no means all new and expanding towns have appointed social development officers; and even when they have done so, their departments have often become the dumping grounds for residual functions such as public relations, attending to visitors and collecting social statistics.

This again is particularly true regarding the situation in Scotland.

The Reith committee (para. 189) also stressed the importance of amenities, such as meeting places being in the 'right situation'. So far there have been few studies trying to evaluate this and thereby test the planning assumptions which decided upon the location in the first place. Thus, as G. Brooke-Taylor [39] stated:

New Towns usually require the creation of a hypothesis, (for a master plan, is a hypothesis), which attempts to project forward an existing social situation and at the same time to forecast a future social situation. While social science has invented techniques for analysing present patterns in society, it has failed as yet to find satisfactory ways of predicting future behaviour. Thus master plans can only be based on hunches and require rigorous testing and analysis.

This study is one such attempt.

Notes

[1]   First Interim Report of New Towns Committee, 1946, HMSO, p. 3.
[2]   Ibid., p. 3.
[3]   Final Report of New Towns Committee, 1946, HMSO, paras. 185 ff.
[4]   Final Report summary, ibid., p. 67.
[5]   J.H. Nicholson, *'New communities in Britain'*, NCSS, London 1961.
[6]   M. Willis, 'Meeting places for hire in new towns – a social survey', Ministry of Housing and Local Government, London 1966.
[7]   A.J.M. Sykes and E. Woldman, 'Irvine new town area – a summary and report on leisure activities', University of Strathclyde, occasional paper no. 2, 1968.
[8]   K. Morley, 'Social activity and social enterprise – a study of voluntary social organisations in the new town of Redditch, 1966'.
[9]   J.H. Nicholson, op.cit., p. 127.
[10]   J.H. Nicholson, op.cit., p. 79.
[11]   New Towns Committee, Final Report, op.cit., pp. 70 and 71.
[12]   Lloyd Rodwin, *The British New Towns Policy,* Harvard University Press, 1956, ch. 5, p. 61.
[13]   'Town and Country Planning, 1943–1951', pp. 165–6.
[14]   Contained in circular Cmnd 8204.
[15]   Sir William Hart, 'Administration and new towns' *Town and Country Planning,* vol. 36, nos. 1–2, 1968.
[16]   Interim Report of the New Towns Committee, March 1946, HMSO, Cmnd 6759.
[17]   Second Interim Report of the New Towns Committee, April 1946, HMSO, Cmnd 6794.
[18]   Final Report of the New Towns Committee, July 1946, HMSO, Cmnd 6876.

[19] F.J. Osborn, in Osborn & Whittick, *The New Towns,* Leonard Hill, London 1969, p. 101.

[20] W.H. Gaunt and F.J. Osborn.

[21] A.W. Kenyon.

[22] F.J. Osborn, op.cit., p. 101.

[23] Ibid., p. 59.

[24] *Hansard,* 8 May 1946.

[25] *Hansard*, 8 May 1946.

[26] New Towns Committee, op.cit., para. 219.

[27] *Hansard* (HL), 11 July 1946.

[28] Ibid.

[29] Lord Reith, 'An essay in civilization' *Town and Country Planning,* vol. 36, nos. 1—2, 1968.

[30] J. Thorpe, ibid., p. 21.

[31] Albermarle Report on the Youth Service, HMSO, 1960.

[32] 'Youth and community work in the 70's', p. 1, para. 2c.

[33] Community of Interests, HMSO, 1968.

[34] Jean Viet, *New Towns — a selected annotated bibliography,* UNESCO no. 12, 1960, p. 11.

[35] Thomas Wyndham, 'In praise of a new town' *The Times*, 4 April 1959.

[36] M. Broady, 'Planning for people', NCSS, 1968, p. 71.

[37] Prof. Roger Wilson in Lomas' 'Social aspects of urban development', NCSS, 1966, pp. 29—30.

[38] M. Broady, op.cit.

[39] G. Brooke-Taylor, 'What price an enlightened social policy?' paper given at conference on 'Social implications of life in new towns', Edinburgh, 7 December 1968.

2 Characteristics of Organisations

2.1 Affiliations

Since new towns offer a new start, and in a sense a new way of life to their residents, it is reasonable to ask whether a new type of social organisation has emerged in this new setting, or whether by and large the people who moved there brought with them well-tried forms of social activity, and simply set about forming the types of organisations they were familiar with.

One way of examining this question is to look at the affiliations of the various organisations.

Tables 2.1, 2.2 and 2.3 illustrate what kind of affiliations, the social organisations of these three new towns have established.

It is of interest to note that in terms of rank order the first two kinds of affiliation were exactly the same in each of the towns. In Glenrothes, 51·5 per cent of all affiliations were with national, and sometimes international bodies, such as Scouts, YMCA, Round Table, Rotary, etc. The percentage for the same category for East Kilbride was almost identical, i.e. 51·1 per cent, whilst in Livingston the corresponding figure was 42·4 per cent. This would suggest that a great many of the organisations, predominantly in the youth category but, as can be seen from the tables, in others too, were integrated into a wider network of organisations, outside the new towns, on a national and, in some cases, international level.

The second largest grouping, in terms of rank order, in each of the three new towns were those organisations with no affiliations of any kind. In Glenrothes these accounted for 17·6 per cent, in East Kilbride for 16·7 per cent and in Livingston for 36·4 per cent. It is of interest to note how closely the figures for Glenrothes and East Kilbride resembled each other, whilst in Livingston the percentage figure for those with no affiliation was more than double that in either of the other two towns. These figures should be seen as no more than an indicator, but it would appear that at that stage in Livingston more groups were 'locally orientated', whilst in the other two towns, as the process of diversification took place, so the incidence of affiliation of one kind or another increased.

Table 2.1

Affiliations — Glenrothes

	Youth organisation		Art and culture		Social service		Women's organisation		Hobby group		Political		Sport		Social and dancing		Old people		Other		Total		Rank order
	no.	%	no.	%	no.	%	no.	%	no.	%	no.	%	no.	%	no.	%	no.	%	no.	%	no.	%	
No affiliation	—	—	2	33·3	—	—	3	23·1	3	30·0	—	—	—	—	2	66·7	1	25·0	1	50·0	12	17·6	2
Church	1	12·5	—	—	—	—	1	7·7	—	—	—	—	—	—	—	—	—	—	—	—	2	2·9	6
Political organisation	1	12·5	—	—	—	—	2	15·4	—	—	4	44·4	—	—	—	—	—	—	—	—	7	10·3	3
National/ international	5	62·5	4	66·7	7	100·0	5	38·5	4	40·0	3	33·3	4	66·7	1	33·3	1	25·0	1	50·0	35	51·5	1
County/ regional	—	—	—	—	—	—	1	7·7	3	30·0	1	11·1	1	16·7	—	—	—	—	—	—	6	8·8	4
Local authority	1	12·5	—	—	—	—	—	—	—	—	—	—	—	—	—	—	—	—	—	—	1	1·5	7
Local affiliation	—	—	—	—	—	—	1	7·7	—	—	1	11·1	1	16·7	—	—	2	50·0	—	—	5	7·4	5
Total	8		6		7		13		10		9		6		3		4		2		68*		

* Exceeds 59 since some are affiliated to more than one organisation.

Table 2.2

Affiliations – East Kilbride

	Youth organisation		Art and culture		Social service		Women's organisation		Hobby group		Political		Sport		Social and dancing		Old people		Other		Total		Rank Order
	no.	%	no.	%	no.	%	no.	%	no.	%	no.	%	no.	%	no.	%	no.	%	no.	%	no.	%	
No affiliation	1	4·8	4	57·1	1	10·0	1	11·1	5	26·3	–	–	–	–	–	–	1	50·0	3	100·0	16	16·7	2
Church	8	38·1	–	–	–	–	1	11·1	–	–	–	–	1	5·6	–	–	–	–	–	–	10	10·4	3
Political organisation	–	–	–	–	–	–	1	11·1	1	5·3	2	40·0	–	–	–	–	–	–	–	–	4	4·2	6
National international	9	42·8	2	28·6	8	80·0	6	66·7	9	47·4	3	60·0	10	55·6	1	50·0	1	50·0	–	–	49	51·1	1
County/regional	2	9·5	–	–	–	–	–	–	3	15·8	–	–	3	16·7	1	50·0	–	–	–	–	9	9·4	4
Local authority	1	4·8	–	–	–	–	–	–	–	–	–	–	1	5·6	–	–	–	–	–	–	2	2·1	7
Local affiliation	–	–	1	14·3	1	10·0	–	–	1	5·3	–	–	3	16·7	–	–	–	–	–	–	6	6·3	5
Total	21		7		10		9		19		5		18		2		2		3		96*		

* Exceeds 82 since some are affiliated to more than one organisation.

Table 2.3

Affiliations – Livingston

	Youth organisation		Art and culture		Social service		Women's organisation		Hobby group		Political		Sport		Social and dancing		Old people		Other		Total		Rank order
	no.	%	no.	%	no.	%	no.	%	no.	%	no.	%	no.	%	no.	%	no.	%	no.	%	no.	%	
No affiliation	2	16·7	2	100·0	–	–	1	20·0	3	75·0	–	–	3	60·0	1	100·0	–	–	–	–	12	36·4	2
Church	1	8·3	–	–	–	–	2	40·0	–	–	–	–	–	–	–	–	–	–	–	–	3	9·1	3
Political organisation	–	–	–	–	–	–	1	20·0	–	–	1	100·0	–	–	–	–	–	–	–	–	2	6·1	4
National/international	7	58·3	–	–	3	100·0	1	20·0	1	25·0	–	–	2	40·0	–	–	–	–	–	–	14	42·4	1
County/regional	–	–	–	–	–	–	–	–	–	–	–	–	–	–	–	–	–	–	–	–	–	–	
Local authority	2	16·7	–	–	–	–	–	–	–	–	–	–	–	–	–	–	–	–	–	–	2	6·1	4
Local affiliation	–	–	–	–	–	–	–	–	–	–	–	–	–	–	–	–	–	–	–	–	–	–	
Total	12		2		3		5		4		1		5		1		–		–		33*		

* Exceeds 32 since one organisation indicated more than one affiliation.

18

The third largest group in East Kilbride and Livingston was found to be affiliated to a given church (10·4 per cent and 9·1 per cent respectively). Although it was stated in the description of the sample used in this study, that organisations specifically associated with any of the churches were not included, in the event, those which were included had in fact featured on the list of organisations available for the town as a whole, and thereby indicated that they were open not only to members of their church.

As will be seen by comparing the rank orders on tables 2.1 and 2.2 relating to Glenrothes and East Kilbride, the patterns in these towns were almost identical with the exception of the affiliations to church and political organisations, which were reversed in rank order; but the remainder of the rank order was identical. It is also of interest to note that the incidence of local affiliations, i.e. offshoots of organisations which are affiliated to a local parent-body, rank fifth in both East Kilbride and Glenrothes, and affiliations to local authorities (such as statutory youth clubs, run by the education authority) rank seventh in both of these towns, and were also last (i.e. equal fourth) in Livingston. This would indicate that the greater number of organisations were voluntary, in the sense that they were not in any way affiliated to a statutory body, such as a local authority. Voluntary organisations can therefore be seen to be making the kind of contribution the Reith report[1] assumed they would.

Although comparative figures for the affiliations of organisations in other new towns do not exist, it is interesting to note how closely the patterns in all three new towns, and in Glenrothes and East Kilbride in particular, resemble each other. The high number of organisations which were affiliated to national/international bodies on the one hand, and the comparatively much lower figure for associations with either no affiliation or a purely local one, would suggest that many organisations operating in the new towns are part of a network of national and international contacts, and would not appear to have become exclusively orientated only towards the new town in which they are operating. Or, put in another way, when new residents were faced with creating for themselves and their children organisations in which they could spend their leisure time, and to which they could belong, to a large extent they formed organisations which also existed elsewhere in the country, and with which many would be familiar. It can therefore be said that the new town residents, coming from diverse cultural backgrounds as they do, brought their culture with them, as was assumed in the Reith report.[2] The list of organisations represented in this study (see Appendix, p.223) will further illustrate this point, in as much as there were in these new towns few, if any, organisations which were not found in other towns up and down the country. In other words, if there is such a phenomenon as a 'new town culture' then it does not appear to have created its own specific 'new town organisation'. Instead, the people who moved into the new town brought with them the culture with which they were familiar, and of which the organisations which they formed were representative.

2.2   Frequency of meetings

It was felt that if an attempt at assessing the contribution of social organisations was to be made, relating to the social life of a new town, 'frequency of meeting' was an important factor, comparable to those relating to total membership and the proportion of members participating at meetings. Secretaries were therefore asked to indicate how frequently their particular organisations met in winter and in summer.

Winter (September–April)

It appeared that the majority of organisations met at least once a week during the winter months. In fact the aggregate figures (as a percentage of the total number of organisations) for groups which held meetings once a week, or more than once a week, were:

Glenrothes:	57·6
East Kilbride:	54·9
Livingston:	78·2

In *Glenrothes* all youth organisations met at least once a week and so did two-thirds of all sports clubs. The arts/cultural groups which met more than once a week were the art club, which has its own premises to which members have access at any time, and the two groups concerned with the performing arts (i.e. the Little Theatre and musical and operatic society), which met for rehearsals more frequently than once a week.

As far as the two organisations in the social/dancing category were concerned, which operate more than once a week, it would appear that availability of premises was a major factor. Both the British Legion and the Glenrothes Recreation & Social Centre have their own premises where members can call in any evening of the week. Only three organisations, 5·1 per cent, met less often than once a month during winter, and of these, one is a committee concerned with the welfare of old people, and the other two are hobby groups, i.e. the pigeon racing club and the angling club.

In *East Kilbride* the pattern was similar to that of Glenrothes. The majority (32·9 per cent of organisations) met once a week and, together with those that met more than once a week, they accounted for over half of all organisations (54·9 per cent). All youth organisations, with the exception of the East Kilbride & District Young Farmers Club, met at least once a week, and so did most of the sports organisations and arts/cultural societies. But the proportion of organisations which met less than once a month was higher than in Glenrothes, 13·4 per cent as compared with 5·1 per cent. One sports organisation, the Boys Football League, never met in winter, which at first appears to be surprising since football is normally regarded as a winter sport. However, in this case, the purpose of the Boys Football League is to occupy boys during the summer vacation, at a time when other activities are not available to them.

In *Livingston* however, the pattern is somewhat different from the other two towns. Virtually every organisation meets at least once a month. In fact, as was seen above, 78·2 per cent of all organisations met once a week or more. This includes all youth groups, except the Calders District Rangers Unit, all sports clubs and all social service organisations. All of these in the other two towns also tended to be among those which met more frequently than the organisations in the other categories.

Summer (May–August)

It became clear that the general assumption that more organised activity takes place during the eight months from September to April was correct, in as much as 'frequency of meetings' is accepted as a factor indicating the scale of social activity. By comparing this with the information relating to winter activities, it will be noted that meetings during the summer months took place less frequently.

Fewer organisations therefore met once a week, or more than once a week, and the aggregate percentage figures for the three towns were as follows:

	Summer	Winter
Glenrothes:	33·9	57·6
East Kilbride:	30·5	54·9
Livingston:	53·2	78·2

At the other end of the 'scale of frequency', it was found that those meeting less often than once a month (including those meeting occasionally or never) accounted for the following proportion of the total number of organisations:

21

	Summer	*Winter*
Glenrothes:	30·5	5·1
East Kilbride:	46·3	13·4
Livingston:	37·4	0·0

Both sets of figures illustrate the same point, namely that in winter the frequency of meetings increases, while in the summer it decreases. It is particularly interesting to note, in each of the towns, the number of organisations which state that they never met in the summer months:

Glenrothes:	20·3
East Kilbride:	14·6
Livingston:	28·1

It is also of interest to note that out of a total of 181 organisations in all three new towns, only one indicated that it never met in winter (0·5 per cent); but 33 (18·1 per cent) indicated that they never met in summer. Among those organisations which never met in summer one particular category stands out, namely the women's organisations. Out of a total of 22 women's groups in all three towns, 10 never met in the summer (45·5 per cent), and all the other categories of organisations have reduced the frequency of their meetings during the summer.

This is to be expected, since the four months, which in this analysis represent summer, also cover the peak holiday months of July and August when many members would be absent from the town at some time. Furthermore, it is also the period during which the hours of daylight in the evenings are longer, and when the garden can be tended, and other outdoor domestic tasks tackled. There is also time for an evening stroll, or a game of golf after work. In other words, it would appear that during these four months there does not exist the same need for organised activity as during the remainder of the year, although there may be a call for special holiday programmes for children. However, within the remit and design of this particular study, it would not be possible to assess whether such a demand for summer activities existed, or whether certain organisations tended to close down during this period, because the 'demand' fell off. However, in the government survey undertaken by K.K. Sillitoe, figures are given relating to participation[3] which clearly show that during the winter months more people actively take part in various activities than during the summer months. Since, in that particular study, the sample was divided into domestic–age categories, strict comparison with the data for Glenrothes, East Kilbride and Livingston was not possible, but the general trend was found to be the same. On the other hand, data which is comparable, such as the findings of Sykes and Woldman's Irvine study,[4] not only confirms the general trend but produces a pattern which is very similar to the one found in the three new towns in this study, i.e. 71·8 per cent of all organisations met at least once a week in winter, as against 40·7 per cent in the summer; 0·9 per cent never met in winter, while 28·8 per cent never met in summer.

It will be noted that these figures correspond very closely to the ones given above, a fact which would suggest that there is a common pattern, as far as this information is concerned, to at least four of the six Scottish new towns.

2.3   Membership of organisations by sex

Tables 2.4, 2.5 and 2.6 show the total membership of the organisations covered by this study in each of the new towns. In Glenrothes this was 6,823 or 26 per cent of the total population, in East Kilbride 10,514 or 16 per cent of the population and in Livingston 1,459 or 21 per cent of the population. However, these figures conceal a certain number of people who hold membership of more than one organisation. It would therefore be more accurate to describe this as the number of units of membership.[5] However, as in T. Bottomore's[6] 'Squirebridge' and in the above mentioned Irvine study, it was thought possible in the three towns covered to assess in this way the degree of involvement and participation in organised activities.

The above tables also give a breakdown of membership by sex. Of the total membership in Glenrothes, 55·6 per cent were males and 44·4 per cent females. The equivalent figures for East Kilbride very closely resembled the Glenrothes ones, i.e. 55·3 per cent males and 44·7 per cent females. In Livingston, however, there was a preponderance of females in membership, i.e. 59·5 per cent as opposed to 40·5 per cent males. Both East Kilbride and Glenrothes showed a pattern which accords with the ones discovered in Irvine,[7] Squirebridge[8] and with the national pattern (including other new towns as shown recently in Sillitoe's study[9]). Livingston would appear to be the exception to a general pattern where men outnumber women in membership of organisations. In Livingston, the opposite was the case. It is conceivable that Livingston was the exception to this pattern at this stage by virtue of being the 'youngest' town of all the examples quoted above. Hume,[10] in her study of neighbourhoods in the towns of East Kilbride, Glenrothes and Livingston, found that frequently the pattern in Livingston was different from the

Table 2.4

Membership of organisations – Glenrothes

	Youth organisation		Art and culture		Social service		Women's organisation		Hobby group		Political		Sport		Social and dancing		Old people		Other		Total	
	no.	%	no.	%	no.	%	no.	%	no.	%	no.	%	no.	%	no.	%	no.	%	no.	%	no.	%
Males	1,222	55·8	155	39·7	118	60·8	0	0·0	323	74·5	589	54·1	573	90·0	728	55·4	67	29·7	17	60·7	3,792	55·6
Females	969	44·2	235	60·2	76	39·1	329	100·0	110	25·4	500	45·9	57	9·9	586	44·6	158	70·2	11	39·2	3,031	44·4
Total membership	2,191		390		194		329		433		1,089		630*		1,314†		225		28		6,823	
Number of organisations	7		6		7		9		9		6		6		3		4		2		59	
Average number of members per organisation	313		65		28		37		48		182		105		438		56		14		116	

* Of that number the golf club alone has 440 members. The remaining 5 clubs therefore share a total of 190 members – the average, excluding the golf club, is 38.
† One of the 3 organisations in this category has only 16 members, the remaining 2 therefore account for 98·7 per cent of the total membership.

Table 2.5

Membership of organisations — East Kilbride

	Youth organisation		Art and culture		Social service		Women's organisation		Hobby group		Political		Sport		Social and dancing		Old people		Other		Total	
	no.	%	no.	%	no.	%	no.	%	no.	%	no.	%	no.	%	no.	%	no.	%	no.	%	no.	%
Males	2,414	48·2	170	51·7	106	34·3	0	0·0	999	92·2	630	48·1	1,021	87·7	194	76·1	160	34·6	119	62·3	5,813	55·2
Females	2,593	51·8	159	48·3	203	65·7	414	100·0	84	7·8	680	51·9	143	12·3	51	23·9	302	65·4	72	37·7	4,701	44·7
Total membership	5,007		329		309		414		1,083		1,310		1,164		245		462		191		10,514	
Number of organisations	17*		7		10		8		14		4		15		2		2		3		82	
Average number of members per organisation	295		47		31		52		77		328		78		123		231		64		128	

* The scouts, who returned questionnaires on a troup basis, were aggregated into one organisation, the East Kilbride Scouts Association, in order to obtain comparability with Glenrothes.

Table 2.6

Membership of organisations – Livingston

	Youth organisation		Art and culture		Social service		Women's organisation		Hobby group		Political		Sport		Social and dancing		Old people		Other		Total	
	no.	%	no.	%	no.	%	no.	%	no.	%	no.	%	no.	%	no.	%	no.	%	no.	%	no.	%
Males	220	34·8	8	12·0	8	18·2	0	0·0	48	57·1	110	73·3	142	91·6	55	47·8	0	0·0	0	0·0	591	40·5
Females	413	65·2	59	88·0	36	81·8	211	100·0	36	42·9	40	26·7	13	8·4	60	52·2	0	0·0	0	0·0	868	59·5
Total membership	633		67		44		211		84		150		155		115		0		0		1,459	
Number of organisations	11		2		3		5		4		1		5		1		0		0		32	
Average number of members per organisation	58		34		15		42		21		150		31		115		0		0		46	

other new towns in a number of respects. She found further that more of the men she interviewed sought their entertainment outside the town than was the case with women, and men also tended to maintain their former social links far longer. The above figures relating to Livingston would tend to support this suggestion.

A closer look at the sex distribution in each category shows that there were some areas where the male preponderance was more complete than in others. As can be seen from the summary table 2·7 which includes the results of the Irvine study, hobby groups and sport organisations were male domains in all four new towns. On the other hand, old people's groups showed a preponderance of females in all three towns where they were in existence. Among the youth organisations however, the distribution was fairly even, i.e. in Irvine and East Kilbride the male and female proportions almost balance, but in Livingston there were decidedly more females and in Glenrothes more males. In the arts and cultural category, in Irvine there was a male preponderance, East Kilbride again was very evenly balanced, whilst in both Livingston and Glenrothes the females outnumbered the males. Among the social service groups, in Irvine the sexes were almost evenly matched, whilst in East Kilbride and Livingston the females outnumbered the males, but in Glenrothes, surprisingly, the situation was reversed. The political organisations, on the other hand, were dominated by male members in both Irvine and Livingston, whilst in East Kilbride the numbers were fairly even, and in Glenrothes too the males outnumbered the females, but to a lesser extent. The social and dancing category again seemed to be a male preserve, except for the case of Livingston where there was a slightly higher proportion of females in membership.

The situation in the Scottish new towns differs from Bottomore's Squirebridge of nearly twenty years ago in as much as in Squirebridge only the arts and cultural organisations showed a preponderance of female membership (although he gave no figures for the 'old people' category). It is also interesting to note that the social service groups in Squirebridge showed a bigger male proportion than females and, in this, Glenrothes and Squirebridge (if these two places are in any way comparable) stand alone.

In Sillitoe's sample which included eight new towns, as far as figures can be adapted from his table 14, [11] the categories where figures were available (i.e. youth, social service, political organisations, sport and social and dancing) indicate that, apart from certain exceptions such as male preponderance in social service category in Glenrothes, the proportions of male and female membership coincide with those shown in the present study.

Table 2.7

Summary — membership of organisations (percentages)

	Glenrothes		East Kilbride		Livingston		Irvine	
	male	female	male	female	male	female	male	female
Youth organisations	55·8	44·2	48·2	51·8	34·8	65·2	51·0	49·0
Art and culture	39·7	60·2	51·7	48·3	12·0	88·0	72·4	25·8
Social service	60·8	39·1	34·3	65·7	18·2	81·8	48·1	51·9
Women's organisations	—	100·0	—	100·0	—	100·0	—	100·0
Hobby groups	74·5	25·4	92·2	7·8	57·1	42·9	84·3	15·7
Political	54·1	45·9	48·1	51·9	73·3	26·7	69·6	30·4
Sport	90·0	9·9	87·7	12·3	91·6	8·4	89·9	10·1
Social and dancing	55·4	44·6	76·1	23·9	47·8	52·2	70·0	30·0
Old people	29·7	70·2	34·5	65·4	—	—	39·6	60·4
Total	55·6	44·4	55·2	44·7	40·5	59·5	62·5	37·5

Notes

[1] Final Report of New Towns Committee, 1946, HMSO, para. 186.

[2] Para. 188, op.cit.

[3] K.K. Sillitoe, 'Planning for leisure', HMSO, London 1969, Table 55, p. 105, and tables A22 and A23, pp. 220–21.

[4] A.J.M. Sykes and E. Woldman, 'Irvine new town area — a summary and report on leisure activities', University of Strathclyde Occasional Paper no. 2, 1968, tables 6, 7.

[5] A term which was also used by Sykes and Woldman, op.cit.

[6] T. Bottomore, 'Social stratification in voluntary organisations' in D.V. Glass (ed.), *Social Mobility in Britain,* Routledge & Kegan Paul, 1954, ch. VIII.

[7] Sykes and Woldman, op.cit.

[8] T. Bottomore, op.cit.

[9] K.K. Sillitoe, op.cit.

[10] V.E. Hume, Neighbourhoods in Scottish New Towns, Ph.D. thesis, Edinburgh University 1969.

[11] P. 56, op.cit.

3 Age Structure of Population/Membership in the Three New Towns - Levels of Participation

People's leisure activities and the degree of participation in organisations can be said to be at least partly determined by the particular stage they have reached in their life cycle. Any policy for provision of facilities and fostering of organisations has therefore to take account of the different age groups to be catered for. It was consequently thought useful to examine the degree of participation in these three towns by age group and sex, in order to assist a more accurate pin-pointing of needs, and relevant policies to meet these.

3.1 Age structure of population

It is one of the demographic features of new towns that the age structure of their populations is more youthful than the national pattern. Cullingworth[1] wrote:

> The earlier new towns consisted predominantly of young married couples with young children. Approximately half were between 20 and 40 years old, compared with about 27 per cent for the rest of England and Wales. Children under 10 years of age formed about a quarter, compared with only 15 per cent for England and Wales. Only a small proportion of the newcomers were in the 15–19 age group or in the over 45 age group. A structure of this kind produces a large school population for the first 10 to 15 years; and during the first ten years a small proportion of teenagers.

Tables 3.1, 3.2 and 3.3 show that by and large the age structures of Glenrothes, East Kilbride and Livingston correspond to this general pattern. However, there were also a number of interesting variations. In Glenrothes and East Kilbride the children under 10 years of age formed just over 26·1 per cent and just under 22 per cent, a quarter of the total population respectively, whereas in Livingston they make up almost a third, 31·8 per cent.

Table 3.1

Age structure of population/age structure of membership – Glenrothes

Males

Age	Number in male population	Percentage of total male population	Membership of organisations in each age group	Percentage membership as a proportion of total population in each age group	No. of memberships per head of population in each age group	Approximate ratio of population to membership
0–9	3,137	26·7	166	5·3	0.05	1:19
10–19	1,965	16·7	770	39·2	0·4	1:3
20–29	2,094	17·8	367	17·5	0·2	1:6
30–39	1,872	15·9	389	20·7	0·2	1:5
40–49	1,422	12·1	336	23·6	0·2	1:4
50–59	698	5·9	119	17·0	0·2	1:6
Over 60	570	4·8	255	44·7	0·5	1:2
Known	(147)*		1,390	(11·8)†		
Total	11,758		3,792			

Females

0–9	3,038	25·4	250	8·2	0·08	1:12
10–19	1,959	16·4	490	25·0	0·3	1:4
20–29	2,360	19·7	173	7·3	0·07	1:14
30–39	1,867	15·6	286	15·3	0·2	1:7
40–49	1,305	10·9	281	21·5	0·2	1:5
50–59	632	5·3	111	17·6	0·2	1:6
Over 60	793	6·6	290	36·6	0·4	1:3
Not known	(147)*		1,150	(9·6)†		
Total	11,954		3,031			

Average membership per head of male population for all age groups: 0·3.
Average membership per head of female population for all age groups: 0·3.
* Not attributable to male or female, therefore omitted from total.
† Percentage of total male/female population for which age group is not known.
Source: Adapted for Household Survey, Glenrothes Development Corporation, 1968.

Table 3.2

Age structure of population/age structure
of membership — East Kilbride

Age	Number in male population	Percentage of total male population	Membership of organisations in each age group	Percentage membership as a proportion of total population in each age group	Number of memberships per head of population in each age group	Approximate ratio of population to membership
Males						
0–9	7,046	22·8	263	3·7	0·04	1:27
10–19	5,661	18·3	2,718	48·0	0·5	1:2
20–29	4,233	13·7	380	9·0	0·1	1:11
30–39	4,609	14·9	470	10·2	0·1	1:10
40–49	4,509	14·6	590	13·1	0·1	1:8
50–59	2,786	9·0	238	8·5	0·1	1:12
Over 60	2,102	6·8	364	17·3	0·2	1:6
Not stated			790	(2·6)		
Total	30,946		5,813			
Females						
0–9	6,656	21·1	996	15·0	0·1	1:7
10–19	5,440	17·3	1,462	26·9	0·3	1:4
20–29	4,727	15·0	254	5·4	0·05	1:18
30–39	5,049	16·0	318	6·3	0·1	1:16
40–49	4,313	13·7	362	8·4	0·1	1:12
50–59	2,617	8·3	194	7·4	0·1	1:13
Over 60	2,749	8·7	451	16·4	0·2	1:6
Not stated			664	(2·1)		
Total	31,551		4,701			

Average membership per head of male population for all age groups: 0·2.
Average membership per head of female population for all age groups: 0·1.

31

Table 3.3

Age structure of population/age structure of
membership — Livingston

Males						
	Number in male population	Percentage of total male population	Membership of organisations in each age group	Percentage membership as a proportion of total population in each age group	Number of memberships per head of population in each age group	Approximate ratio of population to membership
0–9	1,017	32·7	27	2·7	0·03	1:38
10–19	329	10·6	264	80·2	0·8	1:1·25
20–29	799	25·7	44	5·5	0·05	1:18
30–39	549	17·6	31	5·6	0·05	1:18
40–49	227	7·3	30	13·2	0·1	1:8
50–59	101	3·2	18	17·8	0·2	1:6
Over 60	76	2·4	3	3·9	0·04	1:25
Not known	13	0·4	174	(5·6)*		
Total	3,111		591			

Females						
0–9	956	31·0	166	17·4	0·2	1:6
10–19	338	10·9	199	58·9	0·6	1:1·7
20–29	947	30·6	145	15·3	0·2	1:7
30–39	468	15·1	113	24·1	0·2	1:4
40–49	170	5·5	44	25·9	0·3	1:4
50–59	83	2·7	14	16·9	0·2	1:6
Over 60	113	3·7	27	23·9	0·2	1:4
Not stated	15	0·5	160	(5·2)*		
Total	3,090		868			

Average membership per head of male population for all age groups: 0·2.
Average membership per head of female population for all age groups:
0·3.
* Percentage of total male/female population, not age group.

In the age group 10–19 a similar difference appeared. This particular age group in Glenrothes formed 16·5 per cent of the population and in East Kilbride 17·8 per cent, whilst in Livingston the same age group only accounted for 10·7 per cent of the population. Although it was not possible to single out the teenagers in an age group covering ten years at the time, it would nevertheless appear that Livingston, which is a more recent town (designated 1962) than either Glenrothes (designated 1948) or East Kilbride (designated 1947), has a more youthful population still, and for the time being shows this lack of teenagers mentioned by Cullingworth.[2]

The age group 20–29 again showed Livingston to be more youthful than the other two new towns. In Glenrothes this category formed 18·8 per cent of the total population, and in East Kilbride 14·3 per cent, whilst in Livingston the figure was 28·2 per cent. This would again confirm Cullingworth's suggestion that at an early stage of a new town's development the great majority of incomers are young married couples with young children. Schaffer[3] put the same point in a similar way: 'For almost all the young couples moving into a new town, with a new job and a new house, the next priority was a new baby'. It is also interesting to note that in all three towns covered by this study, the females in this particular age group consistently outnumbered their male peers (in Glenrothes by 266 or 6 per cent, in East Kilbride by 494 or 6 per cent and in Livingston by 148 or 8 per cent).

This is a phenomenon which would merit further investigation, particularly since it did not occur again in any other age group except in the case of the over 60's, where presumably female longevity would be the main factor. One can therefore only surmise that it is more likely that single women who work in new towns also live there, whereas single men would commute. The incidence of car-ownership might well be a factor influencing this, as Sillitoe found in his survey.[4] He discovered that in the 23–30 age group only 49 per cent of the single females had a motor car, whereas in the equivalent age group 68 per cent of the males had their own motor cars. It is feasible that this might be one of the factors which could have a bearing on the preponderance of female residents in this age group in the above three towns. Clearly there must be other factors, such as employment opportunities and availability of bachelor flats, and possibly other demographic factors, an investigation of which however would be outside the scope of this particular study.

In the age group 30–39 the difference between the three new towns was less marked than in the preceding group, although the proportion this group represented in the total population was still fractionally higher in Livingston (16·4 per cent) than in East Kilbride (15·4 per cent) and Glenrothes (15·8 per cent).

In the age group 40—49 however, there was again a marked difference between the 'younger' town of Livingston, where only 6·4 per cent of the population fell into this age group, and Glenrothes and East Kilbride, where the figures were 11·5 per cent and 14·2 per cent respectively.

In the age group 50—59, this same trend (i.e. the more recent the town — the younger the population) emerged again. Here, the proportion which this category formed of the total population was 5·6 per cent in Glenrothes, 8·6 per cent in East Kilbride and 3 per cent in Livingston.

This trend was even more marked in the over 60's group, where the proportion in Livingston (3 per cent) was approximately half that of Glenrothes (5·7 per cent) and nearly a third that of East Kilbride (7·8 per cent).

Nowhere was the deviation from the national age structure more marked than in the oldest and the youngest age groups. The preponderance of young people is a characteristic of new towns, as much as the lack of old people. This lack of old people is due to a number of factors, but none more so than the selection procedure, according to which prospective residents usually require to have obtained employment in the town, a policy which naturally favours the more mobile younger people. But new towns generally have a policy of encouraging parents of young couples to move into the town beside them. This is considered to be important, not only from the point of view of a more balanced age structure, but also, as one new town official put it, 'because it makes babysitters more freely available, which in turn will allow the town's social life to grow and flourish'. However, one of the main reasons why this policy has had only a marginal impact on the age structure so far is simply that since the major part of the adult population is between 20 and 30, the parents for the most part are not 'old' at all. They are most likely to be middle-aged, in secure jobs, and settled in an area where they probably have lived for the last twenty years or so, unless of course they themselves are affected by slum clearance and are therefore on the overspill list. Once fifteen or twenty years of development have passed, as is the case with East Kilbride and Glenrothes, many of the parents are around retiring age and would probably be prepared to move, but as Schaffer out it,[5] 'pressing needs of expanding industry meant often that only a small quota of suitable dwellings could be allocated to parents'.

3.2 Age structure of membership

Age group 0–9

Although this was proportionally the largest group in terms of total population, it was also the age group which almost uniformly was least represented in membership. In other words, the proportion of members of that age group who had taken up membership of an organisation was smaller than the proportion who had done so in any other age group in the three new towns.

As can be seen from tables 3.1, 3.2 and 3.3 there were significant differences between each town, and within each town, between the sexes, as to the proportions of that age group, represented in membership:

Table 3.4

Age group 0–9:
proportion of population in membership (percentage)

	Male	Female
Glenrothes	5·3	8·2
East Kilbride	3·7	15·0
Livingston	2·7	17·4

At least two questions would appear to arise out of these figures, namely: (a) Why was there generally such a low proportion of the total population in this age group represented in membership? and (b) Why was there such a marked difference between the figures relating to the different sexes in each of the three new towns? Whilst it would be impossible to furnish categorical answers to these questions, some of the following factors would seem to be particularly relevant.

This age group covers the years 0–9, yet the earliest any of the children could join any actual youth organisation (apart from pre-school play groups and such like), would be at the age of 7½ (cubs and brownies). To all intents and purposes therefore only 1½ years of the period covering this age group were effectively included.

The organisations which they could join, such as cubs and brownies, operated a limited intake per group (twenty-four in the case of brownies, thirty-six in the case of cubs) and were therefore highly 'leadership intensive'. In Livingston for instance, a young teacher started one brownie pack in one school, and when she left it in order to start another one in a second school, her first brownie pack temporarily ceased to operate through lack of leadership.

It is not easy to become a leader in the very organisations which could cater for children of that age, and which tend to be uniformed organisations. The standards of competence and qualifications these organisations set are on the whole very high and recruitment usually takes place from among older scouts and rangers or former members. Again there were not many readily available, since few of the groups will have been established for a long enough time. This also applied to other resources, such as finance, buildings etc. Organisations in new towns cannot rely on the help of a pool of ex-members and contacts which have been built up over generations and who can help in raising finance and finding suitable premises. In the new towns, by contrast most organisations have to start from scratch. More will be said about this question later, but the problem seemed to be particularly acute in this age group.

Another reason for the relatively low proportion of members in this age group could well be the age limit, which was imposed by the Albermarle Report on the Youth Service, and which for purposes of grant-aid was being operated between 14 and 20 years. In other words, a youth organisation wanting to employ a youth leader to run activities for children under the age of 14 strictly speaking could not qualify for grant-aid from the local authority. Although it is true to say that in Scotland anyhow, few organisations have been willing to accept this age differentiation,[6] for purposes of grant-aid it has been operated fairly strictly up to very recently. However, increasingly voices calling for the abolition of these age limits are being heard. The report, 'Youth and community work in the 70's'[7] representing proposals by the Youth Service Development Council of the Department of Education and Sciences, recommended 'in a service designed to meet the needs of individuals it is neither necessary nor desirable to lay down hard and fast dividing lines' (p. 1, para. 2b) and 'The existing age limits of 14 and 20 should disappear and eligibility for grants should be correspondingly widened' (p. 3, para. 6c).[8]

There would appear to be a further important reason for this low proportion which was mentioned frequently in conversation with leaders of youth organisations in the new towns. Some find that, since traditionally their activities are at a peak during the winter months when the evenings are dark, many parents are reluctant to let their children go out of the house and walk for any distance, particularly when, as is the case in the new towns, roads may be unfinished and badly lit, and buses are infrequent.

36

All these factors do not account however for the preponderance of girls in membership. Unfortunately there were no statistics available which divide participation according to sex; indeed, since this age range is outside the youth service age range, there are no statistics available anywhere. It is however possible to speculate that there are more female leaders available due to the reason given above (i.e. 'surplus' of single women in the 20–29 age group).

Age group 10–19

This is the age group which also includes the youth service age range (14–20 years). However, comparison with youth service statistics was only possible in a limited sense, since few were available[9] and those that were available did not cover the same age range as was used in this study. Furthermore, once again multiple membership could not be established, but nevertheless the figures given are an indication of the degree of participation in formal groups.

As in the previous age group, there were again marked differences in the proportions represented in membership between each of the three towns and indeed between the sexes.

Table 3.5

Age group 10–19:
proportion of population in membership (percentage)

	Male	Female
Glenrothes	39·2	25
East Kilbride	40	26·9
Livingston	80·2	58·9

The first general trend which became apparent was that in each town the boys in membership outnumbered the girls. In this these new towns did not appear to differ from any of the other towns in the country which were studied. Pearl Jephcott, [10] for instance, found that in two areas of Glasgow (Dennistoun and Drumchapel) and in the West Lothian town of Armadale the figures for participation in leisure-time activities, which most closely resemble the activities of the organisations in this study showed that 63 per cent of boys and 47 per cent of girls were involved in one way or another. Whilst these figures are not strictly comparable due to differences in sample and survey design, they do nevertheless bear out the above trend. She also demonstrated that many more girls did spend their evenings at home than boys. [11] In answer to the question 'How did you spend yesterday evening?' 38 per cent of the boys and 46 per cent of the girls said they were at home. Similar figures, at least in as much as they confirmed the trend among girls of a lower pattern of participation in club activities, and a higher tendency to spend evenings at home, were given in a report by the Central Advisory Council for Education in England, [12] where it was found that 34·6 per cent of all schoolboys and 62 per cent of all girls had spent three or more evenings at home during the week prior to being interviewed. Pearl Jephcott herself seemed to give a major clue as to the reasons behind these patterns in her report [13] when she said that 'many of the home based interests were connected with feminine skills, such as knitting and dressmaking, cooking and looking after small children at home'. The report by the Youth Service Development Council [14] under appendix 3 [15] drew on the findings of a wide number of committees [16] and showed clearly that a higher proportion of boys than girls belong to youth organisations (36 per cent and 25 per cent respectively). Unfortunately the equivalent figures for Scotland are not available. However in the recent government survey, [17] which included in its sample eight new towns [18] it was found that in the 15–18 age range, 55 per cent of the boys and 43 per cent of the girls were in membership. Although detailed comparison between these different sets of data was almost impossible, mainly because of the differing age criteria being used, nevertheless they did confirm the general trend of male preponderance in that age group, which was observed in Glenrothes, East Kilbride and Livingston.

More specifically, it would appear that the degree of involvement in the new towns was higher than in any of the other areas quoted above. The figures relating to Glenrothes and East Kilbride, although higher than any of those quoted from other studies, did roughly correspond to the third of young people who were said to be involved in voluntary and statutory organisations by the Albemarle report in 1960. [19] However, the percentages which emerged for Livingston for the same age group were exceptional by any standard. Whilst it would be difficult to furnish a comprehensive explanation, from observations and discussion with youth leaders the following factors would appear to be particularly relevant.

Although the percentages are high (i.e. 80·2 per cent and 58·9 per cent for males and females respectively), the actual numbers involved are relatively small, i.e. there were only 329 males and 338 females in the total population of Livingston in this age group at that time. It was therefore reasonable to assume that a great many of the young people would know each other from school and the neighbourhood and they would therefore be under a certain degree of pressure from their peers to join also.

Being a very new town there were few, if any, commercial alternatives for their entertainment in the town itself which at the time of the survey virtually meant Craigshill.

The premises available in the form of youth wings attached to the schools, and the Craigshill Farm were more attractive and up-to-date than any other facilities in the district. This acted both as a disincentive for young local residents to go elsewhere, and as an incentive for young people from the surrounding villages to join new town organisations. This last point, i.e. the influx from outside, may indeed have been an important factor which influenced the high rate of membership. Furthermore, being within the vicinity of the school premises, the children would get to know their age group.

From an early stage in the town development there were two full-time youth leaders working in the town. One of them was employed by the Midlothian County Education Authority and one by the Church of Scotland. Both had an official remit for a wider area, but were based in Craigshill and made a special point of issuing a personal invitation to every young person as he moved into the town. Again, as shown above the numbers involved were such as to make this personal contact still possible. These are some of the factors which would help to account for this high degree of participation which was not found in any other age group or indeed any other of the new towns studied.

Age group 20–29

As was to be expected, young men and women in this age group have different leisure habits from those of people five or ten years their junior. They are very likely to have left full-time education and, other than perhaps in a leadership capacity, they will have lost all contact with youth organisations. Most probably they will have married, moved into a new house and become parents, and are now occupied with activities centred on the home. This 'home-centredness' would appear to be a characteristic not only of the three new towns studied here, but of others also. Ferdynand Zweig in his very short study of Cumbernauld [20] went as far as to call this 'an excessive psychological investment in the family'. Nicholson, [21] however, did not see this necessarily as quite such a negative feature, when he said: 'The retreat to the home, which is sometimes deplored is, at least to some extent, an expression of the satisfaction which the home now gives. Some workers in these communities speak of a "new culture of the home". Others see in it a defence against unfamiliar surroundings and unknown neighbours'.

Cullingworth too in his Swindon social survey [22] found that the garden and the TV set absorbed the interests of at least the adult members of the family. Paradoxically he found that 'there were complaints about the lack of entertainment in the town', and concluded that 'it is difficult to say whether they did not go out because they did not want to – or they did not want to because there was nowhere to go.'

Be that as it may, 'staying in the home' for both the man and the woman of the house is a feature of new communities, much more so than was previously the case in established communities such as Ashton (a mining community), which J. Klein [23] described as a place where a woman's place was in the home, the man's place definitely outside it. She observed that 'After work the men go home for a wash and a meal and then go out again, to meet their friends at the club, the pub, the corner, the sportsground.' In the three new towns concerned, and more specifically in Livingston, at the time of the survey there would not have been a pub or a club nor a sportsground to go to. Quite apart, however, from the special case of the new towns, at a national level Sillitoe's survey [24] has shown that television and gardening are by far the most popular leisure time activities even for this age group, and these activities happen to be 'home and family' centred. Scheuch [25] in an article in the *Sociological Review* suggested that this pattern of leisure-time spending was prevalent in other parts of western Europe too, by demonstrating that in Cologne the majority of leisure time spent by adults was in the home.

This study is of course not primarily about the individual's leisure activities as such, but about the degree of participation in formal groups. The above brief discussion however is relevant, since it would to some extent account in a general sense for the low proportion in membership in the age group 20–29:

Table 3.6

Age group 20–29:

proportion of population in membership (percentage)

	Male	Female
Glenrothes	17·5	7·3
East Kilbride	9·0	5·4
Livingston	5·5	15·3

Once again a number of differences between the above three towns become apparent. Glenrothes had a higher proportion of the male population in membership than either of the other two. On the other hand Livingston showed twice the percentage of females in membership than Glenrothes and nearly three times as many as East Kilbride.

Livingston, being the youngest town of the three, once again showed characteristics which were not found in the other two, in as much as the females would appear to be very much more active in membership in this particular age group. Again these figures cannot be explained totally but there would appear to be some indicators which are particularly relevant.

The general question of the influence of the different stages of the life-cycle and the marital and familial status has already been briefly discussed. The fact that in all three towns this age group was the one in the female category which was least represented in membership would further confirm the notion that a great many young mothers were now completely absorbed with the duties in their home. [26]

In Glenrothes twice as many men (as a proportion of the total population) as in East Kilbride, were members of an organisation. This may partly be attributable to the fact that there had been a social club, which initially was a miners' welfare club, for a number of years. This club had a total membership of 460 male members, some 220 of which were old age pensioners (the over 60's). For the remainder of their membership they were unable to give an age breakdown, but from evidence given by members in Glenrothes it is reasonable to assume that many will be found in the age groups 20–40. It is therefore possible that something of the mining community tradition, which J. Klein [27] described, has survived the closure of the pits in and near Glenrothes.

Furthermore, in the very year in which this research was conducted in Glenrothes a new golf course and clubhouse were opened which caused the number of male club members to rise to 410, of which 125 were in the 20–29 age group, so they too would account for a certain number of members in that age group. It is also interesting to note that the proportion this age group forms of the total population was almost identical to the proportion of that group who are in membership, i.e. 17·8 per cent and 17·5 per cent respectively.

In East Kilbride the picture was different. The 20–29 age group formed a slightly lower proportion of the total population than any other group in the range 0–49, i.e. 13·7 per cent. The proportion of membership was even lower, 9 per cent. Contrary to the situation in Glenrothes there did not appear to be any one organisation in the sample, such as the golf club and social clubs, which would account for a substantial part of the membership. Furthermore, since Glasgow is only six miles away and readily accessible by road and rail, one can assume that a good number of that age group will be able to seek their entertainment there, quite apart from those who were totally absorbed in home and garden. Nevertheless there would appear to be room for organisations in East Kilbride to expand into activities attracting this age group of either sex, particularly since it was the group in East Kilbride which was least represented proportionally of all the age groups.

As already indicated, the pattern in Livingston was the reverse of the other two towns. There were proportionally fewer men in membership, both in relation to male membership in the other towns and in relation to female membership in Livingston itself. On further investigation some of the following factors would appear to be significant in the Livingston context.

As was noted when dealing with the preceding age group, at the start of the new town resources of leadership and efforts were concentrated on activities for young people, with good results. Since these resources were limited, it was neither feasible nor, some would say, necessary, to concentrate equally hard on this age group.

This group is highly mobile and it has been shown that a great many more men than women continue to keep up social contacts in their former area of residence, [28] at least in the initial stages of their 'new life'.

The largest employer of male labour in Livingston is an American iron foundry firm, and at the time of the survey men were asked to work a considerable amount of overtime, which of course curtailed opportunities for leisure time activity. Something of the 'process of americanisation' which Zweig [29] described in Cumbernauld, seemed to have taken place in Livingston also. At the time of the study some sort of 'cohesion' among men in this age group appeared to emerge within the context of 'Forum'. [30] The trend, which was observed elsewhere, namely that the more specialised activities for adults develop at a later stage, certainly would seem to be borne out in Livingston.

As far as female participation is concerned there were a number of factors which would account for the relatively high degree of involvement in Livingston.

The total number of women in the population was considerably smaller than in the other two towns, [31] the 'coverage' which can be achieved with limited resources was therefore higher. Furthermore, the proportion of the total population in that age group was higher than in the other two new towns.

It is generally accepted that young mothers, who can be assumed to

42

form the bulk of the population in their age group, are less mobile than their male counterparts and are therefore to some extent given less choice in their social contacts.

As was the case in Livingston in the age group 10–19, which also had a high degree of involvement, professional leadership was available very early on in the development of the town. The YM/YWCA jointly appointed a worker, who saw her remit as working with young mothers. Furthermore, a district nurse who was working and living in the area organised group meetings for women in that area. In fact, practically every woman living in the same street as the nurse was a member.

The geographical area in which these workers operated was still relatively small and .clearly defined. It was therefore possible for them to know personally, and be known by, most of the residents moving into the new town.

Once again, it would appear that availability of professional leadership at an early stage of the development of the town is a most vital factor in the degree of involvement in organised activities which can be achieved.

Age group 30–39

As the figures in table 3.7 show, the degree of involvement of this age group was markedly different from the one observed for the preceding group.

Table 3.7

Age group 30–39:
proportion of population in membership (percentage)

	Male	Female
Glenrothes	20·7	15·3
East Kilbride	10·2	6·3
Livingston	5·6	24·1

In Glenrothes the proportion of men in membership showed a small increase over the previous age group, but the proportion of women in membership doubled, thus in a sense confirming Sillitoe's 'life cycle theory'. [32] In other words, we can assume that women in this age group no longer had small children and were no longer 'housebound', to the same extent.

In East Kilbride the proportional increase in membership in both sexes was very small, but nevertheless the fact that there was an increase at all would still confirm the general trend of increased participation with increased age, after an initial peak between 10–19, which is then followed by a general falling off towards retirement age and a further increase in participation after retirement. [33]

As in previous age groups the situation in Livingston was different. Again the proportion of female participation was higher than male participation (as has been the case within every age group except the first one). But given that fact, both the male and female proportion showed an increase, a minimal one in the case of the men (from 5·5 per cent to 5·6 per cent), but a sizeable one (from 15·3 per cent to 24·1 per cent) in the case of the women. This last figure would again suggest an increased 'freedom' for the women with slightly older children. A number of the more general factors, such as distance to Glasgow in the case of East Kilbride and overtime at Cameron Ironworks in Livingston, would apply in this age group too. Perhaps splitting the age groups into ten-year spans at this level is no longer quite relevant, particularly since it can be assumed that circumstances affecting one age group, certainly as far as men are concerned, do not necessarily differ radically enough, say between 25 and 35, as to have a significant influence on participation.

Age group 40–49

This would appear to be the age group which records a higher degree of participation in all three towns than any other adult group except the over 60's. The figures for the proportions of membership are shown in table 3.8.

Table 3.8

Age group 40–49:
proportion of population in membership (percentage)

	Male	Female
Glenrothes	23·6	21·5
East Kilbride	13·1	8·4
Livingston	13·2	25·9

It can be noted that in Glenrothes the proportion of memberships among the males was almost twice as high as in the other two towns. Once again, it can be assumed that the Glenrothes Recreation and Social Club and the golf club accounted for a considerable proportion of all the males in membership in this age group. It is also interesting to note that this 23·6 per cent represented twice the proportion this age group accounted for in the total population (i.e. 12·1 per cent). In East Kilbride and Livingston the proportion of male members was remarkably similar. In each case the proportion had risen (with both males and females) for the third successive time starting with the 20−29 age group. The figures for Livingston were again untypical compared with the other two new towns. The highest proportion of both male and female membership participation in this age group was 25·9 per cent. Whilst in both other towns the proportion of male members exceeded that of female, in Livingston the reverse was the case. A comparison with national figures, such as given by Sillitoe, [34] was not possible, since he used different age groups (31−45 and 46−60), but it is interesting to note that in his sample too the same trends appeared, more markedly so among the females. This showed that in this particular age group a higher degree of participation took place than in any other adult age group. This same trend was clearly borne out in the three new towns investigated (see tables 3.1, 3.2 and 3.3). Once again, the stages in the life-cycle would appear to be a relevant factor. The children were now grown up and in some cases have very likely left home. Hence the rise in membership which Sillitoe observed as being a nationwide phenomenon, and which, as was shown, also applied to the three new towns in this study.

Age group 50−59

It is of course arguable whether anything can be gained by separating this age group from the previous one, however, having done so, some interesting characteristics can be shown. As can be seen from the figures in table 3.9, this is the age group in which the proportion of male and female membership differed least from each other, within each town.

Table 3.9

Age group 50−59:
proportion of population in membership (percentage)

	Male	Female
Glenrothes	17	17·6
East Kilbride	8·5	7·4
Livingston	17·8	16·9

In Glenrothes the females only slightly exceeded the males (and then in proportion only, but not in actual figures), and in Livingston, for the first time since the 10–19 age group, the proportion of males very slightly exceeded that of females. This was an age group where the proportion of memberships relative to the proportion in the total population was significantly higher, in the case of Glenrothes and Livingston. In East Kilbride, however, the respective proportions were almost identical.

Age group over 60

This age group was the one in which the total population was least represented. This is to be expected in new towns, for reasons which were already explained. In terms of involvement in membership, however, the situation was different, as the following figures in table 3.10 show.

Table 3.10

Age group over 60:
proportion of population in membership (percentage)

	Male	Female
Glenrothes	44·7	36·6
East Kilbride	17·3	16·4
Livingston	3·9	23·9

The outstanding figure here was the 44·7 per cent male participation in Glenrothes. Once again the recreation and social club seemed to be a most important factor with 100 male and 125 female members listed in the over 60's category. Furthermore, there were three other organisations co-ordinated by one body who specifically looked after the interests of old people.

In East Kilbride too there was an old age pensioners social club, but it would appear to have been less active in recruitment. In Livingston, however, at the time when the fieldwork was done, there was no specific old people's organisation. Table 3.3 shows that the total number of people concerned was of course small, both in terms of total population and the proportion thereof which was involved in any kind of organised activity. Again the proportion of women was significantly higher than that of men, but those who were in membership were not in specific old age pensioners' clubs, but were mainly to be found among the members of such groups as the church women's meeting.

It was stated at the outset that all the figures quoted above demonstrate a degree of involvement in formal organisations without being able to account for multiple membership. [35] Few comparative figures were available, which would allow a reliable comparison with other new towns or even other towns in either this country or elsewhere. It is therefore not possible to say whether participation in these new towns was higher or lower than in any other area. What statistics are available relate mainly to the youth service age range − and where possible, limited comparisons have therefore been made.

One factor, however, seemed to stand out, i.e. where adequate leadership and facilities were available participation was considerably higher than in areas where this was not the case. The 10−19 age group (which incorporates the youth service age range) overall had higher membership figures than any other age group, and it could be claimed that this was largely due to the extent to which full-time leadership was available. Similarly, in Livingston a larger proportion of women was involved in membership (larger in every category except the 10−19 age group). Again this could be said to be due to the leadership given by a trained full-time woman worker. Even the exception (i.e. more boys in membership than girls in the 10−19 age group) would tend to confirm this rule, since two full-time male leaders have been available from a very early time in the new town's development, to further activities for young people.

In Glenrothes too, where more old people over 60 were involved in membership than in any of the other new towns, more facilities would appear to be available for old people, and indeed there was a separate committee which organised activities for old people. It seems clear therefore that where resources, in terms of leadership and facilities, were available the population responded and membership was relatively high. What is less clear, however, is which was the cause and which the effect. In other words, were there less facilities and leaders in a given town, concerning themselves with a given age group, because there was less interest to be found among the population; or was there less interest to be found because there were less facilities available. [36] The fact, however, that apart from one or two youth organisations, no other club had indicated that they had a waiting list, would suggest that on the whole the needs, as far as they have been stimulated, were met satisfactorily.

Notes

[1] Cullingworth et al., 'The needs of new communities', HMSO, 1967. Figures taken from earlier report: 'The first hundred families', HMSO, 1965.

[2] Cullingworth et al., op. cit.

[3] Frank Schaffer, *The New Town Story*, MacGibbon and Kee, London 1970, p. 170.

[4] K.K. Sillitoe, 'Planning for leisure', HMSO, London 1969, tables 4 and 5, pp. 10 and 11.

[5] Schaffer, op.cit., p. 170.

[6] See 'Community of interests', HMSO, 1968, p. 16, para. 21.

[7] 'Youth and community work in the 70's', HMSO, 1969, pp. 1 and 3.

[8] See also paras 175, 176 and 210 in the above report.

[9] See 'Community of interests', para. 21: 'The statistics of membership of the Youth Service as a whole are approximate, and in certain respects, uninformative. They do not, for example, reveal exactly the number of members in each age group, or even the number above or below any particular age'.

[10] Pearl Jephcott, *Time of One's Own*, Oliver and Boyd, Edinburgh 1967, table 19, p. 163.

[11] Ibid., table 14, p. 161.

[12] '15 to 18', report of Central Advisory Council for Education – England, vol. II, HMSO.

[13] Jephcott, op.cit., p. 107.

[14] 'Youth and community work in the 70's', HMSO, 1969.

[15] Youth service involvement of young people in England and Wales.

[16] See p. 167 of that report.

[17] K. Sillitoe, 'Planning for leisure'.

[18] For a list of the towns, see p. 248 of that report.

[19] A figure which more recently in 'Youth and community work' (p. 172, para. 6a) has been declared as being optimistic.

[20] Ferdynand Zweig, 'The Cumbernauld study', Urban Research Bureau, London 1970.

[21] J.H. Nicholson, 'New communities in Britain', NCSS, London 1961, p. 148.

[22] J.B. Cullingworth, 'Swindon social survey: a second report on the social implications of overspill' *Sociological Review*, vol. 9/19.

[23] Josephine Klein, *Samples from English Cultures*, vol I, Routledge and Kegan Paul, London 1965, p. 104.

[24] K.K. Sillitoe, op.cit., tables 9 and 10, pp. 42–3.

[25] E.K. Scheuch, 'Family cohesion in leisure-time' *Sociological Review,* vol. 8, 1960.

[26] For detailed figures see tables 3.1, 3.2 and 3.3, pp. 30, 31 and 32.

[27] J. Klein, op.cit.

[28] The author once gave a lift to a young man in his mid-twenties on his way from Livingston to Edinburgh to attend a Freemasons meeting, and was assured that it was very common for people in that age group to have most of their social life based in Edinburgh. This was later confirmed by other leaders in the community.

[29] Zweig, op.cit., p. 64.

[30] An open group which started as a weekly meeting of new residents and developed into a regular platform on which community affairs are discussed.

[31] See tables 3.1, 3.2 and 3.3 for actual figures.

[32] Op.cit., p. 40.

[33] Strict comparability with other data is problematic since Sillitoe, for instance, starts off with spans of 4 years (15–18, 19–22), then 8 years (23–30) and then 15 years (31–45, 46–60). Nevertheless this is useful, since general trends can be compared.

[34] K.K. Sillitoe, op.cit., pp. 60 and 61.

[35] See also T. Bottomore, in D.V. Glass (ed.), *Social Mobility in Britain,* Routledge and Kegan Paul, 1954, p. 853, who used the same method; and A.J.M. Sykes and E. Woldman, 'Irvine new town area – a summary and report on leisure activities', University of Strathclyde Occasional Paper no. 2, 1968.

[36] This is the same paradox which Cullingworth discovered when reporting on his social survey of Swindon, op.cit.

4 Occupational Status of Membership/Leadership

4.1 The concept of social balance

Some of the most important aspects in the creation of the new towns are expressed in the goal that they should 'be self-contained and balanced communities for working and living'.[1] As its report shows, the Reith committee had very definite assumptions about the desirability of mixing the different social classes. The idea of 'self-containment' was seen as being straightforward. The new towns would not simply contain residential areas, like some of the inter-war local authority housing estates, but were to be designed to encompass within their boundaries 'all of the requirements for day-to-day living'.[2] In this respect the idea of a self-contained town has certain analogous features with the neighbourhood concept, in as much as that within the same small residential area there should be provided shops, nursery and primary schools, and a limited range of other facilities. Self-containment can of course only be a matter of degree, and it would be unrealistic to expect that the 'local facilities should be able to meet all of the requirements of all of the residents all of the time'.[3] The idea of a balanced community, to which the Reith committee devoted a great deal more time and attention, is much more complex than that of self-containment though, as Thomas points out, the origins of the two ideas are partly intertwined. To some extent a town can only be self-contained if it is 'balanced'. Ideally the level of population should more or less match the level of employment or there will be commuting in and out. Similarly the composition of employment must not be dominated by a single industry or occupation, or it will not be possible to attract a sufficient variety of residents. These factors, and many more, are usually subsumed under the heading of a 'balanced community' and to that extent the term is almost synonymous with a self-contained community. In its plans for the new towns, however, the Reith committee took the idea of a balanced community much further than could be attributable to a desire for self-containment alone. The concept, which it held up as an ideal to be followed was that of 'social balance'. Thus the report reads:[4]

So far as the issue is an economic one, balance can be attained by giving opportunity for many sorts of employment which will attract men and women up to a high income level. Beyond that point the problem is not economic at all, or even a vaguely social one, it is to be frank, one of class distinction. So far as these distinctions are based on income, taxation and high costs of living are reducing them. We realise also that there are some who would have us ignore their existence. But the problem remains and must be faced; *if the community is to be truly balanced, so long as social classes exist, all must be represented in it.* A contribution is needed from every type and class of person; the community will be the poorer if all are not there able and willing to make it.

Where possible therefore, businesses and industries established should include not only factories, shops, and the businesses and services meeting local needs, but head offices and administrative and research establishments including sections of government departments and other public offices. It is most desirable that proprietors, directors, executives and other leading workers in the local industries and businesses *should live in the town and take part in its life.* Many professional men and women, writers, artists and other specialists not tied to a particular location should find a new town a good place in which to live and work. So also should retired people from home and overseas, from every kind of occupation, as well as people of independent means. All these should find interest and scope in *playing their part in the development of the social, political artistic and recreational activities of the town.*

According to Thomas[5] however, much of the motivation for balanced communities was more hard-headed than idealistic, since a fair share of higher income groups was thought to generate the kind of success which was particularly important because of the aim of a symbiotic growth of population and employment. How far the various occupational classes were found to be 'playing their part' in the development of the social, political, artistic and recreational activities of the towns of Glenrothes, East Kilbride and Livingston will be discussed in section 4.2 of this chapter. Before doing so however, a further examination of the concept of social balance would appear to be appropriate at this stage.

Lewis Mumford, in his introduction to the 1945 edition of Howard's *Garden Cities of Tomorrow,*[6] expressed the same sentiment as the Reith committee (see above) a year later, but for a different reason, when he stated:

Meanwhile, the need for balanced communities has deepened, for the task of our age is to work out an urban environment that will be just as favourable to fertility, just as encouraging to marriage and parenthood, as rival areas still are.

He obviously wrote this under the immediate postwar impression of the threat, as it was then seen, of a declining population. Lewis Silkin, the minister who had been responsible for steering the new town legislation through Parliament in 1946, again committed himself to the idea of a balanced community on social grounds, when he wrote two years later:[7]

I am very concerned, not merely to get different classes living together in a community, but to get them actually mixing together — unless they do mix freely in their leisure and recreation, the whole purpose of a mixed community disappears.

The reiteration of this principle, after building had barely begun with the first of the new towns following the passing of the New Towns Act in 1946, seemed to have been important at that time. Even Lord Reith himself, in his first report as chairman of the Hemel Hempstead Development Corporation,[8] confessed that he began to doubt whether the object of developing a balanced community could be 'more than an elusive but inspiring concept'. It would appear that Lord Reith was not alone with his doubts as to the practicability of this concept. According to Schaffer,[9] most corporations started off with the intention of mixing the various types of houses and avoiding any suggestions of 'class segregation', but it didn't work out. Harlow, for example, soon found that 'middle-class families liked either to be somewhat isolated and to have big gardens, or to have a large number of their neighbours drawn from similar income groups'.[10] Other corporations reported much the same experience. To many this was a matter of regret because it seemed to represent the failure of a philosophy. But this does not necessarily follow, 'for people still mingle on equal terms in the town's activities'. (At least so Schaffer claims — but it will be seen below how far this is so where the three towns subject to this study are concerned.) He also points out that although it has not been possible to overcome social distinctions and segregation by income groups, nevertheless the new towns can claim to have a 'socially homogeneous society'. A comparison with national figures, as presented by Schaffer,[11] bears this out.

Some people, notably Ruth Glass in an article published in 1955,[12] saw sinister implications in this attempt at achieving social balance. She in fact suggested that this was a 'device for securing middle-class control under the guise of leadership, thus avoiding a threat to the established order'. However, Schaffer[13] dismissed this view as being naïve, since he didn't think that political power was exercised through the 'local community hall, with its bingo and chess club'.

There were others, notably Peter Mann, who were critical of the idea of social balance, particularly as it related to the neighbourhood unit.[14] In his view, Clarence Perry, who popularised the idea of the neighbourhood unit, rather naïvely assumed that 'propinquity produces pals' when he stated:[15] 'when residents are brought together through the use of common recreational facilities they come to know one another better, and friendly relations ensue'. This idea was taken up in Britain, first in the Dudley report[16] and then in a booklet entitled 'The size and social structure of a town', which was published by the National Council of Social Service,[17] who incidentally were also one of the bodies which gave evidence to the Reith committee. This booklet made a case against prewar housing estates on the grounds of lack of social balance. The group which wrote it argued that 'class distinctions have been emphasised to an undesirable extent by the segregation of rigidly divided income groups into separate residential districts. The consequence of this segregation was that the new municipal estates contained relatively few people with varied experience in social leadership.' The group further argued that social barriers will only disappear if people 'in different grades find a unity in common interests and purposes'. This development, they felt, could be accelerated by the provision of adequate neighbourhood facilities. Furthermore, they argued that the problem of social leadership (and particularly the lack of sufficient numbers of leaders) could be overcome by the integration of a number of social groups into one organisation, i.e. a community association. Mann is critical of this approach. The concept of the socially balanced neighbourhood unit, in his view, was based upon an erroneous analysis of the social structure of urban society. He felt that this was an ideal which was unlikely to be attained without a complete change in the structure of our society. He therefore suggested that we should 'bury it quietly (the ideal of social balance) and begin to think again from a sociological rather than an ideological basis'.

More recently Heraud[18] argued too, that class segregation had been a feature of town life ever since the onset of rapid urbanisation in the nineteenth century. He suggests that with the development of municipal housing after the First World War, and the building of housing estates for the working class on the outskirts of large cities, the process had been carried a stage further, and social segregation took on almost an official stamp with the advent of state intervention in housing. However, in due course the view gained prominence that one-class communities were socially undesirable because the presence of large numbers of people with the same life styles, educational expectations and expenditure patterns would have a narrowing effect. Exposure to a mixed environment would, it was argued, enlarge people's horizons and so benefit the community as a whole. Such views were reflected by statements such as the one in the House of Commons during the debate on the new towns, in which the Minister of Town and Country Planning, Mr. Silkin, stated: 'We must not make them towns inhabited by people of one income level, and that the lowest. A new series of Becontrees would be fatal'. [19]

The idea of balance was by now widely canvassed amongst town planners, largely due to the government's increasing assumption of responsibility for housing and planning. Planning was to be the new instrument for mixing different classes together. However, as Heraud point out, the ideal of a socially mixed society should not be confused with the notion of a classless society. Indeed, social balance as defined by the Reith committee explicitly recognised the existence of social classes, but sought through physical proximity and the common use of facilities, such as community centres, to induce them to mix socially. It is of interest to note in this context that in the early days of Stevenage New Town a leading local communist dismissed the whole idea of a socially mixed community as 'not in line with communist principles of a classless society'. [20] Another important argument which was mentioned, among others, by both Heraud and Mann, was the notion that one-class communities would develop a kind of social inertia, and particularly would lack the leadership which it was thought the middle class would provide. This view was said to have gained prominence by the National Council of Social Service report, already mentioned above. Heraud suggests that there can be little doubt that the Reith committee, and thus the subsequent development of the new towns, was strongly influenced by such views, particularly since both the Town and Country Planning Association and the National Council of Social Service gave evidence to the Reith committee.

A mixture of values thus underlies the concept of social balance. A common feature is the belief that the new communities must contain those members who can bring with them and disseminate certain cultural elements considered necessary for the foundation of civilised life. Social balance as such has been defined in various ways, but generally it has been conceived as a reproduction of some standard or average demographic, social and economic structure. [21] The following quotation, taken from the master plan for Livingston New Town, will serve to illustrate the way in which the idea of balance has generally been interpreted by the new towns development corporations. [22]

> The type of town Livingston will become will largely be decided by its population and employment structure — therefore maximum diversity is planned and a positive effort will be made to achieve a balance of population in relation to age groups, family structure and employment.

This of course is a statement of intent, according to which a development corporation hopes to develop the town as a whole, but as far as creating social balance at neighbourhood level is concerned, it is more difficult to see how this could be achieved, in a free society, where mobility exists. The neighbourhood unit originally was to be the cornerstone of planning in the new towns. This was dictated by certain physical, as well as social factors. The road system of most new towns was to be designed on the radial system, which would have the effect of physically defining certain areas. With the addition of facilities such as primary schools, shops and meeting places, these areas could be given social significance as the basis for community life. The neighbourhood was, in the words of the Reith committee, 'a natural and useful conception'. (The maps described in chapter 6, particularly those relating to Glenrothes and East Kilbride, illustrate the way in which this concept has been applied, particularly in the so-called mark 1 new towns, and will also, at least as far as membership of social organisations is concerned, show how far the neighbourhoods form 'a basis for community life'.) The neighbourhood also seemed the appropriate vehicle for the attainment, on a local basis, of 'social balance'. It appears however that a degree of social segregation is a concomitant of most housing developments. Thus Peter Collison [23] summed up the matter as follows:

> although planning policy may do something to modify the degree of (class) segregation, it cannot be expected to eliminate it completely nor can it be expected, of itself, to bring about any profound changes in the social structure. If attempts are made to mix the social classes in close proximity it seems likely that these attempts will be resisted, and, as more dwellings become available, increasingly ineffective.

According to Heraud, 'there has been a gradual slipping away from an ideology which stressed reformist ideas and aims into one which accepted and adapted to what was believed to be a middle class desire for social segregation'. [24] Indeed Nicholson, in his study of housing policy in the new towns concludes that 'most New Towns now accept, though sometimes with reluctance, that an attempt to promote social mixing by building so-called managerial houses, scattered throughout the town and its neighbourhoods, without the alternative of such houses built in groups, has failed'. [25] Some further points emerged from Herauds study of social class and neighbourhood, which are relevant to the discussion of social organisations in the new towns, and which are briefly summarised below.

If the new town neighbourhoods have differing class characteristics, then in view of the fact that the social classes have widely differing patterns of social activities, any one single form of local social provision is unlikely to be successful. The need would appear to be for a variety of forms of local social provision, including opportunities for more informal association with more specialised activities based on the town as a whole. [26] One of the main aims of the whole 'social balance policy' has been the invigoration of social life, through the presence of leadership provided by the middle class, and the mixing of classes through local clubs and associations. In a study of this kind one also has to accept of course, that the number of organisations alone is not in itself an index of social health in a community, since a great many of the social activities are being pursued outside the formal structure of an organisation. However, discussions about the necessity of stimulating 'community life' in the new towns have centred almost entirely on the type of activity accepted and approved of by the professional and middle class in particular, the community associations. However, as was seen in chapter 2, this would not appear to be true in Glenrothes and East Kilbride, since in each of these towns the 'community associations' as such have ceased to make a significant contribution to the life of the community. Heraud further suggests that community associations do not really constitute the kind of 'cross-cutting alliances' which might in fact bring the classes together, because they are not typical of working-class culture. [27] He adds that there is little evidence from elsewhere which would suggest that the degree of class-mixing in clubs and associations is very high. In all this he sees a kind of ideological thread connecting the present new towns with the notions surrounding the eighteenth and nineteenth-century model settlements and overseas emigrations. Traditionally leadership was the responsibility of the upper and middle classes, thus creating the need for 'balanced' groups of migrants. Only in this way, it was thought, would a 'healthy community' together with a degree of social control be built up. Such a notion, he suggests, is in the present day so far from reality that the whole concept of a balanced community based on such arguments must be called into question. The desire to avoid a new series of

Becontrees was understandable in the context of the 1940's, but one can question whether in the sixties and seventies the concept of the socially balanced community as a planning principle has a future, particularly since because of the nature of industry moving to new towns 'fears of a large working-class population were unfounded'. However, as will be seen in section 4.2, whether the concept of social balance is still viable as a planning principle or not, it remains a fact that the upper and middle classes continue to provide leadership to a degree which in most cases far outweighs their proportion in membership of the various organisations. H.J. Gans, in a sense, both sums up the question of social balance as previously discussed, and also provides an answer to Heraud's point. He argues [28] that in any society with clear-cut social divisions of class (and as in America, race) such divisions should be minimised, and this can be effected partly through the medium of town planning. For example in a heterogeneous community, the financial advantages of high rate assessments can be spread to members of all classes in the form of improved educational and other facilities. In his view too therefore the desirability of a balanced community is not merely based on an evasive ideal, but also makes sound economic sense. In this, Gans' view coincides with that of the Reith committee to whom has been attributed hardheaded economic, rather than solely idealistic motivations as the main spring of its desire to create balanced communities.

4.2 Occupational status distribution of membership/leadership of organisations

As was noted above, the Reith committee assumed that 'social organisations could be expected to make a major contribution towards the mixing together of the different social classes'. [29] In order to try and establish how far in fact this assumption has been borne out in the case of the three new towns in this study, the secretaries of the various organisations were asked to indicate the breakdown of their membership into occupational groups. [30] The data obtained was then organised as follows: the membership breakdown of each organisation into five occupational groups is shown in bar-charts for each organisation, according to categories. In order to ascertain how far the leadership of the organisations was distributed among the various status groups, wherever possible separate bar-charts were drawn relating to the leaders of the organisations.

These two sets of figures (i.e. occupational status of members and

58

leaders) were then compared with each other, and the results of these comparisons, expressed in chi-square values (tables 4.1, 4.2 and 4.3). Furthermore, bearing in mind the definition of 'social balance' as given by the Reith committee, and by Heraud (i.e. 'reproduction of some standard or average demographic, social and industrial structure'), the distribution of occupational groups among the membership of organisations was then compared with the distribution for the particular town as a whole (tables 4.4, 4.5 and 4.6). However, not every organisation would appear to maintain a membership record, consequently some secretaries were unable to give figures relating to their membership/leadership.[31] The occupational status distribution for the three new towns concerned and the population of Scotland as a whole are illustrated by bar-charts in fig.4.1.

Fig. 4.1   Occupational status distribution – general population.
(percentage of households–occupational groups 1–5)

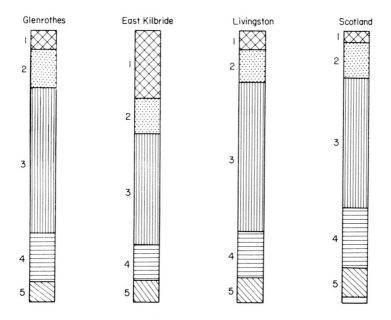

Table 4.1

Glenrothes — comparison of occupational status of membership/leadership

	Number of organisation*	Members' occupational group					Leaders' occupational group					Chi-square value
		1	2	3	4	5	1	2	3	4	5	
Youth	49	16	30	30	14	10	37	27	22	11	3	35·54
organisations	52	20	20	20	20	20	50	10	20	10	10	60·00
	58	20	23	37	13	7	20	25	50	5	0	16·66
Arts and	13	25	40	15	10	10	70	30	0	0	0	118·50
cultural	33	5	75	15	5	0	5	90	5	0	0	14·67
	51	43	28	29	0	0	100	0	0	0	0	132·56
Social	7	70	30	0	0	0	75	25	0	0	0	1·19
services	11	100	0	0	0	0	100	0	0	0	0	0·00
	15	0	100	0	0	0	100	0	0	0	0	999999900·00
	19	9	28	36	9	18	50	0	50	0	0	247·22
	45	9	53	38	0	0	50	50	0	0	0	224·95
Women's	4	50	50	0	0	0	50	50	0	0	0	0·00
organisations	24	10	10	40	40	0	25	25	50	0	0	87·50
	29	0	50	50	0	0	0	50	50	0	0	0·00
	39	1	99	0	0	0	0	100	0	0	0	1·01
	56	0	0	50	50	0	0	0	50	50	0	0·00
Hobby/special	23	40	40	10	5	5	40	20	0	20	20	110·00
interest	25	20	20	50	10	0	30	30	40	0	0	22·00
	30	5	5	45	35	10	0	33	34	33	0	174·60
	53	0	0	100	0	0	0	0	100	0	0	0·00
Political	9	11	18	22	26	23	28	36	7	29	0	77·85
	43	17	8	17	41	17	25	0	50	25	0	99·07
	50	50	0	50	0	0	10	0	90	0	0	64·00
	55	10	5	33	43	9	0	0	75	0	25	139·90
Sports	3	0	0	25	25	50	17	0	83	0	0	28900175·56
	12	50	0	50	0	0	0	0	100	0	0	100·00
	28	0	0	100	0	0	0	0	100	0	0	0·00
	36	30	40	20	5	5	50	30	20	0	0	25·83
	46	62	27	11	0	0	66	17	17	0	0	7·23
Social/	21	0	0	80	20	0	6	0	94	0	0	3600010·45
dancing	32	0	0	100	0	0	0	0	100	0	0	0·00
Old people	18	0	10	50	40	0	33	34	33	0	0	108900037·38
	27	10	20	50	20	0	10	45	45	0	0	51·75
	31	33	20	21	26	0	50	0	50	0	0	94·81
Other	2	33	0	67	0	0	0	0	100	0	0	49·25
	38	19	19	31	31	0	12	12	60	16	0	39·55

* For key to names of organisations see Appendix, p. 223·

Table 4.2

East Kilbride — comparison of occupational status of membership/leadership

	Number of organisation*	Members' occupational group					Leaders' occupational group					Chi-square value
		1	2	3	4	5	1	2	3	4	5	
Youth	68	5	13	65	13	4	18	33	41	8	0	79·35
organisations	69	5	50	40	5	0	5	50	40	5	0	0·00
	81	0	20	60	20	0	50	0	50	0	0	249999941·67
	96	10	30	50	10	0	20	70	10	0	0	105·33
	101	0	0	100	0	0	0	0	100	0	0	0·00
Arts and	84	0	38	55	7	0	0	43	57	0	0	7·73
cultural	94	11	0	63	21	5	0	0	100	0	0	58·73
	149	0	47	49	4	0	0	87	13	0	0	64·49
Social	114	15	0	31	31	23	0	0	100	0	0	222·58
services	117	60	40	0	0	0	60	40	0	0	0	0·00
	123	100	0	0	0	0	100	0	0	0	0	0·00
	127	40	40	20	0	0	100	0	0	0	0	150·00
	128	0	50	25	25	0	25	50	25	0	0	62499975·00
	133	100	0	0	0	0	100	0	0	0	0	0·00
Women's	118	20	0	80	0	0	0	0	100	0	0	25·00
organisations	124	25	75	0	0	0	25	75	0	0	0	0·00
	132	25	25	50	0	0	50	0	50	0	0	50·00
Hobby/special	107	75	10	10	5	0	100	0	0	0	0	33·33
interest	108	1	4	50	20	25	0	1	80	10	9	36·49
	115	45	12	31	12	0	67	33	0	0	0	90·51
	129	10	20	30	5	35	50	0	50	0	0	233·33
	134	40	30	20	10	0	100	0	0	0	0	150·00
	138	10	50	35	5	0	0	33	67	0	0	50·04
	139	5	13	58	24	0	25	25	50	0	0	116·18
Political	72	5	35	40	10	10	10	60	10	15	5	50·36
	91	20	30	30	15	5	70	10	20	0	0	161·67
	109	5	5	20	63	7	0	0	100	0	0	400·00
Sports	71	55	20	20	5	0	100	0	0	0	0	81·82
	74	0	0	70	20	10	10	0	80	10	0	9999996·43
	119	27	59	9	5	0	22	67	11	0	0	7·46
	125	10	60	30	0	0	70	20	10	0	0	400·00
	135	100	0	0	0	0	100	0	0	0	0	0·00
	136	12	18	35	5	30	40	40	20	0	0	133·65
	140	30	10	50	10	0	20	30	50	0	0	53·33
	145	28	47	21	0	4	100	0	0	0	0	257·14
	147	10	20	40	15	15	15	40	45	0	0	53·12
	148	50	0	50	0	0	50	0	50	0	0	0·00
Other	88	24	48	19	9	0	75	25	0	0	0	147·40
	105	50	30	20	0	0	62	38	0	0	0	25·01

* For key to names of organisations see Appendix, p. 223.

Table 4.3

Livingston — comparison of occupational status of
membership/leadership

	Number of organisation*	Members' occupational group					Leaders' occupational group					Chi-square value
		1	2	3	4	5	1	2	3	4	5	
Youth	152	20	20	25	30	5	30	0	40	20	0	42·33
organisations	158	5	0	0	45	50	50	0	0	0	50	450·00
	161	0	0	20	50	30	0	10	70	20	0	10000153·00
Social services	167	15	0	15	0	70	66	0	17	17	0	28900209·67
Women's	169	10	25	50	15	0	10	90	0	0	0	234·00
organisations	170	75	25	0	0	0	100	0	0	0	0	33·33
	172	0	0	55	0	45	0	0	50	0	50	1·01
Hobby/special	173	88	12	0	0	0	100	0	0	0	0	13·64
interest	175	8	32	52	8	0	33	50	17	0	0	119·81
Political	176	4	3	50	20	23	40	33	10	10	7	672·13
Sports	159	0	0	50	50	0	0	0	75	25	0	25·00
	177	0	0	60	40	0	0	0	100	0	0	66·67
	178	62	25	13	0	0	100	0	0	0	0	61·29
	182	15	15	35	8	27	50	40	10	0	0	176·19

* For key to names of organisations see Appendix, p. 223.

Glenrothes: youth organisations

As can be seen from the bar-charts shown in fig. 4.2, in this category every organisation had members from every occupational group, albeit to a different extent. It is of interest, for instance in the case of the Preston Youth Club (no. 26), that groups 1 and 2 were barely represented. (See also fig. 6.3 which might help to explain this in terms of the club's location.) On the other hand the three uniformed organisations, i.e. the Boys Brigade (no. 49), Boys Scouts (no. 52) and Girl Guides (no. 58) would appear to have been able to attract a larger share of children, whose parents were in occupational groups 1, than the other three organisations. However, as can be seen from the respective bar-charts, these were also the three organisations with the highest proportion of representatives of occupational group 5. The graphs in fig. 4.2 relating to the leaders show that there was a considerable difference between the proportion of members and leaders respectively, in the various occupational groups. The

Table 4.4

Glenrothes — comparison of occupational status of membership/population

	Number of organisation*	Occupational group					Chi-square value
		1 (7)	2 (14)	3 (54)	4 (18)	5 (7)†	
Youth	22	5	19	54	16	6	2·72
organisations	26	1	2	72	23	2	26·39
	35	5	25	50	15	5	10·58
	49	16	30	30	14	10	42·70
	52	20	20	20	20	20	72·49
	58	20	23	37	13	7	36·67
Arts and	5	20	30	30	10	10	57·94
cultural	10	10	20	40	25	5	10·78
	13	25	40	15	10	10	127·58
	16	20	58	18	4	0	204·32
	33	5	75	15	5	0	310·91
	51	43	28	29	0	0	235·72
Social	7	70	30	0	0	0	664·29
service	11	100	0	0	0	0	1328·57
	15	0	100	0	0	0	614·29
	19	9	28	36	9	18	42·36
	34	0	33	33	34	0	62·17
	45	9	53	38	0	0	138·96
Women's	4	50	50	0	0	0	435·71
organisations	17	0	17	30	44	9	56·44
	24	10	10	40	40	0	39·95
	29	0	50	50	0	0	124·87
	39	1	99	0	0	0	600·21
	56	0	0	50	50	0	85·19
Hobby/special	14	17	49	17	17	0	134·19
interest	20	11	10	55	19	5	4·07
	23	40	40	10	5	5	249·67
	25	20	20	50	10	0	37·57
	30	5	5	45	35	10	25·20
	48	0	23	48	20	9	14·25
	53	0	0	100	0	0	85·19

Table 4.4 continued

	Number of organisation*	Occupational group					Chi-square value
		1 (7)	2 (14)	3 (54)	4 (18)	5 (7)†	
Political	9	11	18	22	26	23	62·52
	43	17	8	17	41	17	85·88
	50	50	0	50	0	0	303·44
	55	10	5	33	43	9	50·53
Sports	3	0	0	25	25	50	303·44
	12	50	0	50	0	0	303·44
	28	0	0	100	0	0	85·19
	36	30	40	20	5	5	155·22
	46	62	27	11	0	0	503·46
Social and dancing	21	0	0	80	20	0	40·74
	32	0	0	100	0	0	85·19
Old people	18	0	10	50	40	0	42·33
	27	10	20	50	20	0	11·38
	31	33	20	21	26	0	129·87
Other	2	33	0	67	0	0	138·70
	38	19	19	31	31	0	48·54

* For key to names of organisations see Appendix, p. 223.
† Bracketted numbers are the total '000 each occupational group represents in the population of Glenrothes.

Boys Brigade (no. 49) for instance had 16 per cent of its members in occupational group 1, but 37 per cent of the leaders were from that group. More marked still was the difference within the Boy Scouts (no. 52) where 20 per cent of the members, but 50 per cent of the leaders, were in occupational group 1. In the case of the Girl Guides (no. 58) the difference was less marked, in fact the proportions of leaders and members in class 1 was equal, with 20 per cent in each case, but on the other hand groups 4 and 5, which together accounted for 20 per cent of all members were only represented by 5 per cent of the leaders coming from group 4. Group 5 was not represented at all. Whilst it is not possible to compare these figures item by item with Bottomore's findings,[32] it is of interest to note that the general trend, which he observed, of

Table 4.5

East Kilbride – comparison of occupational status of
membership/population

	Number of organisation*	Occupational group					Chi-square value
		1 (25)	2 (13)	3 (41)	4 (13)	5 (8)†	
Youth organisations	68	5	13	65	13	4	32·05
	69	5	50	40	5	0	134·26
	81	0	20	60	20	0	49·34
	96	10	30	50	10	0	41·90
	101	0	0	100	0	0	143·90
	103	2	3	75	15	5	58·48
	112	0	40	40	20	0	92·87
Arts and cultural	80	5	35	50	5	5	61·25
	84	0	38	55	7	0	88·63
	94	11	0	63	21	5	38·69
	149	0	47	49	4	0	129·71
Social service	114	15	0	31	31	23	72·49
	117	60	40	0	0	0	167·08
	123	100	0	0	0	0	300·00
	127	40	40	20	0	0	96·83
	128	0	50	25	25	0	155·63
	133	100	0	0	0	0	300·00
	143	22	56	22	0	0	172·40
Women's organisations	98	10	25	45	15	5	21·90
	118	20	0	80	0	0	72·10
	124	25	75	0	0	0	357·69
	132	25	25	50	0	0	34·05
Hobby/special interest	107	75	10	10	5	0	137·05
	108	1	4	50	20	25	71·14
	115	45	12	31	12	0	26·59
	129	10	20	30	5	35	111·77
	134	40	30	20	10	0	50·68
	138	10	50	35	5	0	128·11
	139	5	13	58	24	0	40.36

Table 4.5 continued

	Number of organisation*	Occupational group					Chi-square value
		1 (25)	2 (13)	3 (41)	4 (13)	5 (8)†	
Political	72	5	35	40	10	10	54·45
	91	20	30	30	15	5	27·61
	109	5	5	20	63	7	224·11
Sports	71	55	20	20	5	0	63·45
	74	0	0	70	20	10	62·78
	119	27	59	9	5	0	200·83
	125	10	60	30	0	0	202·87
	135	100	0	0	0	0	300·00
	136	12	18	35	5	30	74·98
	140	30	10	50	10	0	12·36
	145	28	47	21	0	4	114·04
	147	10	20	40	15	15	19·23
	148	50	0	50	0	0	60·98
Other	88	24	48	19	9	0	115·31
	105	50	30	20	0	0	78·99

* For key to names of organisations see Appendix, p. 223.
† Bracketted numbers are the total '000 each occupational group represents in the population of East Kilbride.

'over-representation' of occupational group 1 in the leadership in relation to the proportion they make up in the membership, is being confirmed in this study as well.

As far as a comparison between the distribution of occupational groups within these youth organisations, and the distribution within the town as a whole, is concerned, it is of interest to note that the non-uniformed organisations, i.e. the Exit Club (no. 22), the Preston Youth Club (no. 26) and the YW/YMCA (no. 35) are showing a pattern of distribution, which more closely resembles that of the town as a whole, than any of the other organisations in this category (see table 4.4).

Table 4.6

Livingston − comparison of occupational status of
membership/population

	Number of organisation*	Occupational group					Chi-square value
		1 (7)	2 (12)	3 (55)	4 (17)	5 (9)†	
Youth	152	20	20	25	30	5	57·56
organisations	158	5	0	0	45	50	300·47
	161	0	0	20	50	30	154·33
Social	167	15	0	15	0	70	480·68
service	168	0	15	75	0	10	32·13
Women's	169	10	25	50	15	0	25·06
organisations	170	75	25	0	0	0	755·65
	172	0	0	55	0	45	180·00
Hobby/special	173	88	12	0	0	0	1018·29
interest	175	8	32	52	8	0	47·40
Political	176	4	3	50	20	23	30.80
Sports	159	0	0	50	50	0	92·51
	177	0	0	60	40	0	59·57
	178	62	25	13	0	0	504·30
	182	15	15	35	8	27	57·93

* For key to names of organisations see Appendix, p. 223.
† Bracketted numbers are the total '000 each occupational group
represents in the population of Livingston.

Glenrothes: arts and cultural organisations

As the bar-charts in fig. 4.3 show, in three of the organisations in this
category, i.e. the Art Club (no. 5), the Gaelic Club (no. 10) and the
Musical and Operatic Society (no. 13) all five occupational groups were
represented, and, as a comparison with fig. 4.1 illustrates, groups 1 and 2
formed a larger proportion of these organisations than they did of the
total population. Two groups, the Film Society (no. 16) and the Little
Theatre (no. 33), had no members in group 5 and the Floral Art Club
(no. 51) consisted entirely of members of occupational groups 1−3. This
club also had the highest proportion (43 per cent) of members in group 1.

Fig. 4.2 Glenrothes: youth organisations—occupational groups

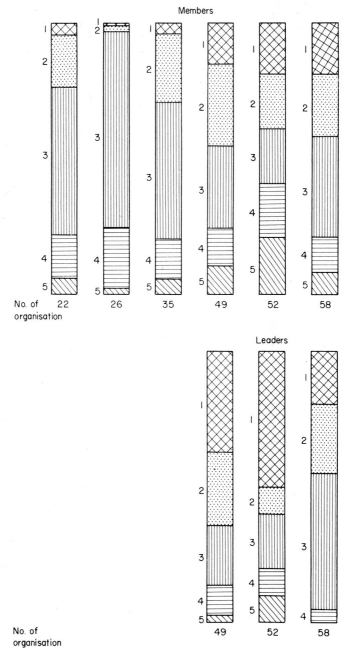

Members

No. of organisation: 22, 26, 35, 49, 52, 58

Leaders

No. of organisation: 49, 52, 58

N.B. For key to names of organisations in figs. 4.2 to 4.25 see Appendix, p. 223

Fig. 4.3   Glenrothes: arts and cultural organisations—occupational groups

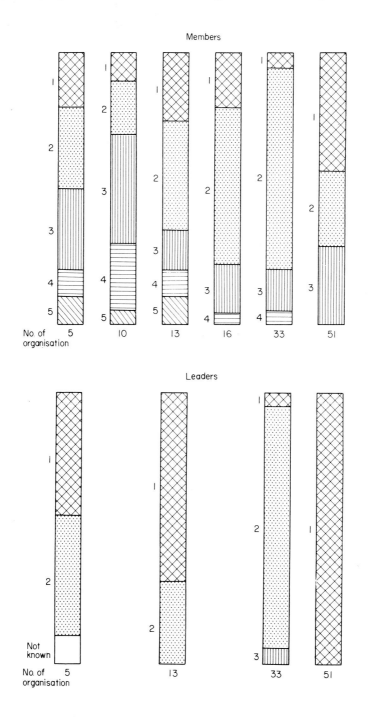

Where figures for the occupational group distribution of the leadership were available they once again illustrate that groups 1 and 2, but particularly group 1, provided proportionately a greater number of leaders than any other group represented in the membership. In terms of 'representativeness' of the total population, it is of interest to note that the occupational class distribution of the Gaelic Club (no. 10) most closely resembled that of the general population, followed by the Art Club (no. 5) and the Musical and Operatic Society (no. 13). On the other hand, membership of the Little Theatre (no. 33) and to a lesser extent of the Floral Art Club (no. 51) and the Film Society (no. 16) would appear to attract predominantly members of occupational groups 1 and 2 (see table 4.4).

Glenrothes: social service organisations

In this category only one organisation, the Social Amenities Council (no. 19) had members from all of the five occupational groups, and as table 4.4 shows is therefore also most 'representative' of the general population. As can be seen from the bar-charts in fig. 4.4, all the other organisations only embraced three occupational groups, i.e. the St. Andrews Ambulance Association (no. 34) and the Toastmasters Club (no. 45), or two, as the Round Table (no. 7), or are made up of members of only one occupational group, as Rotary (no. 11) and the Red Cross (no. 15). In the case of Rotary and the Round Table, the composition of the membership is clearly a function of their respective recruitment policies, which have already been referred to, and to some extent the same would appear to apply to the Toastmasters Club as well.

The bar-charts relating to the composition of the leadership illustrate again the 'dominance' of occupational group 1. This was particularly true of the Red Cross, where the committee consisted entirely of members of group 1 and the members as such (who were all said to be in group 2) were not represented. In a sense it would appear to be true, as Bottomore put it, 'that those who can afford to dispense charity – are the leaders of charitable organisations'. In terms of 'representativeness' of the general population, it is not surprising that Rotary and Round Table least resemble the composition of the general population, since, as was pointed out above, membership of these organisations is by invitation only. On the other hand, the Social Amenities Council most closely followed the occupational distribution of the town's population, from which it seeks its 'representatives' (see table 4.4).

70

Fig. 4.4　Glenrothes: social service organisations—occupational groups

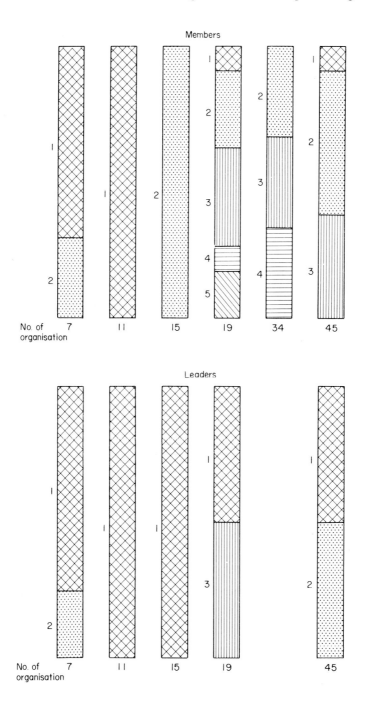

Members

No. of organisation
7　11　15　19　34　45

Leaders

No. of organisation
7　11　15　19　45

Fig. 4.5   Glenrothes: women's organisations—occupational groups

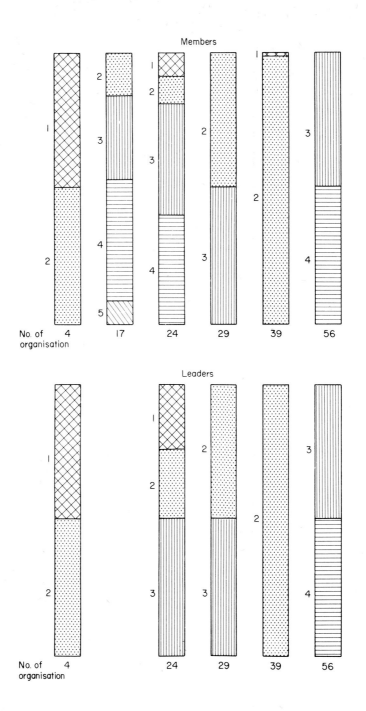

Members

No. of   4   17   24   29   39   56
organisation

Leaders

No. of   4   24   29   39   56
organisation

Glenrothes: women's organisations

As can be seen from the bar-charts in fig. 4.5 not one of the women's organisations drew its membership from all five occupational groups. It would therefore appear that these organisations attracted members from certain occupational status groups only. The exceptions to this were the Co-operative Guild (no. 17), which because of its political affiliation could be said to have at least as part of its purpose the elimination of differences based on occupational status; and the Catholic Women's Guild (no. 24), which was the only organisation specifically for Catholic women and would therefore presumably accept any member who fulfilled the primary conditions for joining (i.e. was a Catholic woman) without any further differentiation on grounds of status.

The bar-charts illustrating the composition of the leadership are particularly interesting in as much as they, perhaps more than in any other category of organisations, reflect the composition of the membership. The exception to this was the Catholic Women's Guild (no. 24) where groups 1 and 2 accounted for 20 per cent of the membership, but for 50 per cent of the leadership, and, at the other end of the scale, the 40 per cent of members said to be in group 4 were not represented at all. However, this exception within this category would tend to confirm the 'rule' found almost everywhere else, regarding the prevalence of higher status groups among the leadership, in disproportion to their numbers in membership (see Table 4.1). Comparing the occupational composition of these organisations with that of the town as a whole, it can be seen from table 4.4 that the Catholic Women's Guild (no. 24) and the Women's Co-operative Guild most closely followed that pattern of the town, whereas the WRI (no. 39) and the Townswomen's Guild (no. 4) would appear to be least representative.

Glenrothes: hobby/special interest groups

A number of interesting factors emerge from the bar-charts in fig. 4.6. In most of the organisations, all five (or at least four of the five) occupational groups were represented in the membership. Only the Angling Club (no. 53) would appear to be attracting members only from occupational group 3. In the Chess Club (no. 14) and the Camera Club (no. 25) there were no members from group 5, and at least as far as the Camera Club is concerned, this may be explained possibly on account of the expense involved in being an amateur photographer. As might be

Fig. 4.6   Glenrothes: hobby/special interest groups—occupational groups

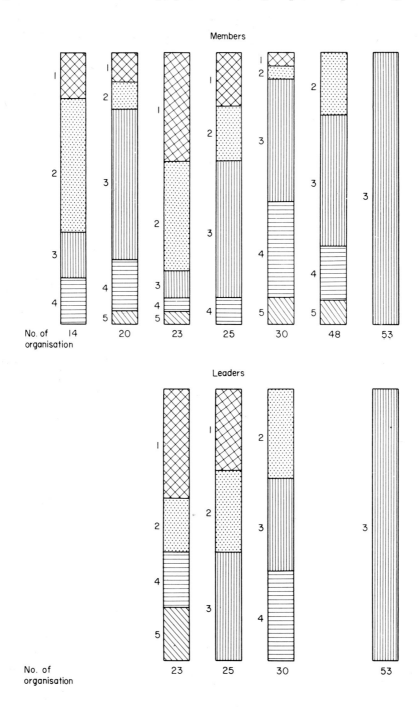

74

expected, the Bridge Club (no. 23) had a large contingent of members (40 per cent) from group 1; what is more interesting however is the fact that 5 per cent of its members were found in occupational group 4 and another 5 per cent in group 5. The club secretary confirmed this, and although he thought this to be unusual, was not able to explain the reason for this. It would appear however that this might be a function of the location and character of the meeting place (Woodside Community Hall), and of the low annual membership fee.

Only four of the seven organisations in this category were able to indicate the occupational group of their leaders. As table 4.1 shows, the proportion of members and leaders per occupational group is identical in the Angling Club (no. 53), followed by the Camera Club (no. 25). It is interesting to note that in the Bridge Club, contrary to the notion of dominance of occupational group 1, which so far has been observed in connection with most of the organisations, groups 4 and 5, which account for 10 per cent of the membership, together provide 40 per cent of the leadership. This can be considered to be an exception, but it would appear that the small group of members in groups 4 and 5 are also very active in providing leadership. [33] In the Camera Club (no. 25), once again the 'rule' to which the Bridge Club provides an exception, would appear to be confirmed again. Groups 1 and 2 provided 40 per cent of the membership, but 60 per cent of the leadership, and group 4, which accounted for 10 per cent of the membership was not represented among the leaders at all. The Rothes Invitation (Racing Pigeons) Club (no. 30) provides a further interesting exception in as much as this was only one of five organisations in this sample (the other four being the Archery Club (no. 12), the Festival Society (no. 2), the Rothes WRI (no. 39) and the Communist Party (no. 55)), in which occupational group 1 was represented in the membership, but did not provide any leaders. However in the case of the Rothes Invitation Club it might possibly be considered to be more suprising to find any members in group 1 at all, since racing pigeons has traditionally been regarded as a 'working-class' leisure pursuit. When comparing the composition of the membership of these organisations with that of the town as a whole (table 4.4) it is of interest to note that the two organisations concerned with gardening (nos. 20 and 48) most closely resemble the pattern of the town as a whole. But then, as Bottomore pointed out, [34] the nature of the activities is of great significance. 'A Rotary Club whose members meet once a week to have lunch together is a very different organisation from a horticultural society whose members cultivate their own gardens and may meet only once a year at the annual show.'

Of the four organisations in this category which were able to supply data on the occupational status of their members, three had members in all five groups. Two of these, the Women's Section of the Communist Party (no. 43) and the Communist Party proper (no. 55), would presumably point out that it is part of their political doctrine to abolish any differences based on occupational status. On the other hand, 50 per cent of the members of the Young Conservatives (no. 50) were found to be in occupational group 1 and the remaining 50 per cent in group 3.

Looking at the bar-charts relating to the composition of the leadership it is interesting to note that in the case of the Scottish National Party (no. 9) and Women's Section of the Communist Party (no. 43) the shift of dominance, which was observed in most other organisations, occurs again. In other words, in the case of the Scottish National Party, occupational group 1 provided 11 per cent of the membership, but 28 per cent of the leadership, whereas group 5, which has 23 per cent of the membership was not represented among the leadership at all. A similar trend, albeit less marked, can be observed in the Women's Section of the Communist Party. There occupational group 1 accounted for 17 per cent of the membership, but for 25 per cent of the leadership, and group 5, which was represented by 17 per cent in the membership, was not found in the leadership at all.

However, with the other two organisations, the Young Conservatives (no. 50) and the Communist Party (no. 55), this shift also took place – but in the opposite direction. In the case of the Young Conservatives, group 1 accounted for 50 per cent of the membership, but only 10 per cent of the leadership. This at first appeared to be surprising, but a possible clue for this situation might be found in Bottomore's observation [35] relating to Conservative organisations in Squirebridge, where he found that the members with high occupational status were less inclined to attend regularly. One of the factors in this, he suggested, was that the Conservative organisations were regarded as conferring prestige, and that those members with a slightly lower occupational status sought, by 'assiduous attendance and whole-hearted participation to raise themselves in the world'. In the case of the Communist Party (no. 55) occupational groups 1 and 2 accounted for 15 per cent of the members, but they were not represented in the leadership at all. On the other hand the skilled workers, which accounted for 33 per cent of the membership provided 75 per cent of the leadership. As table 4.4 illustrates, the Communist Party also happened to be the one organisation in this category, with the occupational status composition, which most closely resembled that of the population of the town.

Fig. 4.7 Glenrothes: political organisations—occupational groups

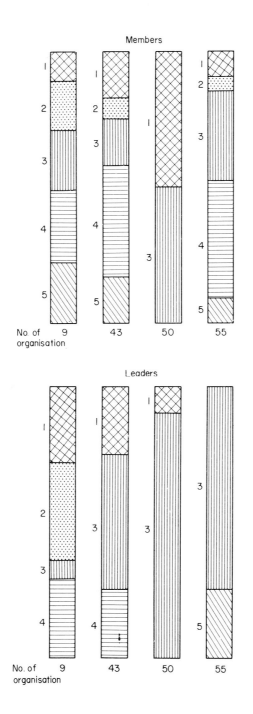

Fig. 4.8   Glenrothes: sports organisations—occupational groups

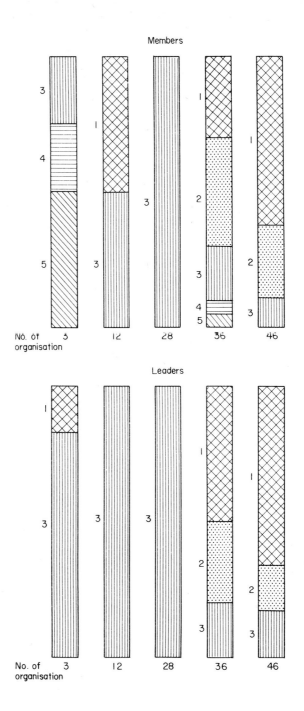

Members

No. of
organisation

Leaders

No. of
organisation

78

Glenrothes: sports organisations

It is of interest to note that only one of the organisations in this category (see fig. 4.8) would appear to cater for members in all five occupational groups, namely the Golf Club (no. 36). The Boxing Club (no. 3), on the other hand, only attracted members from occupational groups 3–5 (50 per cent being in group 5). The Bowling Club, which is attached to the Recreation Centre and Social Club, consisted entirely of members in occupational group 3. When comparing the composition of the leadership with that of the membership, it is found that once again group 1 was more prominently represented in proportion to the actual number of members. For instance, in the Boxing Club (no. 3) there were no members in group 1, but 17 per cent of the leadership belonged to this group. The Archery Club (no. 12), as has already been noted, was an exception to this 'rule'; but in the Golf Club and the Mountaineering Club once again occupational group 1 figured prominently in the leadership. Table 4.4 shows that none of the sports organisations represented here could really be said to resemble in the occupational status structure the town as a whole, although, because of the predominance of group 3 in the general population, the Bowling Club comes nearest to it.

Glenrothes: social/dancing organisations

The two organisations represented by the bar-charts in fig. 4.9, i.e. the Glenrothes Recreation Centre and Social Club (no. 21) and the British Legion (no. 32) are to all intents and purposes the equivalents of 'working men's clubs', and are therefore not catering for members in occupational groups 1 and 2. However it is interesting to note that no members in the British Legion would appear to come from groups 4 and 5, and none in the Recreation Centre and Social Club from group 5.

Glenrothes: old people's organisations

It is of interest to note that not one of the three organisations represented by the bar-charts in fig. 4.10 would appear to cater for members in occupational group 5. On the other hand, group 1 figured more prominently in the leadership than in the membership, except in the case of the Sunshine Club (no. 27) where the proportions were equal as far as group 1 was concerned. Group 4 was represented in all three organisations in the membership, but not in the leadership. Once again, as with every other category, except in a few cases, the leadership tended to be confined to the higher occupational status groups. Table 4.4 illustrates that the

Fig. 4.9   Glenrothes: social/dancing organisations—occupational groups

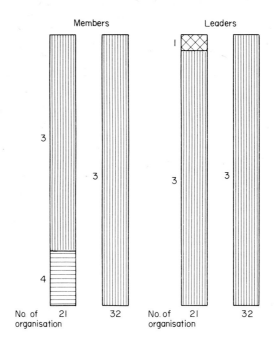

Fig. 4.10   Glenrothes: old people's organisations—occupational groups

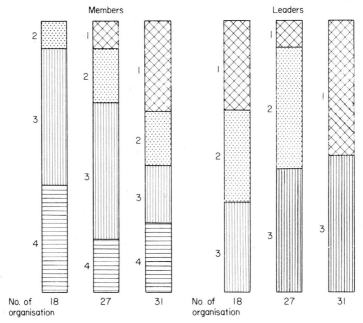

Fig. 4.11   Glenrothes: 'other' organisations—occupational groups

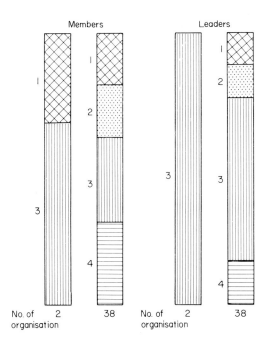

distribution of occupational groups in the Sunshine Club (no. 27) most closely resembled that of the population at large.

Glenrothes: Others

Both organisations represented in fig. 4.11 were 'community associations', the Festival Society and the Glenrothes Community Association.

It is of interest to note, for instance, that although occupational group 1 made up 33 per cent of the membership of the Festival Society (no. 2), none were among its leaders. In Bottomore's terms, one of the factors might be that leadership in this society, particularly since it had been declining for some time, was not seen to be 'status-conferring'. Similarly the community association had proportionately more group 1 members than leaders (19 per cent as opposed to 12 per cent). Both organisations at the time of this study were going through a period of stagnation, and according to their secretaries, it was difficult to find people who were willing to serve as leaders and committee members. However, whether this was the cause, or an effect of this decline would be difficult to determine.

East Kilbride: youth organisations

As the bar-charts in fig. 4.12 illustrate, only two organisations, the Scouts (nos. 60—8) and the Duncanrig Youth Club (no. 103), had members from all five occupational groups. This is in contrast with the situation in Glenrothes, where every youth organisation in the sample comprised members from all five groups. It is also of interest to note that, as was the case in Glenrothes, the uniformed organisations (i.e. the Scouts, the Venture Scouts and the Girl Guides) attracted the highest proportion of children of parents in occupational group 1. The bar-charts relating to the composition of the leadership once again confirm the general trend, which has been observed throughout the Glenrothes sample, namely the disproportionate representation of occupational group 1 within the leadership as compared with the number of members in that group. Two exceptions to this however have to be noted, i.e. the Venture Scouts (no. 69) and the Murray Youth Club (no. 101), where the proportions were exactly equal in both the membership and leadership. In the case of the other three organisations, where such a comparison was possible the proportions varied considerably. For instance, in the case of the Scouts (nos. 60—8) occupational group 1 accounted for 5 per cent of the members, but for 18 per cent of the leaders, and group 5, although represented in membership, did not provide any leaders. This shift was even more marked in the case of the South Parish Youth Club (no. 81) where occupational group 1 was not represented among the membership, but provided 50 per cent of the leaders; and again in the Girl Guides (no. 96) where groups 1 and 2 accounted for 40 per cent of the members and constituted 90 per cent of the leadership. Finally, when comparing the composition in terms of occupational groups within the membership of these organisations, with that of the town at large (see table 4.5), it is of interest to note that the uniformed organisations most closely resembled the composition of the town's population, whereas in Glenrothes it was the non-uniformed organisations which did so.

East Kilbride: arts and cultural organisations

The bar-charts in fig. 4.13 show that two of the organisations in this category had members from all five occupational groups, namely the Light Opera Club (no. 80) and the Burgh Pipe Band (no. 94). The other two organisations, the Rolls Royce Male Choir (no. 84) and the Repertory Theatre Club (no. 149) would appear to be catering for occupational groups 2—4 only. As far as representation among the leaders was concerned, however, in each of the organisations, for which figures were

82

Fig. 4.12   East Kilbride: youth organisations—occupational groups

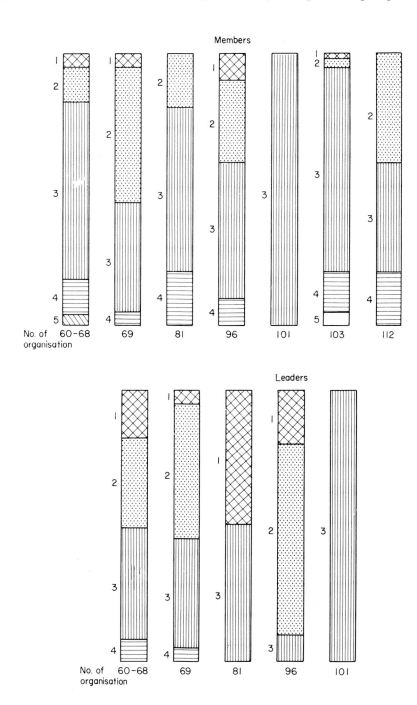

Fig. 4.13   East Kilbride: arts and cultural organisations—occupational groups

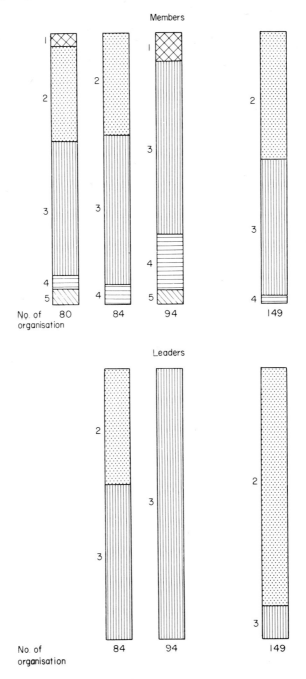

available, the lower status groups 4 and 5 were not found in the leadership. However, it is of interest to note that in the case of the Burgh Pipe Band, although all five groups were reputed to be in membership, the leadership consisted entirely of members in group 3. A shift of this kind however, as has been shown, was an exception. In fact in the East Kilbride sample there were only six organisations which had members in group 1, which were not represented in the leadership. A comparison of the composition of the leadership with that of the membership shows that the Rolls Royce Male Choir (no. 84) most closely reflected the composition of its membership in the leadership (see table 4.2). On the other hand, it would appear from table 4.5 that the membership of the Burgh Pipe Band resembled the general population more closely than any other organisation in this category.

East Kilbride: social service organisations

Once again, as was found with the organisations in this category in Glenrothes, membership (and even more so, leadership) of social service organisations was to a large degree the domain of the higher status occupational groups (see fig. 4.14). Only one organisation, the St Andrews Ambulance Association (no. 114), had members in all five groups. The Red Cross (no. 128) also, the only other 'first aid' organisation in the sample, had members in occupational group 4, but the remainder would appear to be very much more exclusive. The Round Table (no. 117) consisted entirely of members in groups 1 and 2, the Inner Wheel (no. 123) (the wives of Rotarians), and the Royal National Life Boat Institution (no. 133) had only members from group 1. However, in the strict sense of the word, the RNLI has no 'membership', but exists as a committee to raise funds. Once again it would appear that Bottomore's dictum about membership (and leadership) of charitable organisations – consisting of those who could afford to dispense charity – is shown to be correct.

As far as leadership is concerned, there would appear to be only one exception to the trend of 'higher-status dominance', which has been observed with the St Andrews Ambulance Association (no. 114). The bar-chart shows that all five groups were represented among the membership, but only group 3 provided leadership. On the other hand, just as was the case in Glenrothes, the Red Cross (no. 128) has no members in group 1, but 25 per cent of the leaders were from that group. Table 4.2 illustrates that there was in fact only one other organisation in the East Kilbride sample (South Parish Youth Club, no. 81) where the

Fig. 4.14   East Kilbride: social service organisations—occupational groups

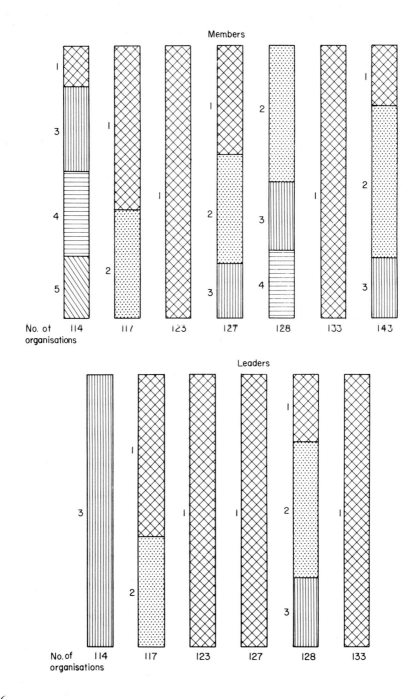

difference in composition between membership and leadership was greater. The comparison between membership and the population at large, as contained in table 4.5 shows that the St Andrews Ambulance Association (no. 114) most closely resembled the pattern of the town, followed by the Educational Association (no. 127).

East Kilbride: women's organisations

As can be seen from the bar-charts in fig. 4.15, only one of the women's organisations catered for all five occupational groups, i.e. the Calderwood Ladies Club (no. 98). In Glenrothes no women's organisation embraced all five groups — as far as it is possible to generalise from these two samples, it would therefore appear that there are very few women's organisations which cater for women in all occupational groups, and particularly those in low-status groups. Of the remaining three organisations, the Business and Professional Women's Club of course specifically incorporated in its name that it only caters for a given group. The composition of its membership was therefore a function of its recruiting policy. It is also of interest to note that, as was the case in Glenrothes, by and large the leadership of organisations in this category reflected the composition of the membership closely, although the Auldhouse WRI (no. 118) was another one of the few exceptions where group 1 was represented in the membership, but not in the leadership. Table 4.5 illustrates that the Calderwood Ladies Club (no. 98) resembled the composition of the general population most closely, followed by the Townswomen's Guild (no. 132).

East Kilbride: hobby/special interest groups

As fig. 4.16 illustrates, each one of the organisations represented in this sample embraced members from at least four occupational groups, and two of them, the Freemasons (no. 108) and the Photographic Club (no. 129), had 25 per cent and 35 per cent respectively of their members in group 5. It was also observed in Glenrothes that organisations in this category appear to be able to attract a wide cross-section of the community, with members from the various occupational groups mixing in the same clubs, in pursuit of a specific hobby or special interest. However, once again the bar-charts relating to the leadership of these organisations show that with the exception of two organisations, the higher status occupational groups accounted in every case for a higher proportion among the leaders than among the members. The two exceptions were the St Andrews Lodge (Freemasons, no. 108) and the

Fig. 4.15　East Kilbride: women's organisations—occupational groups

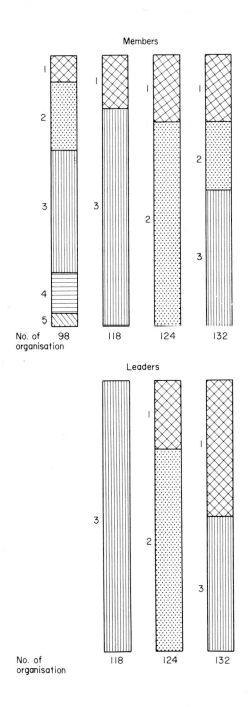

Fig. 4.16   East Kilbride: hobby/special interests groups—occupational groups

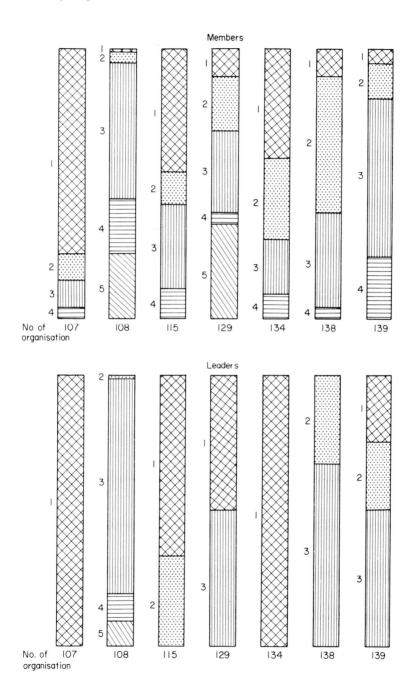

Chess Club (no. 138) where group 1 was represented in the membership, but not in the leadership. On the other hand, in both the Bridge Club (no. 134) and the United Nations Association (no. 107) four occupational groups were represented in the membership, but all the leaders were drawn from group 1. With the remaining organisations in this category, the same shift of emphasis can be observed. Table 4.5 indicates that in this category the membership of the Savings Committee (no. 115) and the Motor Club (no. 139) more closely resembles the composition of the population at large.

East Kilbride: political organisations

As was the case in the Glenrothes sample (see fig. 4.7), each of the political parties represented by the bar-charts in fig. 4.17 drew its membership from all five occupational groups. Furthermore, a number of factors emerged which are of interest. For instance the Westwood Ward Labour Party (no. 91) had 20 per cent of its members in occupational group 1 and 20 per cent in groups 4 and 5 combined. The 20 per cent of members in group 1, however, provided 70 per cent of the leadership and groups 4 and 5 were not represented at all. In the neighbouring ward of West Mains, which is older and also incorporates parts of the old village of East Kilbride, the Ward Labour Party (no. 109) had members in all five groups, but the 20 per cent found in group 3 provided virtually all the leadership. Details for the occupational group compositions of the various wards that make up East Kilbride were not available, but it might be possible to surmise that the different compositions of these two ward associations of the Labour Party are a function of the two different phases of development of the towns which they represent. (The bulk of West Mains was completed in the period 1955–59, whereas a major part of Westwood was not completed till the period 1965–70.) It is also of interest to note that of these three organisations, the Conservative and Unionist Association had the kind of leadership structure which most closely resembled the pattern of the membership. Although group 1 had only 5 per cent of the membership and provided 10 per cent of the leadership, and group 5 had 10 per cent of the membership and only 5 per cent represented in the leadership, the 'shift of dominance' was not as marked as, for instance, in the Westwood Ward Labour Party (no. 91). It was also a relatively rare occurrence to find that all five groups, which made up the membership, were also found in the leadership.

Comparing the membership composition with the population at large, as in table 4.5, it was found that the Westwood Ward Labour Party most

Fig. 4.17 East Kilbride: political organisations—occupational groups

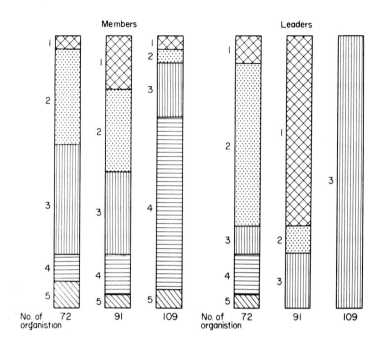

closely reflected the pattern prevailing in East Kilbride as a whole.

East Kilbride: sports organisations

From the bar-charts in fig. 4.18 it would appear that, with a few exceptions, organised sports activities were mainly pursued by the first three occupational groups. Of the organisations for which information was available, only two would appear to cater for all five occupational groups, namely the Sub-Aqua Club (no. 136) and the East Kilbride Hamilton and District Gun Club (no. 147). In the case of all the other organisations groups 1—3 would appear to provide the majority of members, except in the case of the Rugby Club (no. 74) where groups 1 and 2 were not represented in the membership at all.

Given therefore the preponderance of members in the higher status occupational groups in membership, it is not surprising to find that group 1 once again provided a higher proportion of leaders than members. For instance, the Ladies Hockey Club (no. 125) had 10 per cent of its members in group 1, but this group provided 70 per cent of the leaders. Or, in the case of the East Kilbride Sports Council (no. 145) which

91

Fig. 4.18   East Kilbride: sports organisations—occupational groups

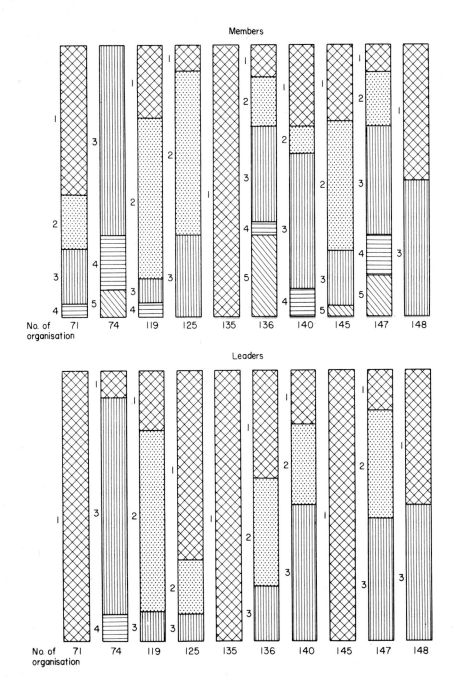

92

consisted of delegates from various sports organisations, group 1 accounted for 28 per cent of the membership, but for 100 per cent of the leadership. There were some exceptions to this, where the composition of the leadership was identical with that of the membership – as in the Torrance Rifle Club (no. 135) and the Bowling Club (no. 148), or the Cricket Club (no. 119) where the difference was minimal. The overall tendency, however, would appear to be that the majority of the officials of sports organisations were of high occupational status. Bottomore[36] observed the same phenomenon in Squirebridge, and stated that the organisations themselves considered it to be desirable that their affairs should be in the hands of officials of some standing, who did not have to account for every minute of their time, and who possibly could make use of clerical assistance and had ready access to a telephone. To some extent of course, this could be said to apply to officials in any one of the categories into which organisations have been put in this study – however, it would seem that this comment is particularly relevant in the case of sports organisations, which, at least during the playing season, require a great deal of day-to-day administration, such as arranging fixtures, notifying teams, booking playing fields, finding referees etc.

It is also of interest that the three sports organisations which according to table 4.5 would appear to reflect most closely in their membership the composition of the town's population were the Curling Club (no. 140), the Gun Club (no. 147) and the Bowling Club (no. 148), which are all minor sports but can be pursued by members of almost all ages.

East Kilbride: others

As was the case in Glenrothes, both organisations represented by the bar-charts in fig. 4.19 were 'community associations'. As can be seen, the East Kilbride Civics Association (no. 88) had members in four occupational groups and the Whitemoss Residents Association (no. 105), which confined its membership to a clearly defined geographical area, consisted of members from occupational groups 1–3 only. In both cases, only members from groups 1 and 2 were represented in the leadership, thus once again bearing out the tendency of higher status members to be 'over-represented' in the leadership, a tendency which has been observed throughout this, and the Glenrothes sample.

Livingston

Since Livingston is a very much younger new town than either Glenrothes or East Kilbride, naturally fewer organisations were in existence at the

Fig. 4.19   East Kilbride: 'other' organisations—occupational groups

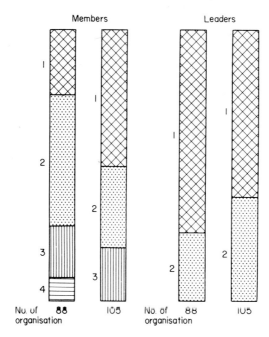

time of this study, although their number is growing all the time. Furthermore, with some of the organisations the membership had not been consolidated yet to the extent which would have allowed the secretaries to compile reliable membership records, or indeed supply a breakdown of the membership into occupational groups. Consequently the sample for which it was possible to draw up bar-charts is smaller than in the other two towns, which in turn does not allow for detailed comparisons, other than at the level of general trends.

Livingston: youth organisations

The bar-charts in fig. 4.20 represent the YMCA/YWCA (no. 152), the 1st Calders District Rangers Unit (no. 158) and the Riverside Youth Wing Over 15's Club (no. 161). Each of these in a sense represents a different category of organisation according to a distinction which is frequently made in the youth service, namely a voluntary organisation, a uniformed organisation and a local authority youth club. Whilst it would be difficult to generalise from such a small sample, it is of interest to note that the local authority youth club (no. 161) would not appear to attract any

Fig. 4.20   Livingston: youth organisations—occupational groups

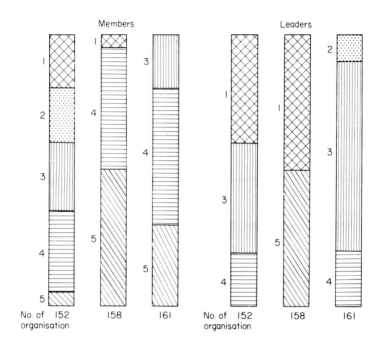

members in occupational group 1 and 2. The YMCA/YWCA (no. 152) was in fact the only organisation in this category which would appear to be able to attract members from all five occupational groups. In this respect this category would appear to differ from the sample in Glenrothes, where every organisation contained members from all five groups. In East Kilbride, however, as fig. 4.12 illustrates, the majority of clubs did not cater for all five occupational groups. The trend, according to which the higher status occupational groups were found to be more prominent in the leadership in comparison with the proportion they made up of the membership, was once again apparent. This was particularly marked in the case of the Rangers Unit (no. 158) where 5 per cent in group 1 in the membership, provide 50 per cent of the leadership. Table 4.3 illustrates that the pattern of distribution of occupational groups in the membership, compared with that of the leadership, was almost similar in the case of the YMCA/YWCA (no. 152). As table 4.6 shows, this is also the organisation in which the membership most closely resembled the composition of the population of Livingston.

Fig. 4.21   Livingston: social service organisations—occupational groups

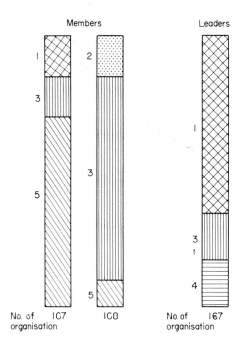

Livingston: social service organisations

The two organisations represented in this category, see fig. 4.21, were the Citizens Advice Bureau (no. 167) and the St Andrews Ambulance Association (no. 168). It would appear that, as in Glenrothes, the St Andrews Ambulance Association did not have any members in occupational group 1. A comparison, however, between the membership and the leadership was not possible, since figures for the leadership were not available. In the case of the Citizens Advice Bureau (no. 167) it is of interest to note that 15 per cent of the membership in group 1 accounted for 66 per cent of the leadership. On the other hand, 70 per cent of the members [37] were in group 5, which was not represented in the leadership at all.

Livingston: women's organisations

Two points of interest appear to emerge from the bar-charts in this category, see fig. 4.22. First, as was the case in Glenrothes and East Kilbride (with one exception), in Livingston, too, not one of the women's organisations catered for members from all five occupational groups. In

96

Fig. 4.22   Livingston: women's organisations—occupational groups

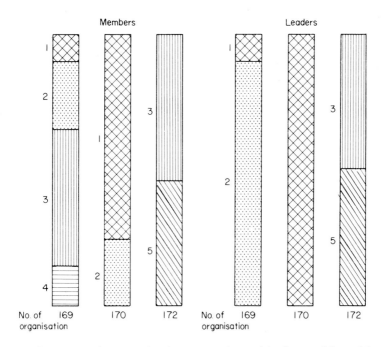

other words women's organisations can be said, from this evidence, to attract members from specific status groups. The Craigshill SWRI (no. 169) catered for four occupational groups and would therefore appear to embrace a fairly wide cross-section of the community. The Howden Ladies Club (no. 170) on the other hand, drew its membership entirely from occupational groups 1 and 2, which also happens to be concentrated in one geographical area (see also fig. 6.28 on p. 183). The Co-operative Women's Guild, by contrast, attracted members from groups 3 and 5 only. Secondly, a further observation, which would appear to be applicable to women's organisations in all three new towns, relates to the 'representativeness' of the leadership. In each of the towns it would appear that the composition of the leadership more closely resembled that of the membership than in any other category of organisation. In other words, although the 'shift of dominance' which took place in most organisations also took place in the case of women's organisations, it was less marked than anywhere else. Of the women's organisations represented in fig. 4.22, it would appear from table 4.6 that the Craigshill SWRI (no. 169) resembled in its composition the population at large, more so than any other organisation in this sample.

Livingston: hobby/special interest groups

The two organisations represented in this category were the Bridge Club (no. 173) and the Camera Club (no. 175). It is interesting to note that whereas in Glenrothes the bridge club (see fig. 4.6, no. 23) had members from all five occupational groups, and in East Kilbride (see fig. 4.16, no. 134) it had members from groups 1–4, in Livingston only two groups were represented (see fig. 4.23). In fact, 88 per cent of the members were from group 1 and 12 per cent from group 2. In Glenrothes and East Kilbride, these two occupational groups accounted for 80 per cent and 70 per cent of the membership respectively. On the other hand, the leadership consisted of members of group 1 only, both in Livingston and East Kilbride, whereas in Glenrothes, as was noted earlier, group 1 only accounted for 40 per cent of the leadership. A comparison between the camera clubs in these three towns shows that the composition of the Livingston club and the Glenrothes club were very similar. Occupational groups 1 and 2 accounted for 40 per cent in each case, group 3 for 50 per cent and 52 per cent respectively, and group 4 for 10 per cent and 8 per cent in each case. Group 5 was not represented in either of these two. In

Fig. 4.23   Livingston: hobby/special interest groups—occupational groups

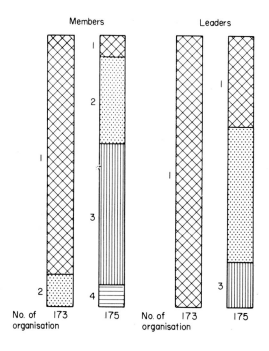

East Kilbride however, the Camera Club (no. 129) had over a third of its members (35 per cent) in group 5. This marked difference in composition may possibly be accounted for by the following factors: first, the East Kilbride club asked for a lower annual subscription (£1) than the two clubs in Glenrothes and Livingston, where the annual subscription was £1.50 and £2.10 respectively. Second, the East Kilbride club met in public premises, a school which was readily accessible for members, even without cars, whereas the Glenrothes club had its own premises and the Livingston club met at Howden House – and both of these meeting places were readily accessible by car only. It would therefore appear to be possible from this evidence to support the suggestion that cost of membership and accessibility of the premises are important factors, which determine whether certain occupational groups are to be found in the membership of a particular organisation or not – perhaps much more so than the actual type of activity which is offered.

Livingston: political organisations

The only organisation for which information was available was the Craigshill Branch of the Scottish National Party (no. 176). Only limited comparisons were therefore possible, particularly since the East Kilbride sample did not include a Scottish National Party Branch. However, it is interesting to compare the composition of the Livingston Craigshill Branch (see fig. 4.24, no. 176) with that of the SNP in Glenrothes (see fig. 4.7) both for their similarities and dissimilarities. The respective bar-charts show that in Glenrothes there was a higher proportion of members in groups 1 and 2, namely 11 per cent and 18 per cent respectively. Group 3 accounted for twice as many members in Livingston than in Glenrothes, i.e. 50 per cent as opposed to 22 per cent, but the proportions of members in group 4 turned out to be remarkably similar (20 per cent and 26 per cent respectively), and indeed in both SNP branches the proportion of members in group 5 was identical with 23 per cent in each case. This also happens to be the highest proportion of members in occupational group 5 noted with any of the political organisations in all three towns, which would suggest that at the time of the study, at least in terms of membership, the Scottish National Party had more support proportionately among the members of occupational group 5 than any other political party.

Livingston: sports organisations

Once again, as with sports organisations in Glenrothes and East Kilbride,

Fig. 4.24   Livingston: political organisations—occupational groups

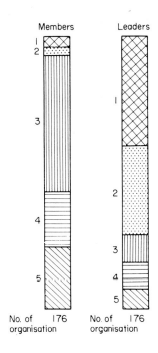

most clubs in Livingston tended to cater for one or two specific occupational groups, and those attracting members from all five occupational groups were a minority (see fig. 4.25). In Livingston only the Rugby Club (no. 182) had members in all five groups. The Riverside Table Tennis Club (no. 159) had 50 per cent of its members in group 3 and the remaining 50 per cent in group 4. A comparison between the two badminton clubs, the Grove (no. 177) and the Riverside Badminton Club (no. 178) is particularly interesting in as much as it supports the suggestion that different clubs cater for different occupational status groups, sometimes even if they pursue the same activity. For instance, the Grove Badminton Club had 60 per cent of its members in group 3 and 40 per cent in group 4, whereas the Riverside Club had 62 per cent in group 1, 25 per cent in group 2 and 13 per cent in group 3. The bar-charts relating to the leadership again illustrate that the higher status groups provide most of the leadership. (See also discussion of this point under 'East Kilbride: sports organisations' above.)

100

Fig. 4.25   Livingston: sports organisations—occupational groups

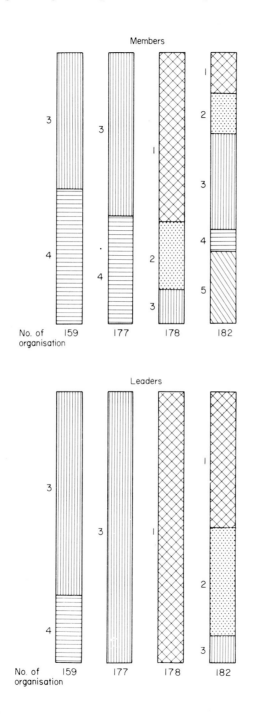

Summary

As noted in the introduction to this chapter, the Reith committee assumed that the various occupational classes would all play their part in the social organisations of the new towns. Lewis Silkin reiterated this aspiration when he stated that it was his hope 'that the different classes would mix freely in their leisure'. One must now ask how far these expectations have been fulfilled in the three new towns subject to this study. Table 4.7 shows the proportion of organisations in each of the three towns which contain members of a given number of occupational classes. This in turn can be taken to be an indication as to the extent to which organisations do act as 'meeting grounds' for all sections of the community.

Table 4.7

Number of occupational groups represented in organisations

	Percentage of organisations containing				
	at least 5 occupational groups	at least 4 occupational groups	at least 3 occupational groups	at least 2 occupational groups	1 occupational group only
Glenrothes	30·6	47·2	61·1	86·1	13·9
East Kilbride	17·9	53·8	76·9	87·2	12·8
Livingston	21·4	35·7	64·3	100·0	—

It is of interest to note that in all three towns less than a third of all organisations catered for all five occupational classes.[38] On the other hand, in Glenrothes slightly less, and in East Kilbride slightly more, than half (47·2 per cent and 53·8 per cent respectively) cater for at least four occupational classes. In fact, as the table illustrates, as the minimum number of occupational groups catered for decreases, so the proportion of organisations in that particular category rises. For instance, in Glenrothes 61·1 per cent of all organisations had within their membership people from at least three occupational classes, and 86·1 per cent from at least two classes. A similar development can be observed both in East Kilbride and Livingston.

At the other end of this particular scale it is found that in Glenrothes and East Kilbride 13·9 per cent and 12·8 per cent of the organisations cater for one occupational class only. However, the bar-charts illustrate that it would be wrong to assume that one-class organisations necessarily cater for class 1 (see, for instance, fig. 4.12, no. 101, or fig. 4.6, no. 53). On the other hand, in Livingston all organisations in this sample had at least two occupational classes among their members.

Since there were some differences in the occupational class composition of the population of these three new towns (see fig. 4.1), it was thought to be useful to compare the composition of the various organisations with that of the particular town in which they operated, in order to achieve some measurement of the 'representativeness' of the membership. This, it was felt, would give a further indication as to how far these organisations fulfilled a function as meeting grounds for the different sections of each of these three communities. Table 4.8 summarises, by categories, the results given in tables 4.4, 4.5 and 4.6, which indicate the chi-square value of this comparison for every organisation.

From this table a number of interesting factors emerge. It would appear that judging by the above criteria of 'representativeness' the youth organisations in each of the three new towns were more representative of the general population in terms of occupational groups than any other category of organisation (except in Livingston, where they were no. 2 in the rank order). It would therefore appear that the youth organisations above all provided the kind of meeting ground where every section of the community was represented. However, beyond this definite statement, applying to all three towns, a number of trends appear to be discernible, particularly when Glenrothes and East Kilbride are compared with each other (Livingston more often than not provides an exception in cases where the different stage of development of that town would appear to be significant). For instance, it has already been pointed out that social service organisations tend to cater for those who are in a position to 'dispense charity'. Table 4.8 would tend to confirm this in as much as both in Glenrothes and East Kilbride the social service organisations ranked last in their particular order (nos 10 and 8 respectively). The women's organisations too have been found to cater for specific occupational classes only, frequently leaving out the lower status groups. It is therefore significant that in all three towns they rank low in the particular ranking order. On the other hand, the hobby/special interest groups, at least in Glenrothes and East Kilbride, would appear to be able to provide a meeting ground for a cross-section of the community. In Livingston however, it was too early to draw conclusions, since the type

Table 4.8

Summary comparison of occupational status of membership/population in all three towns (average chi-square value* per category)

	Glenrothes	Rank order	East Kilbride	Rank order	Livingston	Rank order
Youth organisations	31·93	1	78·97	1	70·79	2
Arts and cultural	157·88	7	79·57	2	–	–
Social service	475·10	10	180·63	8	256·41	4
Women's organisations	223·73	8	121·44	7	320·24	5
Hobby/special interest	78·59	4	80·81	3	532·85	6
Political	125·60	6	102·05	5	30·80	1
Sports	270·15	9	111·15	6	149·02	3
Social/dancing	62·96	3	–	–	–	–
Old people's	61·19	2	–	–	–	–
Other	93·62	5	97·15	4	–	–
Overall average chi-square value for all organisations	175·15		109·07		255·11	

* If composition of membership were identical with composition of general population, then chi-square value = 0·00.

of organisation found in this category is among those which can only get under way once a given catchment has been developed up to a given point. It is also of interest that in Glenrothes and East Kilbride the political parties, taken as a category, rather than individually (for individual scores see tables 4.4 and 4.5), were no more than 'moderately' representative of the population in their membership. The exception to this was found in Livingston, where however the sample only consisted of one organisation, i.e. the Scottish National Party, which at the time of the study was in fact one of the organisations with a membership composition which most closely resembled that of the town at large. The sports organisations would appear to be less significant as instruments of 'mixing' all sections of the community than might have been assumed, at least as far as the samples for Glenrothes and East Kilbride are concerned. It is however conceivable that they might play a more important role in this respect at an earlier stage of the development of a new town, since in Livingston they rank third, as compared with ninth and sixth in Glenrothes and East Kilbride respectively. The social/dancing and old people's organisations were in this instance only represented in the Glenrothes sample – the community associations, listed under category 'others' in Glenrothes and East Kilbride both figure at mid-point in their respective ranking orders.

As far as it is meaningful to calculate an average chi-square value, measuring the 'representativeness' of all the organisations in these three new towns, it is interesting to note that generally the organisations in East Kilbride were more akin in the composition of their membership to the composition of the general population, than Glenrothes and Livingston. Whether or not there is a relationship between the 'maturity' (i.e. stage of development) of a town, and the degree to which its organisations become 'representative' would be difficult to demonstrate conclusively within the remit of this study, although it is of interest that according to table 4.8 it happens to turn out that way. In other words, East Kilbride, which is the town in the sample which is nearest to completion, provided the lowest chi-square value in this comparison, followed by Glenrothes, which is not as near yet to its eventual target; and the highest chi-square value (more than twice that of East Kilbride) is indicated by Livingston, which is the most recent development.

Apart from ascertaining the incidence of different occupational groups within the membership, an attempt has been made in this chapter to establish how far the leadership was representative (proportionately) of the membership. The results of this part of the investigation, which have been discussed above in more detail, are summarised in table 4.9 by categories according to town.

Again this table is of interest, both because of the parallels between the new towns and the differences which emerge. For instance, it is striking that in both Glenrothes and East Kilbride the category with the lowest recorded chi-square value (and therefore those most suitable in terms of composition of leadership compared with the membership) was the women's organisations. Also in Livingston this category ranked among the first three.

Table 4.9

Summary comparison of occupational status of membership and leadership in all three towns (average chi-square value per category)

	Glenrothes	Rank order	East Kilbride	Rank order	Livingston	Rank order
Youth organisations	37·40	3	46·17	3	164·11	4
Arts and cultural	88·57	7	43·65	2	—	—
Social service	118·34	9	74·52	4	—	—
Women's organisations	17·70	1	25·00	1	89·44	3
Hobby/special interest	76·65	6	101·41	6	66·72	1
Political	95·21	8	204·01	8	672·13	5
Sports	33·27	2	109·61	7	82·28	2
Social/dancing	—	—	—	—	—	—
Old people's	73·28	5	—	—	—	—
Other	44·40	4	86·20	5	—	—

Furthermore, the youth organisations in both Glenrothes and East Kilbride ranked third, the hobby/special interest group ranked sixth in both, and the political organisations, again in both, ranked eighth; and in Livingston too, the discrepancy between the composition of leadership and membership was greatest in this category. With only a few exceptions which have been referred to above, these differences were accounted for by the 'shift of dominance' towards the higher status groups. It has been shown that they tended to be represented in the leadership to a greater extent, proportionately, than in membership. It is therefore possible to state that a relationship exists between high occupational status and the exercise of leadership, without however being able to specify the precise nature of this relationship.

In this respect the findings of this study, as they relate to participation and leadership, would seem to concur with those of a number of other studies in this field. Bottomore, for instance, found the same to be true in

Squirebridge. [39] Similarly, L. Reissmann, referring to a number of American studies [40] stated:

> the combined findings of a number of separate studies seemed clearly to support the existence of a positive relationship between social class position on the one hand, and the character and extent of leisure activity and social participation on the other. Those in 'higher' class positions were more active and diverse in their participation than those in 'lower' positions. Phrased in somewhat less rigorous terms, this can be interpreted to mean that middle class generally tends to dominate the organisational activity, the intellectual life and the leadership of the community.

Further evidence pointing in the same direction, at least as far as the link between high occupational status and holding office in associations is concerned, comes from W. Bell and M. Force who wrote (again in the *American Sociological Review*): [41] 'Men living in the high economic status neighbourhoods belong to the greater number of associations, attend more frequently and hold office more often than men living in low economic status neighbourhoods.' From within the United Kingdom too there are a number of examples which would tend to support the above findings. Vereker and Mays, for instance, found in their study of social conditions in central Liverpool that the working class were less frequent 'joiners' and that areas in which working class predominated were characterised by a paucity of formal activities. [42] Willmott and Young too found that in Woodford [43] 'clubs and other organisations plainly attracted middle class people more than working class'. Similarly, Cauter and Downham [44] found in Derby that the middle-class people 'were easily more interested in joining clubs'. Josephine Klein [45] in *Samples from English Cultures* comments on the question of leadership as follows: 'The history of working class associational life is bedevilled by the fact that leadership in many associations comes from the same classes who are thought of as "they".' In other words there exists a *de haut en bas* relationship. As far as the tendency of 'joining' as a middle-class peculiarity is concerned, she warns that there are certain difficulties of interpretation, i.e. there are forms of association, say emanating from an informal gathering in a pub, such as darts clubs and domino leagues, etc., which are not readily listed by (middle-class) social scientists as formal associations. The fact that this particular study does not claim to include all forms of social activity in these three new towns, has already been stated. However, having sounded this warning, Klein did not doubt the validity of the findings of Young and Willmott and Cauter and Downham referred to above. Furthermore,

Peter Willmott, in another article, [46] which is more closely relevant to the present research than any of the other studies quoted as examples, compared East Kilbride with Stevenage and wrote:

> The residents of both new towns, after a little more than a decade, enjoy a good deal more of this kind of organised activity than do those of the 40 year old housing estate (i.e. Becontree estate at Dagenham). This contrast with Dagenham is partly explained by social class differences between the new towns and the estate. Whereas the population of the latter is overwhelmingly working class in occupation, both new towns have fairly high proportions of professional, managerial and white collar people. And in both new towns, more of what might be called the middle classes belong to clubs than do in other parts of the country.

This statement suggests that there is a relationship between social class and membership (and therefore incidence) of social organisations; and also makes clear that in terms of the image which 'haunted' the Reith committee, 'a series of new Becontrees' has indeed been avoided. Furthermore, this chapter shows that mixing of different sections of these communities does take place to a certain extent within social organisations, and to varying degrees. However, whether or not it can be said to have met the ideals and assumptions of the Reith committee, and indeed the postwar Labour government, responsible for passing the appropriate legislation, largely depends on the political and ideological standpoint of the reader interpreting these figures.

Notes

[1] This quotation is from the terms of reference of the New Towns Committee — see Final Report of the New Towns Committee Cmnd 6876, HMSO, London 1946.

[2] R. Thomas, 'London's new towns', PEP no. 510, London 1969, p. 381.

[3] Ibid., p. 382.

[4] Final Report of the New Towns Committee, op.cit., p. 10.

[5] R. Thomas, op.cit., p. 383.

[6] Ebenezer Howard, *Garden Cities of Tomorrow*, Faber & Faber, London 1945.

[7] Lewis Silkin, *Journal of the National Institute of British Architects*, 1948.

[8] Report of Hemel Hempstead Development Corporation 1947/48, PP. 1948–49 (113) xviii HMSO, p. 65.

[9] Frank Schaffer, *The New Town Story*, MacGibbon and Kee, London 1970, p. 166.

[10] See also Report of Harlow Development Corporation 1953/54, PP 1953/54 (230) xvii HMSO, p. 247.

[11] Op.cit., fig. 1, p. 168.

[12] Ruth Glass, 'Urban sociology', *Current Sociology*, no. 4, 1955, pp. 14–19.

[13] Op.cit., p. 167.

[14] Peter Mann, 'A socially balanced neighbourhood unit', *Town Planning Review*, no. 29, 1958/59.

[15] Clarence Perry, *Housing for the Machine Age*, New York 1920.

[16] 'Design of dwellings', Ministry of Health, HMSO, 1944.

[17] 'Size and social structure of a town', National Council of Social Service, London 1943.

[18] B.J. Heraud in *Urban Studies*, vol. 5, no. 1, February 1968.

[19] House of Commons Debates, sessions 1945/6, vol. 422, col. 1088, 8 May 1946.

[20] H. Orlans, *Stevenage – a Sociological Study of a New Town*, Routledge & Kegan Paul, 1952.

[21] Smailes, for instance, defines a balanced community as one with a representative economic or social structure, i.e. 'one which conforms to that of the country as a whole'. See 'Balanced towns', *Journal of the Town Planning Institute* vol. 32, 1945.

[22] 'Livingston Master Plan', 1963, p. 74.

[23] P. Collison, 'Neighbourhood and class', *Town and Country Planning*, July 1955, p. 337.

[24] Heraud, op.cit., p. 54.

[25] J.H. Nicholson, 'New communities in Britain', NCSS, London 1961, p. 132.

[26] See also finding of this present study on preference of locality for clubs, etc., p. 122.

[27] He does so on the basis of his study of Crawley quoted in *Urban Studies*, vol. 5, no. 1, February 1961.

[28] H.J. Gans, 'The balanced community – homogeneity or heterogeneity in residential areas', *Journal of the American Institute of Planning*, vol. XXVII, no. 3, 1961.

[29] See the Final Report of the New Towns Committee, op.cit., p. 10, para. 23.

[30] These figures were based on the secretaries' records. In the case of

Glenrothes it was possible to corroborate the figures given by the secretaries with the aid of address lists, with the results of a household survey which the GDR conducted at the time.

[31] The chi-square comparison leadership/membership was possible for 61·0 per cent of the Glenrothes sample, 47·6 per cent of East Kilbride sample and 43·8 per cent of Livingston sample. The proportion of organisations for which comparison membership/towns population was possible is as follows: Glenrothes – 79·7 per cent; East Kilbride – 53·7 per cent; Livingston – 46·9 per cent.

[32] T.B. Bottomore, *Social Mobility in Britain,* Routledge and Kegan Paul, 1954, table 5, p. 358.

[33] Perhaps this is one of these situations which Bottomore is referring to when he wrote: 'The high occupational status of the members of an organisation may on the other hand, be an attraction to the individual whose own status is low if he is anxious to climb'. Op.cit., p. 368.

[34] T.B. Bottomore, op.cit., p. 370.

[35] T.B. Bottomore, op.cit., p. 363.

[36] T.B. Bottomore, op.cit., pp. 365–6.

[37] The term 'members' here denotes people who have undergone training courses for volunteers staffing CAB enquiry desks.

[38] As was also the case in Bottomore's Squirebridge (see p. 368, op.cit.), but it has to be noted that he used only three categories which make a more detailed comparison with his findings impossible.

[39] T.B. Bottomore, op.cit., p. 369.

[40] L. Reissmann, *American Sociological Review,* vol. 19, 1954.

[41] W. Bell and M. Force, 'Urban neighbourhood type and participation in formal associations' *American Sociological Review,* vol. 21, no. 1, February 1956, p. 333.

[42] C. Vereker and J.B. Mays, *Urban Redevelopment and Social Change: a study of social conditions in central Liverpool, 1955–56,* Liverpool University Press, 1961.

[43] P. Willmott and M. Young, *Family and Class in a London Suburb,* Routledge & Kegan Paul, 1960.

[44] T. Cauter and J.S. Downham, *The communication of ideas, a study of contemporary influences on urban life,* Chatto and Windus London 1954, pp. 64–6.

[45] Josephine Klein, *Samples from English Cultures,* vol. I, Routledge and Kegan Paul, London 1965, pp. 206–7.

[46] Peter Willmott, 'Some social characteristics of a Scottish and an English new town' *Town Planning Review,* vol. XXIV, 1963–64, p. 314.

5 Social Facilities

In established towns, numerous social facilities such as clubs, swimming pools, sports halls, pubs, cinemas, theatres etc., are part and parcel of the provisions which often have come to be taken for granted. Many of these provisions have been created over a long period, and are now maintained by local authorities, membership-based voluntary organisations or commercial enterprises. Often traditions have grown up which make it possible for former pupils, ex-members and the public at large to provide financial support for the creation, renovation or maintenance of social facilities of all kinds. By contrast, a new town has to start from scratch. Facilities, which elsewhere have developed over long periods, have to be created over a much shorter space of time, in other words, time needs to be 'telescoped'. When the building of a new town coincides with a time of financial stringency, it is tempting to put provision of social facilities aside as a luxury and concentrate on the building of houses and factories. Yet it can be argued that such provisions, far from being a luxury, are in fact essential to the success of a new town. In a free society, where freedom of mobility exists, new towns can only grow if people wish to move and settle there. If successions of new residents fail to be able to put down roots for themselves and their families, they will leave, and if they left in sufficient numbers the new towns programme would be in serious jeopardy. If it is therefore accepted that social organisations are a means by which people are helped to put down roots in a new community, then it follows that meeting places and other social facilities need to be made available as essential to the development of a new town, rather than tacked on as a frill at some date in the distant future.

In this chapter the types of premises available, their suitability and ideal location from the consumers' point of view will be examined, not only by way of evaluation of what has already been provided, but perhaps also some useful pointers regarding future policies might emerge, which have a wider application than the three new towns in which the field work for this study was undertaken.

5.1 Premises used by organisations

Tables 5.1, 5.2 and 5.3 give a summary of the various kinds of accommodation available to organisations in the three new towns, and also show the differing extent to which they were being used.

Glenrothes

In Glenrothes for instance, it was found that fifteen organisations (25·4 per cent) had exclusive use of their own premises and a further nine (15·3 per cent) hired accommodation from a club which owned its own building. The relative importance of the contribution to the provision of social facilities which commercial undertakings, such as public houses and hotels, can make is illustrated by the fact that they shared third place with the 'large community centre'. Both of these types of accommodation were being used by seven organisations (i.e. 11·9 per cent).

The apparent lack of popularity of school buildings as meeting places for social organisations in Glenrothes is illustrated by the fact that only four organisations (6·8 per cent) used them. The reason for the limited use of church halls can be explained by the fact that frequently these are mainly used by organisations attached to churches as such, which, as has been pointed out, have not been included in this sample.

East Kilbride

One of the interesting factors which emerges from table 5.2 is the smaller proportion of organisations which own their premises in East Kilbride, compared with Glenrothes. There, some 25 per cent of all organisations owned their buildings, whereas in East Kilbride the proportion was only 18·3 per cent of the total, although the actual number (15) was identical in both of these towns. Furthermore, the largest proportion of the premises owned by all organisations were found among the youth organisations in East Kilbride and Glenrothes. This would support the notion that youth organisations in particular attach a good deal of importance to owning their premises, to give them maximum independence and flexibility in the running of their activities.

On the other hand, a considerably higher proportion of groups in East Kilbride used school premises as meeting places than in Glenrothes (20·8 per cent as compared with 6·8 per cent). The contribution of commercial premises again was evident in the East Kilbride sample, where 14·6 per cent of all organisations met in such places.

Livingston

The most striking contrast between Livingston and the other two new

Table 5.1

Premises used – Glenrothes

	Youth organisations		Arts and cultural		Social service		Women's organisation		Hobby groups		Political		Sport		Social/ dancing		Old people		Other		Total	
	no.	%	no.	%	no.	%	no.	%	no.	%	no.	%	no.	%	no.	%	no.	%	no.	%	no.	%
Room in large community centre or social centre	–	–	1	16·7	–	–	3	33·3	3	33·3	–	–	–	–	–	–	–	–	–	–	7	11·9
Entire small community building, tenants' meeting room	–	–	2	33·3	–	–	2	22·2	–	–	1	16·7	–	–	–	–	1	25·0	–	–	6	10·2
Room belonging to another organisation	–	–	1	16·7	2	28·6	2	22·2	1	11·1	1	16·7	–	–	1	33·3	–	–	1	50·0	9	15·3
Room in pub or hotel	–	–	–	–	3	42·9	–	–	1	11·1	2	33·3	1	16·7	–	–	–	–	–	–	7	11·9
Church hall or room	1	14·3	–	–	–	–	–	–	–	–	–	–	–	–	–	–	1	25·0	–	–	2	3·4
Room/hall in school or college	2	28·6	1	16·7	–	–	–	–	–	–	–	–	1	16·7	–	–	–	–	–	–	4	6·8
Room in public building (e.g. library, council offices etc.)	–	–	–	–	–	–	1	11·1	2	22·2	–	–	2	33·3	–	–	–	–	1	50·0	6	10·2
Private house	–	–	–	–	1	14·3	–	–	–	–	2	33·3	–	–	–	–	–	–	–	–	3	5·1
Club owns/rents its own premises	4	57·1	1	16·7	1	14·3	1	11·1	2	22·2	–	–	2	33·3	2	66·7	2	50·0	–	–	15	25·4
Total	7		6		7		9		9		6		6		3		4		2		59	

Table 5.2

Premises used – East Kilbride

	Youth organisations		Arts and cultural		Social service		Women's organisations		Hobby groups		Political		Sport		Social/ dancing		Old people		Other		Total	
	no.	%	no.	%	no.	%	no.	%	no.	%	no.	%	no.	%	no.	%	no.	%	no.	%	no.	%
Room in large community or social centre	–	–	–	–	2	18·2	–	–	1	6·7	3	75·0	–	–	1	50·0	1	50·0	–	–	8	9·8
Entire small community building, tenants' meeting room	–	–	–	–	1	9·1	1	12·5	–	–	–	–	–	–	–	–	–	–	–	–	2	2·4
Room belonging to another organisation	–	–	1	14·3	–	–	–	–	3	20·0	–	–	2	13·3	–	–	–	–	1	33·3	7	8·5
Room in pub or hotel	1	5·8	1	14·3	3	17·3	2	25·0	2	13·3	1	25·0	3	20·0	–	–	–	–	–	–	13	15·1
Church hall or room	5	29·4	–	–	–	–	1	12·5	1	6·7	–	–	1	6·7	–	–	–	–	–	–	8	9·8
Room/hall in school or college	5	29·4	2	28·6	2	18·2	3	37·5	3	20·0	–	–	1	6·7	1	50·0	–	–	–	–	17	20·8
Room in public building (e.g. library, council offices etc.)	–	–	–	–	1	9·1	–	–	1	13·3	–	–	2	13·3	–	–	1	50·0	2	66·7	7	8·5
Private house	–	–	1	14·3	1	9·1	–	–	–	–	–	–	3	20·0	–	–	–	–	–	–	5	6·1
Club owns/rents its own premises	6	35·3	2	28·6	–	–	1	12·5	3	20·0	–	–	3	20·0	–	–	–	–	–	–	15	18·3
Total	17		7		10		8		14		4		15		2		2		3		82	

Table 5.3

Premises used – Livingston

	Youth organisations no.	%	Arts and cultural no.	%	Social service no.	%	Women's organisations no.	%	Hobby groups no.	%	Political no.	%	Sport no.	%	Social dancing no.	%	Old people no.	%	Other no.	%	Total no.	%
Room in large community or social centre	–	–	2	100·0	1	33·3	1	20·0	3	75·0	–	–	–	–	–	–	–	–	–	–	7	21·9
Entire small community building, tenants' meeting room	–	–	–	–	–	–	–	–	–	–	–	–	–	–	–	–	–	–	–	–	–	–
Room belonging to another organisation	–	–	–	–	–	–	–	–	–	–	–	–	–	–	–	–	–	–	–	–	–	–
Room in pub or hotel	–	–	–	–	–	–	–	–	–	–	–	–	–	–	–	–	–	–	–	–	–	–
Church hall or room	–	–	–	–	–	–	–	–	–	–	–	–	–	–	–	–	–	–	–	–	–	–
Room/hall in school or college	11	100·0	–	–	2	66·7	3	60·0	1	25·0	1	100·0	5	100·0	1	100·0	–	–	–	–	24	75·0
Room in public building (e.g. library, council offices etc.)	–	–	–	–	–	–	–	–	–	–	–	–	–	–	–	–	–	–	–	–	–	–
Private house	–	–	–	–	–	–	1	20·0	–	–	–	–	–	–	–	–	–	–	–	–	1	3·1
Club owns/rents its own premises	–	–	–	–	–	–	–	–	–	–	–	–	–	–	–	–	–	–	–	–	–	–
Total	11		2		3		5		4		1		5		1		0		0		32	

115

towns in this part of the study is to be found in the lack of choice of premises available at the time to the Livingston clubs. Obviously, this is to a considerable extent a function of time over which these towns have been in existence. Livingston is the newest of these three towns; nevertheless, as table 5.3 illustrates, it is interesting to note that only three different types of premises were available for use. These were Howden House, a former country mansion, which was adapted by the development corporation with the aid of funds from a major charitable fund (21·9 per cent of sample), the youth wings attached to the two primary schools in the area (7·5 per cent) and a private house, which was used by only one organisation.

It is entirely consistent with the findings of this and other studies that in a very young new town no organisation had so far been able to acquire its own premises, although almost by way of the exception confirming the 'rule' a group of people were then in the process of trying to buy an old farm and convert it into a community centre. The long drawn out and hard financial struggle this involved confirms the view that, unless premises can be inherited from an existing village, as was the case in some instances in East Kilbride, in the initial stages of a new town the new residents' resources are usually absorbed in equipping the new home, and very little spare finance or even time can be devoted to the creation of individual club premises, such as exist in traditional towns.

As will be noted, neither was there a public house or a hotel at that time, which would have been available as a meeting place. By the frequency with which they were being used, one might be led to believe that the policy of providing youth wings attached to schools, rather than separate community centres, had proved to be successful, however, as will be noted below, this was not the case. Looking at table 5.3, it may also appear to be surprising that no use was being made of church halls. This was simply because at the time no church buildings had been completed — in fact, the churches themselves held their services in school premises, which again illustrates the key position school buildings occupy in the provision of facilities available for social organisations in the early days of a new town.

5.2   Suitability of premises used

Glenrothes

Table 5.4 shows that in Glenrothes 71·2 per cent of all organisations considered the accommodation available for their use as suitable. As can

116

be seen however, the proportion of those satisfied in each category varied considerably. For instance, in three of the categories (i.e. social service, hobby and others) all organisations considered their premises to be suitable. At the other end of the scale, the level of satisfaction was lowest with the categories relating to arts and culture and political organisations, where in each case only a third of the organisations concerned found their premises to be suitable.

Table 5.4

Suitability of premises — Glenrothes

	Suitable		Unsuitable		No answer		Total
	no.	%	no	%	no.	%	no.
Youth organisations	5	71·4	2	28·6	—	—	7
Arts and cultural	2	33·3	4	66·7	—	—	6
Social service	7	100·0	—	—	—	—	7
Women's organisations	5	55·6	4	44·4	—	—	9
Hobby	9	100·0	—	—	—	—	9
Political	2	33·3	4	66·7	—	—	6
Sport	5	83·3	1	16·7	—	—	6
Social/dancing	2	66·7	1	33·3	—	—	3
Old people	3	75·0	1	25·0	—	—	4
Other	2	100·0	—	—	—	—	2
Total	42	71·2	17	28·8	—	—	59

The reasons advanced by organisations for their dissatisfaction with their premises were as varied as their respective activities and would be too numerous to mention here, but the following examples may serve as useful illustrations[1] of the kind of factors which, in the eyes of a particular organisation, renders premises unsuitable for their purpose.

One of the youth organisations, for instance, felt that their own building was no longer suitable on the grounds that it lacked shower facilities and a specific arts/crafts area, the absence of which was considered to be limiting the scope of their programme. This case also illustrates that it would be wrong to assume that the ownership of a separate building, which is what most youth organisations want, does not automatically mean that the needs in terms of facilities of a particular club will now be satisfied.

Among the categories for whom the provision of purpose-built accommodation was a high priority were the arts and cultural organisations. The only group who had exclusive use of their own premises in this category, was the art club. Every member has access at any time to the cottage/studio in which it was housed, and therefore did not have to remove an unfinished painting and store it away till the next opportunity to work on it arose, as might be the case, say, in an art class run on school premises.

The other groups in this category were mainly concerned with the performing arts in one form or another, such as the film society, the theatre group, and the musical and operatic society, who all felt that their facilities to rehearse and perform were not adequate for their purpose, these being a hall in a community centre, a works canteen and a school hall respectively.

By contrast, the hobby/special interest groups all found their premises suitable, largely because the main activity was not based on a building, such as gardening, angling, 'advanced motoring'. Where a regular and easily accessible base was essential, such as in the case of a camera club or an aero-modelling club, it was found that they had exclusive use of their premises.

The majority of the local political organisations found that particularly at election times, they missed having their own headquarters which could be used as a permanent base from which to recruit and campaign. One must add, of course, that perhaps unlike other categories it could be argued that the authorities conceivably do have a responsibility to help groups to find suitable premises from which to operate and make a contribution to the social fabric of the new town; that same responsibility perhaps does not extend in the same way to political organisations, important though their contribution is.

Given the great variety of activities which was pursued by the social organisations in general, and therefore the diverse needs which societies have to cater for, it is remarkable to find that over 70 per cent of the organisations found the premises available to them suitable.

East Kilbride

Table 5.5 indicates that overall 69·5 per cent of all organisations considered the premises they used suitable for their purposes. It is striking to note the similarity of these figures with the ones relating to Glenrothes (see table 5.4), where 71·2 per cent considered their premises suitable. Again the proportion of those which were satisfied varied from category to category, and in three of them (i.e. political, old people and other) all organisations were satisfied with the accommodation available to them. The lowest level of satisfaction was recorded by the sports organisations, where only a third found the facilities available to them suitable.

Table 5.5

Suitability of premises — East Kilbride

	Suitable		Unsuitable		No answer		Total
	no.	%	no.	%	no.	%	no.
Youth organisations	12	70·5	5	29·4	—	—	17
Arts and cultural	5	71·4	2	28·6	—	—	7
Social service	9	90·0	1	10·0	—	—	10
Women's organisations	6	75·0	2	25·0	—	—	8
Hobby	10	71·4	3	21·4	1	7·1	14
Political	4	100·0	—	—	—	—	4
Sport	5	33·3	9	60·0	1	6·7	15
Social/dancing	1	50·0	1	50·0	—	—	2
Old people	2	100·0	—	—	—	—	2
Other	3	100·0	—	—	—	—	3
Total	57	69·5	23	28·0	2	2·5	82

Comparing the two overall figures for Glenrothes with those of East Kilbride, it is particularly interesting to note that there should be differences between the same categories without any apparent reasons. For instance, in Glenrothes only a third of the political groups found their accommodation suitable, whereas in East Kilbride everyone of the parties accepted their premises as suitable, and yet the type of accommodation used in each town was very similar. The picture was also reversed in East

Kilbride in the case of the arts and cultural organisations. In Glenrothes two-thirds of the groups in this category found their accommodation unsuitable, whereas in East Kilbride over 70 per cent found theirs suitable, although again the range of premises available to these respective groups was similar. In the other categories, the differences between these two towns did not appear to be significant, as a comparison between tables 5.4 and 5.5 shows.

It would therefore appear that in both these towns, which were mark 1 new towns and among the first to be started, the 'maturing process' had brought in its wake a range of facilities which were considered to be suitable by 70 per cent of all the organisations in this sample. Whilst this does not provide reasons for complacency, it could be said that with the exception of some areas, such as cultural facilities in Glenrothes and sports facilities in East Kilbride, the general need for suitable premises by now had been met in both of these towns.

Livingston

As table 5.6 illustrates, the pattern in Livingston differed significantly from the ones found in the two older new towns. Only 56·3 per cent of all the organisations considered the accommodation available to them as suitable, whereas some 43·7 per cent looked upon theirs as unsuitable. These figures differ considerably from the ones found in the other new towns, where, as was noted above, in each case approximately 70 per cent of the organisations found their premises suitable. Given the very much more limited choice of venues available to the groups in Livingston (see table 5.3), it is perhaps more surprising to find over half the groups were accepting their accommodation as suitable.

However, as table 5.6 shows, the proportions differ from category to category, but due to the limited number of organisations in existence at the time in some categories, comparison with the other two new towns is not always feasible; nor is it sensible to talk in terms of 100 per cent suitable or unsuitable where there is only one organisation represented in a given category, as was the case with two of them.

In Glenrothes and East Kilbride it was possible to indicate ways in which the number of organisations which found their accommodation unsuitable could be reduced. In the case of Glenrothes it was the building of an arts centre cum theatre which would fill an obvious gap. In East Kilbride it was the provision of more and better sports facilities which would make a significant contribution to improve the situation.

In Livingston, on the other hand, the largest number of groups whose

Table 5.6

Suitability of premises – Livingston

	Suitable		Unsuitable		No answer		Total
	no.	%	no.	%	no.	%	no.
Youth organisations	7	63·6	4	36·4	–	–	11
Arts and cultural	1	50·0	1	50·0	–	–	2
Social service	2	66·7	1	33·3	–	–	3
Women's organisations	3	60·0	2	40·0	–	–	5
Hobby	1	25·0	3	75·0	–	–	4
Political	–	–	1	100·0	–	–	1
Sport	4	80·0	1	20·0	–	–	5
Social/dancing	–	–	1	100·0	–	–	1
Old people	–	–	–	–	–	–	–
Other	–	–	–	–	–	–	–
Total	18	56·3	14	43·7	–	–	32

needs were, at the time, not satisfactorily met were found in the youth category. In Glenrothes over half of all the youth groups had premises of their own, and in East Kilbride more than a third were in that position. It is therefore reasonable to assume that in Livingston too, the trend will be for youth groups to want to have their own premises. Since there is a reluctance to share accommodation with other youth organisations, it is unlikely that the provision of one centre for them all to use would meet the bill entirely. It is particularly interesting to note that the youth clubs, which started in the specially provided youth wings of the primary schools (and derived their names from these), were wanting to get premises of their own in spite of the fact that in a real sense the youth wings were 'their own premises'. It may therefore be, that a more flexible approach to the design and use of these youth wings, including the provision of more storage facilities and longer opening hours (which might for instance entail employing another part-time janitor), would help to solve some of the problems which arise and lead to dissatisfaction with their use.

In time also, national organisations such as the YMCA and YWCA, who traditionally have their own buildings, will want to build their own facilities. The scouts and guides will want to have their own headquarters, even if it is only a modest hut somewhere in the neighbourhood which they can call their own, although such a building might incur the planners' displeasure on aesthetic grounds.

These few comments should illustrate that, at least as far as the youth organisations are concerned, there is no single overall remedy available which would drastically alter the position. A variety of facilities would be required to meet diverse needs. However, drawing on the experience of the other two new towns, it would appear that in the case of the sports category the provision of a multi-purpose sports centre would not only be able to satisfy the needs of the existing clubs, but also help to meet demands which as yet might not have been fully formulated. Experience, however, in places like Glenrothes, Billingham, Edinburgh etc. has shown that imaginative sports complexes are able to attract a wide cross-section of the population, including whole families, who are keen to pursue their respective interests or learn new skills. The risk of creating a 'white elephant', which might be underused over a long period because it was built too far in advance of demand, is lessened, particularly if the kind of architectural approach is used which allows perhaps for a more modest beginning and expansion of the building as the demand grows.

An arts centre however, which seemed to commend itself in the other two, longer-established new towns, would at least on the evidence of this sample, not appear to be an immediate need, since there were only two groups in this category at the time. Of course, this is not to say that over a longer period of time, when more arts-oriented groups have emerged, such a centre might well become a real need, just as it had in larger established new towns.

5.3   Ideal location

Not only is it important that the actual premises available to organisations should be suitable for their purpose, frequently their location is a significant determining factor as to whether or not they are being used fully. It is therefore crucial that more should be known about the users' own comments and preferences regarding the location of certain facilities. However, at the time when some of these buildings are required, it is not necessarily already possible to predict their ideal location, particularly if a pattern of usage has not had time to emerge. This part of the study is therefore relevant to the situation of these new towns only in a limited, but nevertheless important, way.

Glenrothes

Table 5.7 illustrates that there is a great deal of variation, as to what would be considered to be the ideal location, even within the same categories. However the most striking feature in this table is the fact that twenty-seven organisations (i.e. 45·8 per cent) considered the ideal lcoation to be in the town centre. The second largest group, i.e. nine organisations (15·3 per cent) saw the ideal location for their facilities to be 'on the edge of the town or by an open space'. To a further eight organisations (13·6 per cent) the actual location did not matter. (Presumably as long as the premises as such were suitable.) Only seven organisations (11·9 per cent) felt that the local centre (i.e. the neighbourhood centre) was the ideal location for them. This is particularly interesting in a town like Glenrothes which has been planned and built largely on the neighbourhood principle. The report 'The needs of new communities'[2] introduced the idea of the 'concept of a hierarchy of social facilities' in the context of planning for a city such as Liverpool, but went on to suggest that this concept might also usefully be applied to expanded towns. Bearing the differences between an expanded town and a new town in mind, this study would suggest that the application of this concept might also be usefully considered in the context of new towns. It is true of course, that to some extent, such a hierarchy already exists, but the idea merits further examination and development both in principle and practice.

As already pointed out, nearly half of the *organisations* (i.e. 45·8 per cent) considered the centre of the town to be the ideal location for their meeting place. Furthermore, in half of the *categories* the majority of groups indicated the town centre as the ideal location. In a further two categories, the town centre ranked equal first as the ideal location. The exceptions to this pattern however are of particular interest. The majority of youth organisations and sports clubs placed a location 'on the edge of the town/by an open space' first. To them a central location would not appear to be of the same importance as in some of the other categories. Similarly, to the hobby groups the location is of less importance than to any other category, since the majority stated that the location did not matter to them. In the light of the growing tendency to add 'community facilities' or so-called 'youth wings' to school buildings, it is also of interest to note that not one of a total of fifty-nine organisations looked

Table 5.7

Ideal location – Glenrothes

	Youth organisations		Arts and cultural		Social service		Women's organisations		Hobby		Political		Sport		Social/ dancing		Old people		Other		Total		Rank order
	no.	%	no.	%	no.	%	no.	%	no.	%	no.	%	no.	%	no.	%	no.	%	no.	%	no.	%	
No answer	–	–	–	–	–	–	–	–	1	11·1	–	–	–	–	1	33·3	–	–	–	–	2	3·4	6
In town centre	1	14·3	4	66·7	4	57·1	4	44·4	2	22·2	5	83·3	2	33·3	1	33·3	2	50·0	2	100·0	27	45·8	1
In local centre, by shops	1	14·3	–	–	2	28·6	2	22·2	–	–	–	–	2	–	–	–	–	–	–	–	7	11·9	4
In residential area	1	14·3	1	16·7	–	–	–	–	–	–	–	–	–	–	–	–	2	50·0	–	–	2	3·4	6
In industrial area (works canteen)	–	–	–	–	–	–	–	–	–	–	–	–	–	–	–	–	–	–	–	–	–	–	8
On edge of town or by open space	3	42·9	–	–	–	–	–	–	2	22·2	1	16·7	3	50·0	–	–	–	–	–	–	9	15·3	2
Attached to school	–	–	–	–	–	–	–	–	–	–	–	–	–	–	–	–	–	–	–	–	–	–	8
Elsewhere	–	–	–	–	–	–	–	–	–	–	–	–	–	–	–	–	–	–	–	–	–	–	7
Does not matter	–	–	1	16·7	1	14·3	1	11·1	4	44·4	–	–	–	–	1	33·3	–	–	–	–	8	13·6	3
Current meeting place suitable	1	14·3	–	–	–	–	2	22·2	–	–	–	–	1	16·7	–	–	–	–	–	–	4	6·8	5
Total	7		6		7		9		9		6		6		3		4		2		59		

upon premises attached to a school as an ideal location. Considering however that Glenrothes was planned and built on the basis of the 'neighbourhood pattern', possibly the most significant point to emerge from table 5.7, apart from the overwhelming majority of both categories and groups within them, which considered the centre of the town to be the ideal location, is the small number of organisations which looked upon the local neighbourhood centre as their ideal location. Those which did would seem to fall into distinct and significant categories: youth, social service, women's organisations and those catering for old people. Table 5.7 shows that in all except one of these categories the town centre was the predominantly favoured ideal location. However, it would seem to be possible to generalise and claim that only some of the organisations catering for young people, women and old people in a town the size of Glenrothes have any desire for their meeting place to be in the centre of a particular neighbourhood, rather than the centre of the town itself. Since the two organisations in the category social service (i.e. Red Cross and WRVS) were also effectively women's organisations, they can readily be included in this generalisation. This would appear to support the notion of providing facilities on a 'hierarchical' basis, e.g. instead of distributing social facilities of every kind into every separate neighbourhood, as far as possible the establishment of meeting rooms, sufficient to meet the needs of some youth groups (particularly those catering for young children), women's groups and old people's clubs, would appear to be satisfactory, and would safeguard scarce resources to be used on providing multi-purpose facilities on a generous scale in the centre of the town.

East Kilbride

Table 5.8 illustrates that, as was the case in Glenrothes, the town centre was considered by far the most popular location for meeting places. Thirty-five organisations (i.e. 42·7 per cent of total) listed this as their ideal location. Again the proportion of organisations in each category which gave the town centre top preference varied, but it is striking to note that in every one but the old people's category, a location in the centre of the town was given first (or equal first) preference. Furthermore, as was the case in Glenrothes, apart from the old people's groups, the youth organisations did not opt for town centre locations to the same extent as other categories. In fact, in both East Kilbride and Glenrothes, a location on the 'edge of town/by open space' was just as important.

Overall, the local centre (i.e. neighbourhood) was considered to be the ideal location by twelve organisations (i.e. 14·6 per cent) followed by a

Table 5.8

Ideal location — East Kilbride

	Youth organisations		Arts and cultural		Social service		Women's organisations		Hobby groups		Political		Sport		Social/ dancing		Old people		Other		Total		Rank order
	no.	%	no.	%	no.	%	no.	%	no.	%	no.	%	no.	%	no.	%	no.	%	no.	%	no.	%	
No answer	1	5·9	—	—	1	10·0	1	12·5	1	7·1	—	—	1	6·7	—	—	—	—	—	—	5	6·1	5
In town centre	4	23·5	3	42·9	6	60·0	3	37·5	9	64·3	2	50·0	6	40·0	1	50·0	—	—	1	33·3	35	42·7	1
In local centre, by shops	3	17·6	1	14·3	1	10·0	1	12·5	2	14·2	1	25·0	—	—	—	—	2	100·0	1	33·3	12	14·6	2
In residential area	2	11·8	—	—	—	—	—	—	—	—	1	25·0	—	—	—	—	—	—	—	—	3	3·6	7
In industrial area (works canteen)	—	—	1	14·3	—	—	—	—	—	—	—	—	—	—	—	—	—	—	—	—	1	1·2	9
On edge of town or by open space	4	23·5	1	14·3	—	—	—	—	1	7·1	—	—	5	33·3	—	—	—	—	—	—	11	13·4	3
Attached to school	—	—	—	—	1	10·0	1	12·5	—	—	—	—	—	—	—	—	—	—	—	—	2	2·4	8
Elsewhere	—	—	—	—	—	—	1	12·5	1	7·1	—	—	1	6·7	—	—	—	—	—	—	3	3·6	7
Does not matter	—	—	—	—	—	—	1	12·5	—	—	—	—	1	6·7	1	50·0	—	—	1	33·3	4	4·9	6
Current meeting place suitable	3	17·6	1	14·3	1	10·0	—	—	—	—	—	—	1	6·7	—	—	—	—	—	—	6	7·1	4
Total	17		7		10		8		14		4		15		2		2		3		82		

location on the edge of the town, which was the preferred location of eleven organisations (i.e. 13·4 per cent). It would, therefore, appear that of the first three most popular locations in both these new towns, two are the same. The centre of the town was given first preference in both. And the 'edge of town' followed third in rank order in East Kilbride, and second in Glenrothes. Since both of these towns were designed to follow the neighbourhood principle which incorporated most of the kind of facilities social organisations were thought to want at neighbourhood level, it is of interest to note that in East Kilbride only 14·6 per cent, and in Glenrothes 11·9 per cent of all organisations would consider the local centre the ideal location for their activities.

The salient features regarding 'ideal location' which emerged from the East Kilbride sample can be summarised as follows. The centre of the town was again, as was the case in Glenrothes, regarded as the ideal location by a majority of organisations. In fact the proportions in both towns which gave this as their first preference were strikingly similar (i.e. Glenrothes 45·8 per cent and East Kilbride 42·7 per cent). Although the overall percentage was slightly higher in Glenrothes, in East Kilbride the actual number of categories which either ranked ideal location first or as equal first preference, was higher (9 out of 10 compared with 7 out of 10).

Old people's groups in both towns were the strongest supporters of the local centre as the ideal location, and in both towns attachment to a school was not considered to be ideal. In fact of the 141 organisations which made up the combined sample of both towns, only two listed this as their ideal location. On the other hand a considerably higher proportion (13·6 per cent) stated in Glenrothes that location to them did not matter, compared with East Kilbride where the equivalent figure was 4·9 per cent. This was most strongly apparent in the case of the respective hobby/ special interest categories, and it could be argued that this might partly be a function of the different sizes of these two towns.

Finally, the proportions relating to preferences for location in a 'residential area' were remarkably similar, i.e. 3·6 per cent in East Kilbride and 3·4 per cent in Glenrothes, as indeed were the proportions of those which indicated that their actual location was suitable, where the figures were 7·1 per cent and 6·8 per cent respectively.

Livingston

Table 5.9 summarises the views on 'ideal location' as expressed by the organisations in the Livingston sample. Although, as was the case in the

Table 5.9

Ideal location – Livingston

	Youth organisations no.	%	Arts and cultural no.	%	Social service no.	%	Women's organisations no.	%	Hobby no.	%	Political no.	%	Sport no.	%	Social/ dancing no.	%	Old people no.	%	Other no.	%	Total no.	%	Rank order
No answer	—	—	—	—	—	—	—	—	—	—	—	—	—	—	—	—	—	—	—	—	—	—	—
In town centre	2	18·2	—	—	2	66·7	—	—	1	25·0	—	—	1	20·0	1	100·0	—	—	—	—	7	21·9	1
In local centre, by shops	2	18·2	—	—	—	—	—	—	—	—	1	100·0	2	40·0	—	—	—	—	—	—	5	15·6	3
In residential area	2	18·2	—	—	1	33·3	1	20·0	—	—	—	—	—	—	—	—	—	—	—	—	4	12·5	4
In industrial area (works canteen)	—	—	—	—	—	—	—	—	—	—	—	—	—	—	—	—	—	—	—	—	—	—	—
On edge of town or by open space	2	18·2	—	—	—	—	—	—	—	—	—	—	1	20·0	—	—	—	—	—	—	3	9·4	5
Attached to school	3	27·3	1	50·0	—	—	2	40·0	—	—	—	—	—	—	—	—	—	—	—	—	6	18·8	2
Elsewhere	—	—	—	—	—	—	1	20·0	—	—	—	—	—	—	—	—	—	—	—	—	1	3·1	6
Does not matter	—	—	1	50·0	—	—	—	—	3	75·0	—	—	1	20·0	—	—	—	—	—	—	5	15·6	3
Current meeting place suitable	—	—	—	—	—	—	1	20·0	—	—	—	—	—	—	—	—	—	—	—	—	1	3·1	6
Total	11		2		3		5		4		1		5		1		0		0		32		

other two new towns, the town centre once again emerged as the location which attracted most support, the distribution of preferences turned out to be much more even in Livingston. Only seven organisations (i.e. 21·9 per cent) chose the town centre as their ideal location, which was approximately half the proportion found in the other two new towns. However, it also needs to be stressed that in Livingston the 'town centre' did not exist yet, other than on the master plan. Organisations were, therefore, dealing with an abstract alternative when choosing the town centre as an ideal location, whereas in both Glenrothes and East Kilbride the towns were substantially completed, and a town centre towards which some of the social activities tended to gravitate, had emerged. Therefore, as in previous comparisons, it was found that whilst it was possible to draw parallels in many instances between Glenrothes and East Kilbride, the case of Livingston frequently had to be considered separately, due to the different circumstances which prevailed.

The second most popular location, which was named by six organisations (18.8 per cent) was 'attached to a school'. In this respect, the pattern in Livingston differs markedly from that of the other two towns. However, this figure has to be seen in the light of the fact that four times as many organisations actually used school premises (twenty-four organisations, i.e. 75 per cent). The lack of 'popularity' which school premises enjoyed in the other two towns has, therefore, been confirmed in Livingston, in spite of the fact that youth wings have been added to some of the schools.

Third place in the rank order was shared by 'the local centre' and 'does not matter'. Each of these was mentioned by five organisations (i.e. 15·6 per cent). In connection with Glenrothes and East Kilbride the suggestion was put forward that the importance for certain categories of location was related to the size of the town. This was illustrated by the fact that in Glenrothes (which is smaller than East Kilbride) a larger proportion indicated location did not matter. This was particularly so in the case of the hobby groups. In Livingston too, the proportion for whom location did not matter was higher than in East Kilbride, and similar to the one found in Glenrothes – and again it was particularly the hobby category for whom location was not important. Again, the preferences indicated varied from category to category, as in the other two towns, although in marked contrast to tables 5.7 and 5.8, it was found that only two out of eight categories in fact put 'in the town centre' first. A further two categories preferred the local centre, and three (two plus one joint first) preferred a location attached to a school. Lastly, a further two (one plus one joint first) felt that location did not matter. This illustrates again the fact that the preferences for the various locations were very much more evenly distributed among the categories in Livingston than was the case in the other two new towns.

The findings of this part of the study in three of the Scottish new towns have shown that a great many social organisations, which are expected to make an important contribution to the success of a new town, desire to be able to operate from a reasonably central position. It may, therefore, be that in the interest of the social development of these communities, purely commercial considerations might have to take second place to important, social considerations, when sites are being allocated for their respective purposes. This is not to say that all social facilities, for every type of activity and every age group, have to be in the centre of the town to be successful and make a contribution to the life of the community. Hopefully, this study has shown that this is not required, but that it might be desirable to put into operation the kind of 'hierarchy of social facilities' Cullingworth mentioned. However, in the view of the author, the case for more facilities to be centrally located has been made, if the views and preferences of users of such facilities are to be taken into account in the planning of future facilities.

Notes

[1] For full details see chapter 12 of the author's Ph. D. thesis, 'A Comparative Study of Social Organisations in three Scottish New Towns', Edinburgh University 1972.

[2] Cullingworth et al., 'The needs of new communities', Ministry of Housing and Local Government, HMSO, 1967, p. 28.

6 Geographical Distribution of Membership/Location of Meeting Places

In the previous chapter the premises available to organisations were listed, and their views regarding suitability and ideal location of social facilities recounted. In this chapter a further dimension to the question of location of premises will be added. Many planners in this field are exercised by the question as to whether or not the siting of community facilities has a direct bearing on the recruitment of membership of organisations which use these facilities. It was therefore hoped that further light might be shed on this question by mapping the home addresses of the membership of individual organisations. A selection only will be presented here, representing various categories in each of the three towns, and where the pattern of membership distribution was thought to be significant in one way or another.

It has also been widely assumed that new towns would act as a focus for various activities for the area which surrounds them. This is indeed the case, to a lesser or greater degree, depending on the activity involved, as will be shown in this chapter.

6.1 Description of sites/catchment areas

Glenrothes

The site chosen when Glenrothes was designated to become a new town in October 1948 was an area of 5,730 acres immediately north of the East Fife Coalfield, between the parishes of Markinch in the east, and Leslie and Kinglassie in the west. The River Leven flows west—east through the area. The main railway line from Edinburgh to Aberdeen runs along the eastern boundary, while the A911 road runs east—west through the town north of the river. The A92 road from Edinburgh to Dundee (via the Forth Road Bridge and the Tay Bridge) runs south—north a little west of the eastern boundary. This brings Glenrothes within approximately an hour's journey of either city. The region is one of undulating land and wooded hills, with the Lomond Hills to the north and the Goatmilk Hills to the west, and it has been described as one of the most beautiful of the new town sites.[1] The altitude of the area is around 200–300 feet, and most of the site slopes gradually towards the Leven Valley on the north. The nearest major urban centre is Kirkcaldy, six miles south of Glenrothes.

East Kilbride

The town of East Kilbride is only eight miles south–east of the centre of Glasgow, and the built-up areas of Rutherglen extend to within one mile of the northern boundary of the site. However, the separation from the outskirts of Glasgow is more distinct than distance alone would suggest, by virtue of the fact that it is formed by a rugged ridge, the Cathkin Braes, rising to nearly 700 feet. Furthermore, there is a gap of approximately two miles between the boundary of the designated area and the developed part of the town. The designated area comprised 10,250 acres, which makes this one of the largest sites of any new town. This was done to enable the development corporation to preserve a green belt under its own control. The altitude of the site is around 500 feet, predominantly hilly, with several winding valleys draining into the Calder Water, which is a tributary of the Clyde. The town straddles the A749 road leading to Glasgow in a south–north direction, and the A726 to Strathaven on a north–west to south–east axis.

Livingston

Livingston is being built on a site of 6,700 acres straddling the Almond Valley. The designated area extends roughly five miles from the main Edinburgh–Glasgow road (M8) on the north to the outlying slopes of the Pentland Hills in the south. The site measures about 3½ miles from east to west, and is divided by the River Almond into a northern and southern section of approximately equal size. The area rises from 300 feet along the river channel, to about 700 feet at the northern and southern boundaries. Livingston's main road pattern gives the town its basic shape. It is enclosed to the north by the new M8 and to the south by the A71. By the Glasgow–Edinburgh road, it is thirty miles to the former, and fifteen miles to the latter. Furthermore, there are good routes to the north via the Forth Road Bridge and through the Bathgate Hills to Linlithgow and the Falkirk–Grangemouth growth area, and southwards across the Slamannan Plateau to Lanark and Carlisle. Two rail lines pass through the site, and the surrounding region, containing Bathgate and Broxburn in West Lothian, and the Calders area of Midlothian, is readily accessible.

132

Secretaries of organisations were asked to indicate whether any of their members lived outside the actual new town and travelled in to join in a particular activity, but no specific details as to how far members were prepared to travel have been ascertained. Tables 6.1, 6.2 and 6.3 summarise the proportion of clubs in each category which indicated that they had members who resided outside the new towns. Comparing the total proportions in these three towns with each other, it is interesting to note that in each case approximately half the number of organisations had members resident outside the new town as well. This should not be looked upon as surprising, since each of these new towns has within its immediate proximity villages such as Leslie, Thornton, Markinch in the case of Glenrothes, Busby, Eaglesham, Auldhouse in the case of East Kilbride, and Uphall, Midcalder and Pumpherston near Livingston. By and large, these villages did not have the same standard of facilities which the new towns can offer, nor was there the same diversity of activities available. Some of the organisations in the new towns, therefore, can be said to act as a kind of magnet, attracting members from the surrounding districts to join in its activities.

According to the tables, this would appear to be particularly true in relation to activities in the three categories arts and cultural (excepting Livingston in this instance), hobby/special interest and sport. The women's groups, old people's clubs and social service organisations, however, would appear to be much more 'localised'. In other words, since on the whole these organisations only required a straightforward meeting room, and were not dependent on the availability of sophisticated equipment, it is very likely that such rooms are also available in the surrounding villages to cater for similar local groups there. Furthermore, as found in chapter 5, dealing with the 'ideal location' the women's and old people's groups were also among those which preferred to meet in the local centre. The youth organisations, at least in Glenrothes and Livingston, were fairly evenly split between those which had members resident in the new town only, and those which also attracted members from outside. Usually the chief determining factor was the particular age group for which an organisation was catering, i.e. the younger age groups were more localised than those dealing with the more mobile teenagers. The exception to this pattern was found in East Kilbride where only four organisations also had members resident outside the town. Three of these, however, were of a more specialised nature, and therefore not likely to be found elsewhere in the district. These were the Young Farmers' Club, the Air Training Corps and the Girl Guides Association (i.e.

Table 6.1

Catchment area — Glenrothes

	Youth organisations		Arts and cultural		Social service		Women's organisations		Hobby		Political		Sport		Social/ dancing		Old people		Other		Total	
	no.	%	no.	%	no.	%	no.	%	no.	%	no.	%	no.	%	no.	%	no.	%	no.	%	no.	%
Members resident in new town only	3	42·9	1	16·7	4	57·1	5	55·6	1	11·1	2	33·3	2	33·3	2	66·7	3	75·0	2	100·0	25	42·4
Members resident outside new town as well	4	57·1	5	83·3	3	42·9	4	44·4	8	88·9	4	66·7	4	66·7	1	33·3	1	25·0	—	–	34	57·6
Total	7		6		7		9		9		6		6		3		4		2		59	

Table 6.2

Catchment area – East Kilbride

	Youth organisations		Arts and cultural		Social service		Women's organisations		Hobby		Political		Sport		Social/dancing		Old People		Other		Total	
	no.	%	no.	%	no.	%	no.	%	no.	%	no.	%	no.	%	no.	%	no.	%	no.	%	no.	%
Members resident in new town only	12	70·6	6	85·7	5	50·0	7	87·5	6	42·9	3	75·0	5	33·3	–	–	2	100·0	2	66·7	42	51·2
Members resident outside new town as well	4	23·5	1	14·3	5	50·0	1	12·5	8	57·1	1	25·0	10	66·7	2	100·0	–	–	1	33·3	38	46·3
Not stated	1	5·9																			2	2·4
Total	17		7		10		8		14		4		15		2		2		3		82	

Table 6.3

Catchment area – Livingston

	Youth organisations		Arts and cultural		Social service		Women's organisations		Hobby		Political		Sport		Social/ dancing		Old people		Other		Total	
	no.	%	no.	%	no.	%	no.	%	no.	%	no.	%	no.	%	no.	%	no.	%	no.	%	no.	%
Members resident in new town only	5	45·5	2	100·0	2	66·7	4	80·0	–	–	1	100·0	1	20·0	–	–	–	–	–	–	15	46·9
Members resident outside new town as well	6	54·5	–	–	1	33·3	1	20·0	4	100·0	–	–	4	80·0	1	100·0	–	–	–	–	17	53·1
Total	11		2		3		5		4		1		5		1		–		–		32	

the 'supporters' of the guide movement). More details referring to the proportion of members resident outside the new towns can be found in the pie-graphs which are inset into the maps.

6.2 Distribution of membership in relation to location of meeting place(s) in Glenrothes

In chapter 5 the preferences of organisations for the location of their premises were discussed in detail. Furthermore tables 6.1, 6.2 and 6.3, which were summarised above, indicated the catchment areas of the various organisations by categories. Both these aspects are further illustrated by the selection of maps which now follow. Whilst it would be impossible to establish a rationale behind the distribution of membership in the case of every organisation, it can nevertheless be said that frequently their statements about ideal location were borne out by the illustration of the maps.[2] Furthermore, the pie-graphs, featured on every map, indicate the proportion of the membership which is represented in these maps.

Glenrothes

Figure 6.1 illustrates the different forms of tenure which prevailed in Glenrothes at the time of the study. As can be seen, the number of owner-occupied houses is very small (see details in table 6.4) and all of them were concentrated in three distinct areas. Again, the houses owned and let by Fife County Council were all located in one area (Woodside), where they formed part of the earlier development of the new town. In addition to those areas, relating to a specific form of tenure, the development corporation designated a specific part of the town in which they were pursuing a policy of selling GDC houses to sitting tenants. However, as the table illustrates, the vast majority of houses in the new town were owned and factored by the Glenrothes Development Corporation.

Table 6.4
Forms of tenure — Glenrothes

Forms of tenure	No. of houses	Percentage
GDC houses	7,755	91·7
Owner-occupied houses	152	1·8
Fife County Council	347	4·1
Cadham and farms[3]	199	2·4
Total	8,453	100·0

Fig. 6.1 Forms of tenure: Glenrothes

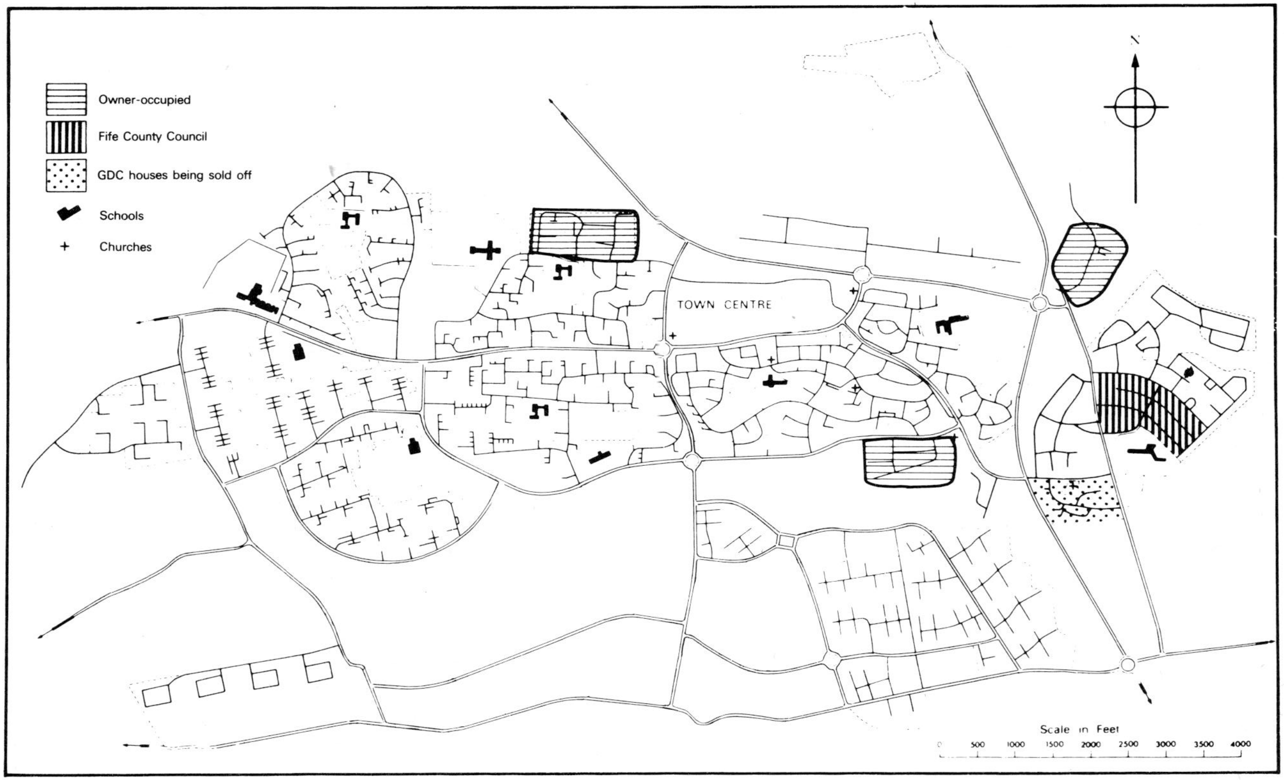

Owner-occupied
Fife County Council
GDC houses being sold off
Schools
Churches

TOWN CENTRE

Scale in Feet
0 500 1000 1500 2000 2500 3000 3500 4000

138

Figure 6.2 indicates the approximate periods during which the development of the respective parts of Glenrothes were completed, at five-yearly intervals. As can be seen, the town was developed basically along an east—west axis, starting with Woodside in the east and Tanshall in the west. The precincts of Newcastle (westernmost area in maps) and Pitteuchar (southernmost area in maps) were at the time of the study not developed, that is, only the road network existed, which is indicated on the maps as such.

Youth organisations in general were found to recruit more of their members in the immediate neighbourhood of their meeting place. However, a further distinction has to be made between various youth organisations according to the age range they cater for and the type of activities they pursue. The two groups which are described below are representative of these two different strands, and these differences were noticeable in the pattern of membership distribution they produced.

1   PRESTON YOUTH CLUB
    Founded 1965
    Membership: 594
    Proportion in new town: 80 per cent
    Meeting place: Preston Youth Centre (see fig. 6.3)

This centre is a converted school. Again, its membership consisted mainly of teenagers, most of whom lived in the Auchmuty and Woodside precinct (to the west and east of the centre respectively). As fig. 6.2 illustrates, these two precincts were among the first housing areas to be built in the new town and are, therefore, the areas in which the highest proportion of teenagers are to be found. However, it is also interesting to note that the area to the north of the Preston Centre, Alburne Park, which is entirely populated by owner-occupiers (see fig. 6.1), has only produced one member. This may be partly explained by the fact that there were only eighteen children (including both sexes) in the 10—19 age group in that area, and partly maybe a function of occupational class. The leader was unable to supply an actual breakdown of the occupational class structure of his centre, but did indicate that very 'few members came from professional homes'. Alburne Park, however, almost entirely consists of 'professional homes', since this was the area which the development corporation had developed early on to accommodate its executive staff on an owner-occupier basis.

2   GIRL GUIDES
    Founded 1954
    Membership: 520
    Proportion in new town: 70 per cent

Fig. 6.2   Housing completion dates: Glenrothes

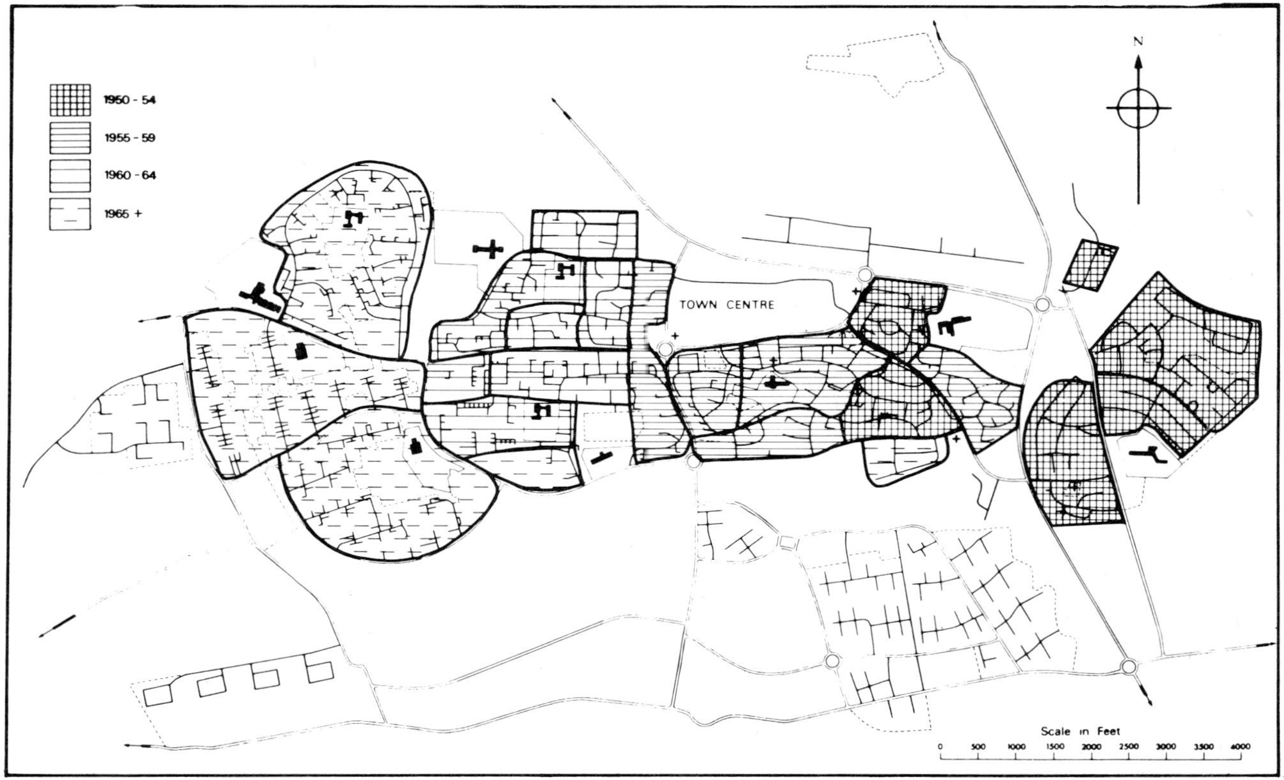

Fig. 6.3   Preston Youth Club: location of members/premises

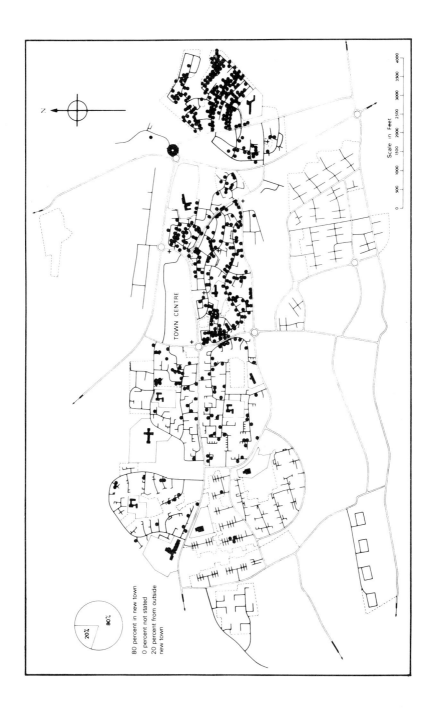

TOWN CENTRE

80 percent in new town
0 percent not stated
20 percent from outside
new town

20%

80%

N

Scale in Feet

0 500 1000 1500 2000 2500 3000 3500 4000

Meeting places: Carleton Primary School, St. Margaret's Parish Church, Warout Primary School, YM/YWCA, St. Columba's Church, Rimbleton Primary, South Parks Primary, Macedonia Community Centre (see fig. 6.4)

At the time of the study there were eleven Brownie Packs, nine Guide Companies and one Ranger Unit attached to the Glenrothes Girl Guide Association. They were the largest uniformed organisation in town. They met in the above halls (see fig. 6.4 from east to west). The pattern of membership distribution was very similar to that of the scouts, and both are examples of groups which are 'localised' (which is also further supported by the fact that only a small proportion of the membership (1 per cent) comes from outside the town). Furthermore, as was the case with the scouts, the 'owner-occupied' areas, i.e. Willow Crescent, Braid Drive and Alburne Park, were areas in which a significant number of members were found. This was also the youth organisation which catered for the largest number of children under the age of ten. This factor might serve to explain, if the 'age structure theory' regarding the west side of the town is correct, why they would seem to be more heavily represented in Macedonia.

Whereas most of the youth organisations were seen to draw their membership almost entirely from the new town itself and more particularly from the immediate locality in which their meeting place was situated, the organisations in the arts and cultural category tended to draw a sizeable proportion of their members from outside the new town. In other words, the new town would appear to act as a focal point for cultural activities for a wider area than is covered by the town itself. In the discussion of 'ideal location' (see ch. 5, p. 122), it was seen that the centre of the town was the location most of the groups in this category preferred — but this remained a hitherto unattained aspiration. However, it would also appear that the fact that none has so far obtained a meeting place in what it considered to be its 'ideal location', did not prevent members from being recruited in parts of the town which were furthest away from the meeting place, as fig. 6.5 illustrates.

1 ART CLUB
   Founded 1955
   Membership: 116
   Proportion in new town: 51 per cent
   Meeting place: own premises

This club had the exclusive use of a converted farmhouse in Alburne Park

Fig. 6.4   Girl Guides: location of members/premises

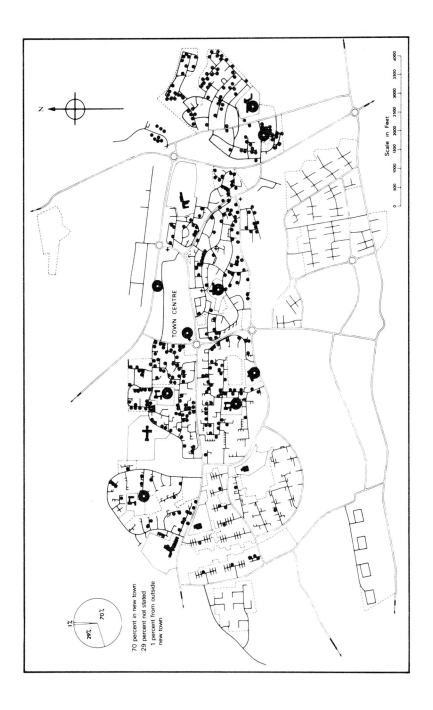

TOWN CENTRE

70 percent in new town
29 percent not stated
1 percent from outside
new town

70%
29%
1%

Scale in Feet
0 500 1000 1500 2000 2500 3000 3500 4000

N

143

Fig. 6.5 Art Club: location of members/premises

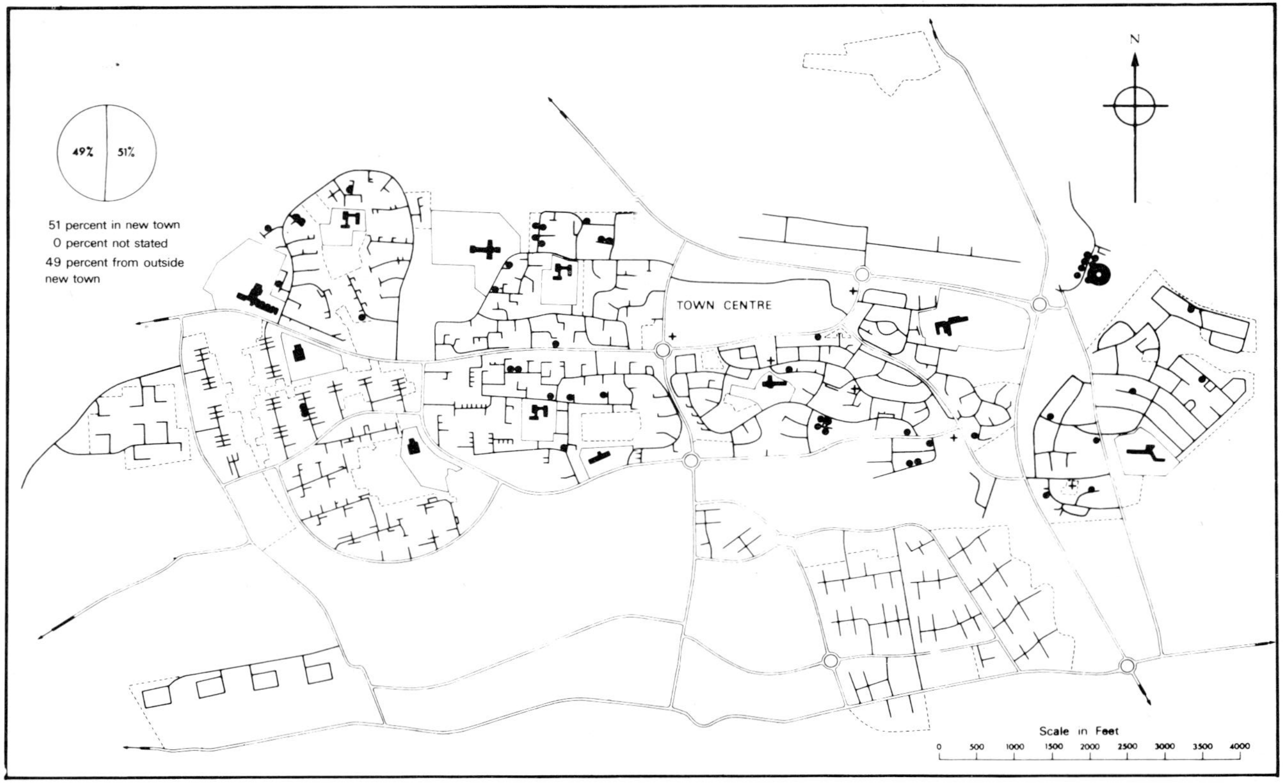

144

which they leased from the Glenrothes Development Corporation. From the start, this club has had strong links with the staff of the GDC, many of whom live in Alburne Park. Apart from this 'link with the firm' factor, there is another attraction for members who live in the immediate vicinity of the studio. Every member is given a key to the premises and can, therefore, make use of the facilities at any time of the day, which is particularly convenient for those who live near the premises. The high-status emphasis on the membership of this club (see also chapter 4) is further illustrated by the fact that, apart from Alburne Park, the other two 'owner-occupied zones', namely Braid Drive and the northern part of South Parks, were particularly well represented in the membership. Furthermore, the membership distribution in the remainder of the town would tend to reflect the notion of 'neighbour-recruitment', whereby one neighbour tells the other about his hobby and occasionally the neighbour then follows suit. The most striking feature, however, of the geographical distribution of the membership of this club, is the fact that 49 per cent of the members travel to the studio from outside Glenrothes. According to the secretary this was largely due to the fact that the premises were very suitable for this kind of activity and members had access to them at any time. Furthermore, the art club in a neighbouring town had recently lost their premises due to redevelopment and some of their members joined Glenrothes Art Club. This, therefore, seems a good example, where a club situated in the new town has, in fact, a much wider sphere of influence. It also illustrates a further point, namely that art is one of the more specialised leisure pursuits, which may not find sufficient supporters to form a viable club among a population of 25,000. In a real sense, therefore, one could say that the club depends on a wider area for its support, and this was illustrated by the high proportion of members who resided outside the actual new town.

2   FILM SOCIETY
    Founded 1962
    Membership: 88
    Proportion in new town: 82 per cent
    Meeting place: Woodside Community Hall

The membership of this society (see fig. 6.6) seems to be fairly evenly distributed throughout the town, with slightly more members to be found in the newer precincts in the western part of the town. However, what stands out is the number of localised clusters of membership. Many are two members of the same household (represented by this symbol 𝟴) or then they are neighbours. This pattern reflects the method of recruitment open

145

Fig. 6.6   Film Society: location of members/premises

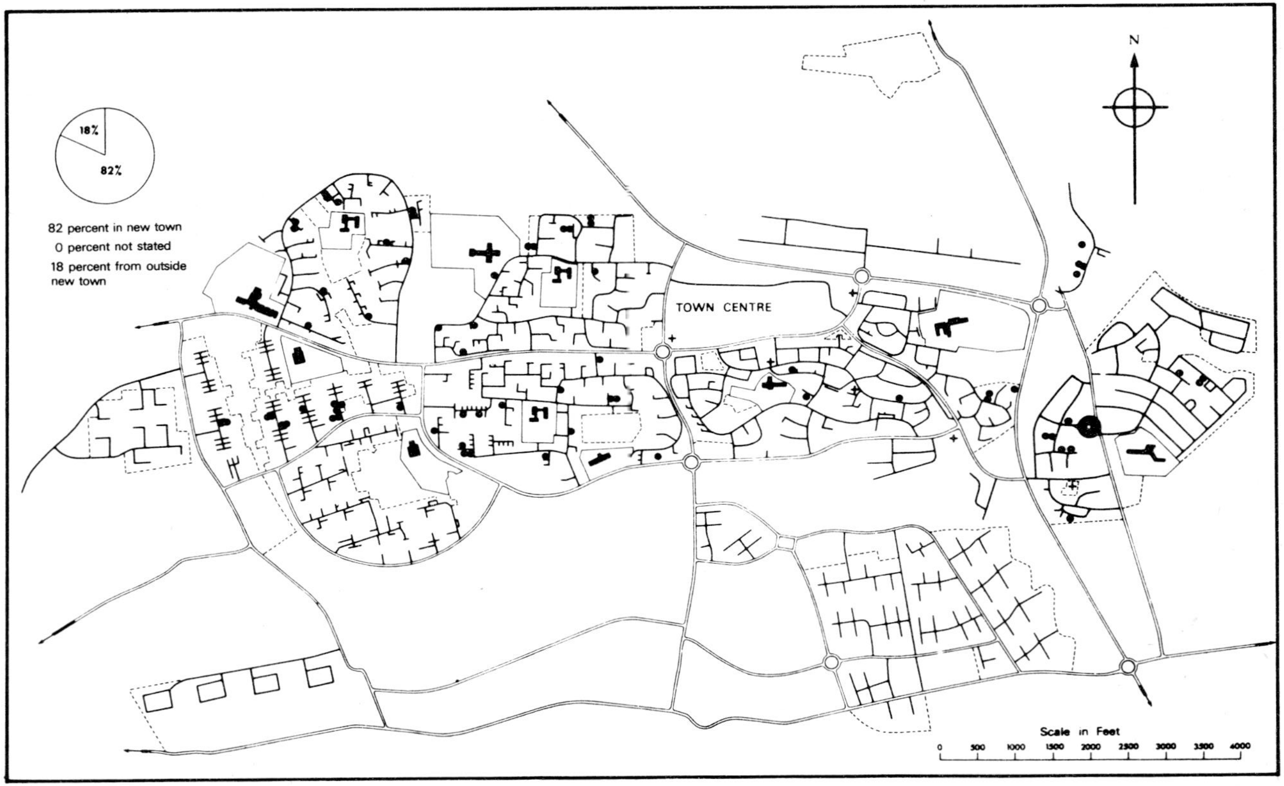

82 percent in new town
0 percent not stated
18 percent from outside
new town

82%

18%

TOWN CENTRE

N

Scale in Feet

0   500   1000   1500   2000   2500   3000   3500   4000

146

to this kind of society. All film societies within the Federation of Scottish Film Societies are party to an agreement with the commercial cinema trade, whereby they are not permitted to advertise their activities by way of press or poster publicity. The society, therefore, relies entirely on word-of-mouth publicity. Once again this is a special interest where the location of the meeting place, almost on the periphery of the town on one side, would not appear to deter the recruitment of membership at the other end of the town. However, just because there are members in every precinct of the town, it is understandable that this club indicated that they would prefer a more central location to the one they were using, because there was no other hall available in the town with adequate seating and projection facilities.

3   FLORAL ART CLUB
    Founded 1965
    Membership: 70
    Proportion in new town: 69 per cent
    Meeting place: Woodside Community Hall
The most striking feature relating to the pattern of membership distribution becomes obvious when fig. 6.7 is compared with fig. 6.1, which indicates the location of owner-occupied houses. Owner-occupation in Glenrothes, as in much of the rest of the country, is status-linked, and according to the secretary of this club, 43 per cent of the members belong to occupational class 1, and the remainder are equally divided between classes 2 and 3. Figure 6.7 shows that the majority of members who live in the town, live in the owner-occupied areas in Willow Crescent (South Parks), Alburne Park and Braid Drive, with a further cluster to be found south of St. Margaret's Church, where the corporation had been selling off houses. When this map was shown to the demographic research office of GDC, she immediately suggested that 'the ladies of the town' all seemed to be members. In other words, membership of this particular group is status-linked, and although the meeting place is conveniently situated for some members, the fact that so many members live in precincts some distance away, and indeed travel from outside the town, would suggest that the actual location of the meeting place is not of any importance, or at least is not seen to have a marked influence on recruitment.

4   ROTARY CLUB
    Founded 1957
    Membership: 40
    Proportion in new town: 17.5 per cent
    Meeting place: Golden Acorn Hotel

Fig. 6.7 Floral Art Club: location of members/premises

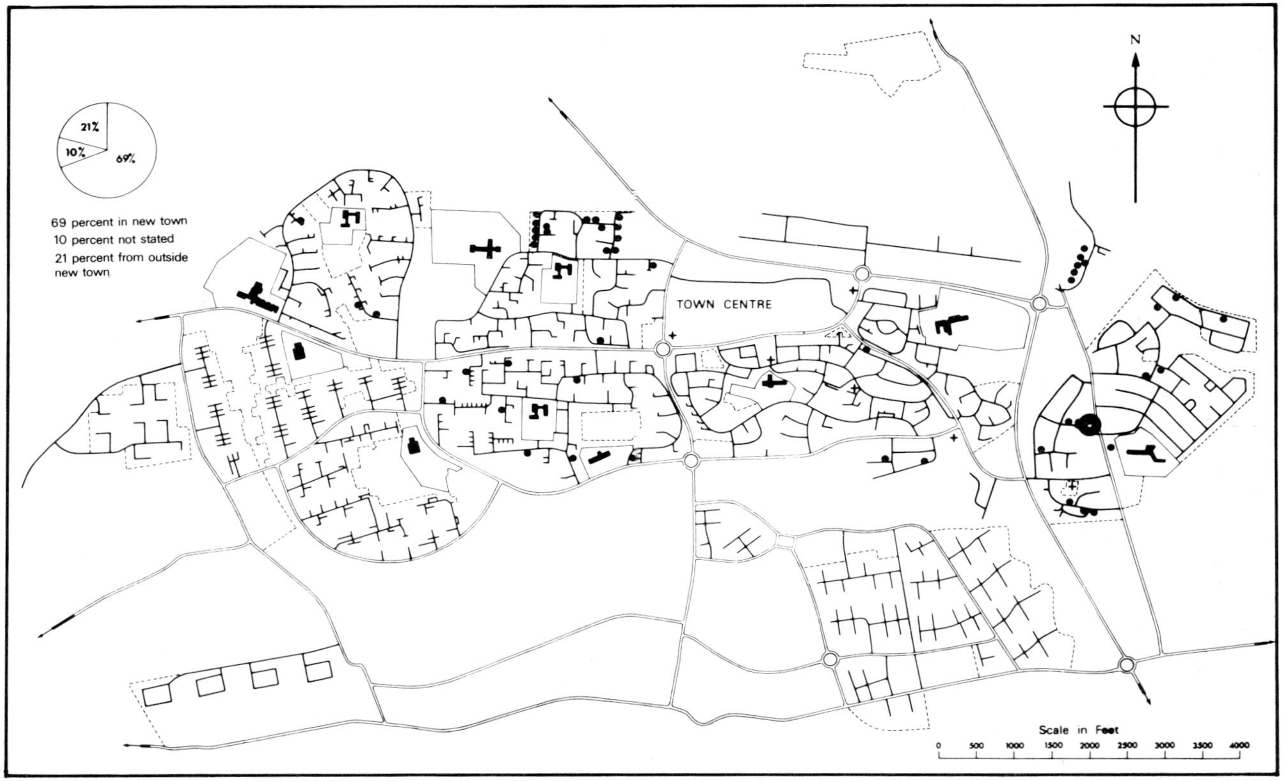
21%
10%
69%
69 percent in new town
10 percent not stated
21 percent from outside new town
TOWN CENTRE
N
Scale in Feet
0 500 1000 1500 2000 2500 3000 3500 4000

This particular map (see fig. 6.8) is not so much of interest because of its pattern of membership distribution, but rather because it would seem to illustrate a phenomenon which was referred to as follows in an annual report of the development corporation:[4]

> One of the most intransigent problems with which the New Town is faced is the 'five o'clock executive exit'. In the surrounding country of Fife, with its cosy villages and little pantiled seaports, there are within easy reach of Glenrothes numerous attractive places in which to set up home. This appeals to many executives who have come to work in the town; yet socially there is a need to encourage such people and their families to live within its boundaries.

The report went on to state that for this reason alone, they would welcome private builders to the town to provide more suitable executive housing.

This was obviously the type of organisation which mostly had executives of one kind or another within its membership. The proportion of members living within the town itself were found in owner-occupied areas, and two-thirds of all the members lived outside the town.

In chapter 5, as already stated, it was found that next to youth organisations dealing particularly with small children, the women's organisations were more 'localised' than any other category, with the possible exception of old people's groups. The exact extent to which this was the case can be seen from the distribution of membership in relation to the meeting places as plotted on the map in fig. 6.9.

1   SOUTH PARKS FARMHOUSE LADIES SOCIAL CLUB
    Founded 1964
    Membership: 60
    Proportion in new town: 100 per cent
    Meeting place: South Parks Farmhouse tenants' meeting room.

This club was formed shortly after the South Parks precinct was completed and, as can be seen from fig. 6.9, this is a good example of a localised women's organisation. The great majority of members are drawn from the immediate geographical vicinity of the actual meeting place. The 'localised' character of this club is further underlined by the fact that no member resides outside the town, and by the absence of any affiliation to another organisation, local or even national. In many ways, therefore, this is a good example of a typical 'neighbourhood club', of the kind most women's groups turned out to be.

When discussing 'ideal location' in the previous chapter, the hobby/

Fig. 6.8 Rotary Club: location of members/premises

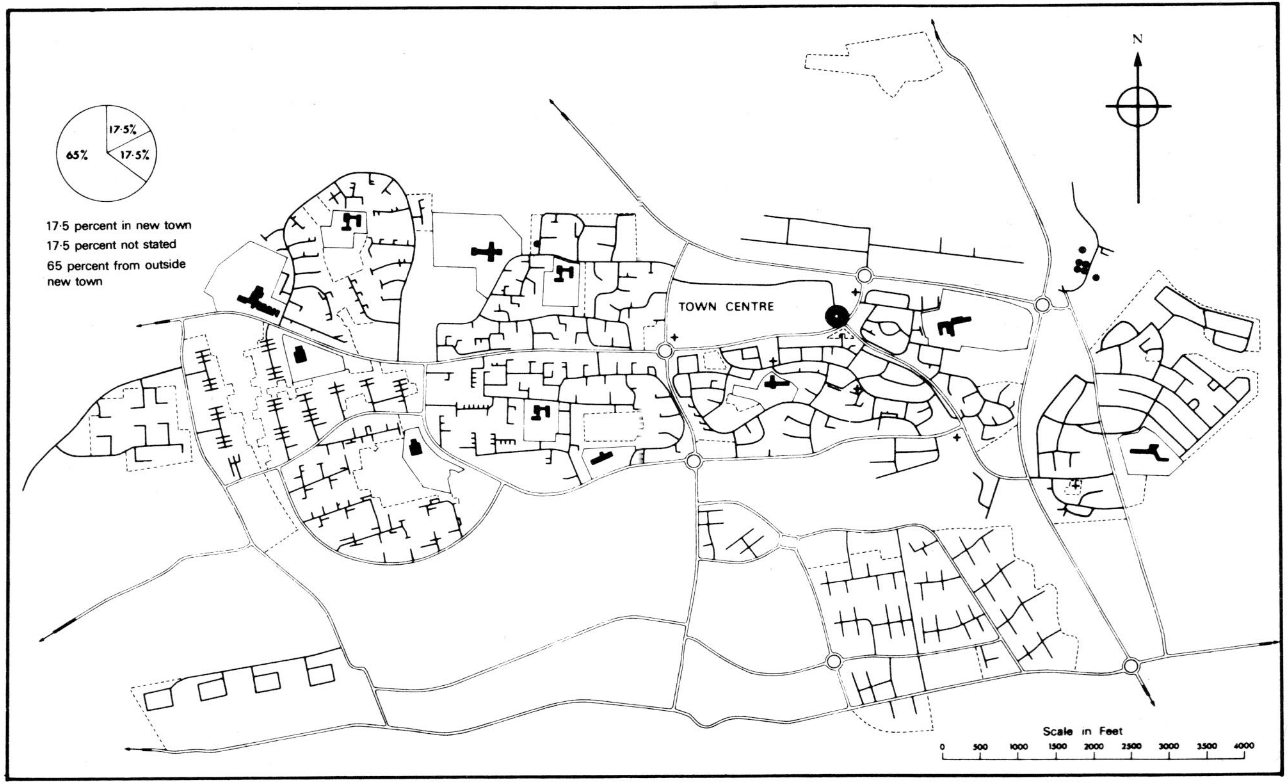

17·5 percent in new town
17·5 percent not stated
65 percent from outside
new town

65%   17·5%   17·5%

TOWN CENTRE

Scale in Feet
0   500   1000   1500   2000   2500   3000   3500   4000

150

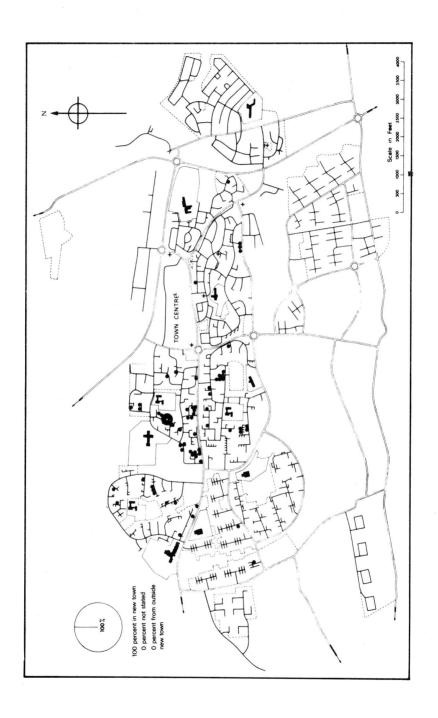

Fig. 6.9 South Parks Farmhouse Ladies Social Club: location of members/premises

100 percent in new town
0 percent not stated
0 percent from outside
new town

100%

TOWN CENTRE

N

Scale in Feet

0 500 1000 1500 2000 2500 3000 3500 4000

special interest groups as a category seemed to be somewhat less concerned about the actual location, and more about the suitability of the accommodation for their purpose. Furthermore, since frequently theirs was a fairly specialised interest, they tended to draw their membership from a wider area than the new town itself. The map in fig. 6.10 would seem to be fairly representative of that category.

1   CAMERA CLUB
    Founded 1965
    Membership: 30
    Proportion in new town: 80 per cent
    Meeting place: own clubrooms

Once again, this is a more specialised interest where, judging by the distribution of the membership as shown on the map, the actual location of the meeting place would not appear to be an important factor; certainly not as important as the suitability of the actual premises which are available. (The club has exclusive use of its own.) This is further borne out by the fact that 20 per cent of the members are attracted to this club from outside the town.

The last map to be included from the Glenrothes sample is fig. 6.11 representing a social club which, due to its size and peculiar history, is in many ways unique, and in that form, has not been found in any of the other Scottish new towns.

1   RECREATION CENTRE AND SOCIAL CLUB
    Founded 1959
    Membership: 885
    Proportion in new town: 99·5 per cent
    Meeting place: own premises (CISWO building)

The club originated as a miners' welfare club, and for the first few years of its existence there were 1,500 members on the roll. This was largely due to the fact that all miners in the area were automatically members, paying a weekly subscription which was deducted from their wages. When the Rothes pit closed and miners left the district membership fell, and as a consequence the composition of the club changed. Among the 885 members the proportion of miners is now relatively small. According to comments received, one of the big attractions of this club was the fact that it was licensed and provided very pleasant bar facilities. Although there is, inevitably, a mass of symbols in parts which might slightly obscure this, a closer examination will show a great many households, usually husbands and wives, which are represented thus by the symbol ⁸.

Fig. 6.10 Camera Club: location of members/premises

153

Fig. 6.11   Recreation Centre and Social Club: location of members/premises

99·5 percent in new town
0 percent not stated
0·5 percent from outside
new town

0·5%
99·5%

TOWN CENTRE

N

Scale in Feet
0   500   1000   1500   2000   2500   3000   3500   4000

The map also illustrates that the greatest concentration of members was to be found in Auchmuty. In that general area the only other licensed premises available were found in a hotel, where the bars were considered something of a 'male preserve'.

The recreation centre however, apart from the bar facilities, offers recreational opportunities such as bowling and tennis. Again, there were no other such facilities in Auchmuty. Furthermore, traditionally, Auchmuty was one of the areas in which the miners were housed when coalmining was the mainstay of industry in Glenrothes. There existed, therefore, in that precinct a tradition of going to the recreation centre, which was just a few hundred yards walk away across a piece of open ground. All this helps to explain the dense cluster of members resident in Auchmuty. It may, however, be more surprising to find so many members in Macedonia on the one hand, and so relatively few in Woodside. An explanation for this would appear to be along the following lines: Macedonia, at the time, did not have any licensed premises, nor were there similar recreational facilities available. The recreation centre had, therefore, a great deal to offer to anyone living there, particularly couples. In Woodside, on the other hand, there were already two public houses, and a recreational park built by the District Council, which offers tennis and bowling facilities; quite apart from the extra distance which would have to be covered to get to the Recreation Centre & Social Club.

6.3   East Kilbride

Figure 6.12 illustrates the different forms of tenure found in East Kilbride. Again, as was the case in Glenrothes (see fig. 6.1) the number of houses which were owner-occupied was relatively small (see details in table 6.5) and all were concentrated in three district areas, i.e. Whitemoss, within, or alongside the boundaries of the old, pre-new town village and on the western periphery of Westwood precinct. Again, as in the case of Glenrothes, however, the great majority of houses were owned and let by the East Kilbride Development Corporation. (Incidentally, the proportion of corporation-owned houses in East Kilbride and Glenrothes was identical, 91·7 per cent).

Figure 6.13 indicates the various phases of the development of the new town at five-yearly intervals. Whereas it was noted that Glenrothes developed along an east—west axis, this particular map illustrates that the growth pattern in East Kilbride was from the centre (i.e. the old village) outwards. However, as the map indicates, the growth pattern was not a

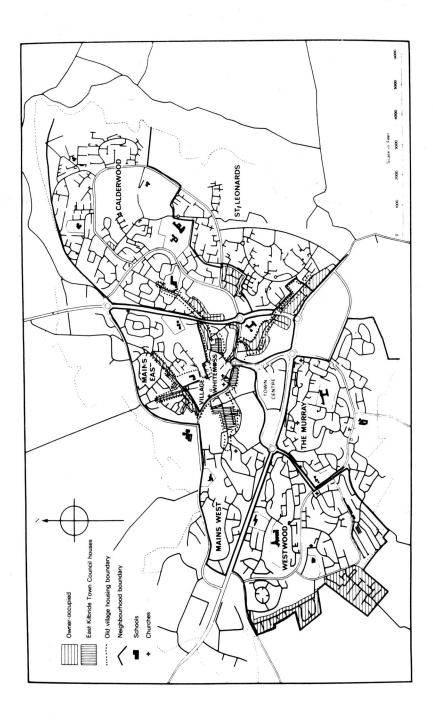

Fig. 6.12   Forms of tenure: East Kilbride

156

Fig. 6.13   Housing completion dates: East Kilbride

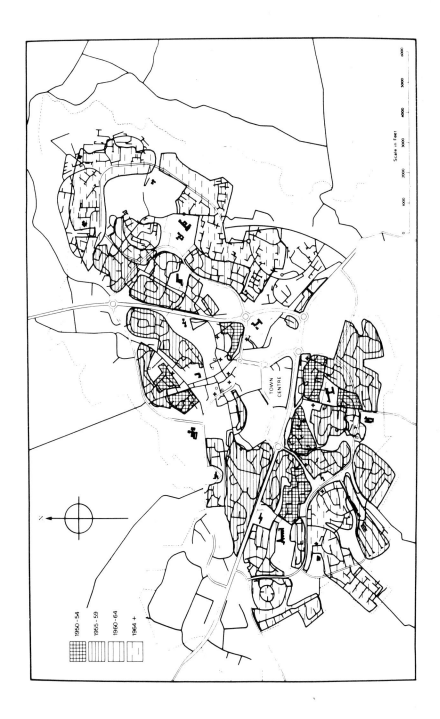

1950 - 54

1955 - 59

1960 - 64

1964 +

TOWN
CENTRE

Scale in Feet

Table 6.5

Forms of tenure − East Kilbride

Forms of tenure	No. of houses	Percentage
EKDC houses	16,942	91·7
Owner-occupied	1,113	6·0
EK Town Council houses	315	1·7
Privately rented	103	0·6
Total	18,473	100

regular one, in the sense that very few of the neighbourhoods were completed in one five-year period. (See for instance, Murray, East Mains, and also Westwood, where one area was completed by 1954, one by 1959, and one by 1964; the westernmost part of Westwood was only just being completed at the time of this study.) In other words, the process of building continued from the early fifties to the late sixties within the one neighbourhood, which in turn meant that newcomers into this neighbourhood continued to arrive over a longer period. On the other hand there are areas, particularly on the eastern and northeastern periphery of the town (Calderwood and St Leonards), which form part of a uniform, post-1964 development, and in which there were no houses built in earlier phases.

The maps chosen from among the East Kilbride youth organisations are typical of three different types of groups, each with a somewhat different emphasis. The Scouts and Guides, as in Glenrothes (see fig. 6.4), work on a very localised basis. On the other hand, a very specialised organisation dealing with teenage boys, such as the Air Training Corps does not rely on premises within the immediate vicinity of a given neighbourhood. Lastly in this category, again as was the case in Glenrothes (see fig. 6.3), a youth club for teenagers recruits a substantial proportion of members in the neighbourhood, but due to the higher mobility of teenagers, as compared with smaller children, also has some members from other parts of the town.

1   10th EAST KILBRIDE ST LEONARDS SCOUT GROUP
     Founded 1968
     Membership: 42
     Proportion in new town: 98 per cent
     Meeting place: St Leonards School

This seems to be a particularly good example of a 'localised' organisation, dealing mainly with young children. St Leonards and Calderwood are relatively new areas in East Kilbride (see fig. 6.13) and this scout group was the most recent to be started, because there was a need in this area. The distribution of the membership as seen in fig. 6.14 shows that all the members were recruited locally and within easy walking distance of the meeting place, which, in turn, bears out the preference voiced by such organisations regarding ideal location.

2   AIR TRAINING CORPS
    Founded 1959
    Membership: 56
    Proportion in new town: 95 per cent
    Meeting place: own headquarters/Rolls Royce

The East Kilbride Squadron of the Air Training Corps was started as a detached flight in 1959 and made into a squadron in 1964. This organisation caters for the 13–18 age group, a fact which may help, to some extent, to account for the distribution of membership. As fig. 6.15 illustrates, the village, which has an older population, and the newer areas, such as parts of Westwood, Calderwood and St Leonards, where the newcomers who typically have young families are found, do not provide any members. This was particularly apparent in Calderwood where the bulk of the members was found in those parts completed before 1964 (see fig. 6.13) and again in Westwood and the Murray, where there would appear to be an almost invisible dividing line between the pre-1964 areas in which members are found, and the more recent areas in which there are hardly any members. So it would appear that the age structure of neighbourhood (which in turn is connected to the completion dates)[5] may be a factor in the membership distribution. On the other hand, along with other more specialised pursuits, where there was only one organisation of its kind available in town, the actual location of the meeting place would not appear to matter, since a large proportion of the members lived in areas as far removed from the meeting place as was possible within the boundaries of the town.

3   HEATHERY KNOWE CO-OPERATIVE YOUTH CLUB
    Founded 1957
    Membership: 200
    Proportion in new town: 67 per cent
    Meeting place: Heathery Knowe Primary School

As fig. 6.16 illustrates, the great bulk of the members live in the immediate vicinity of the school which is the meeting place. In its

Fig. 6.14 10th East Kilbride St. Leonards Scout Group: location of members/premises

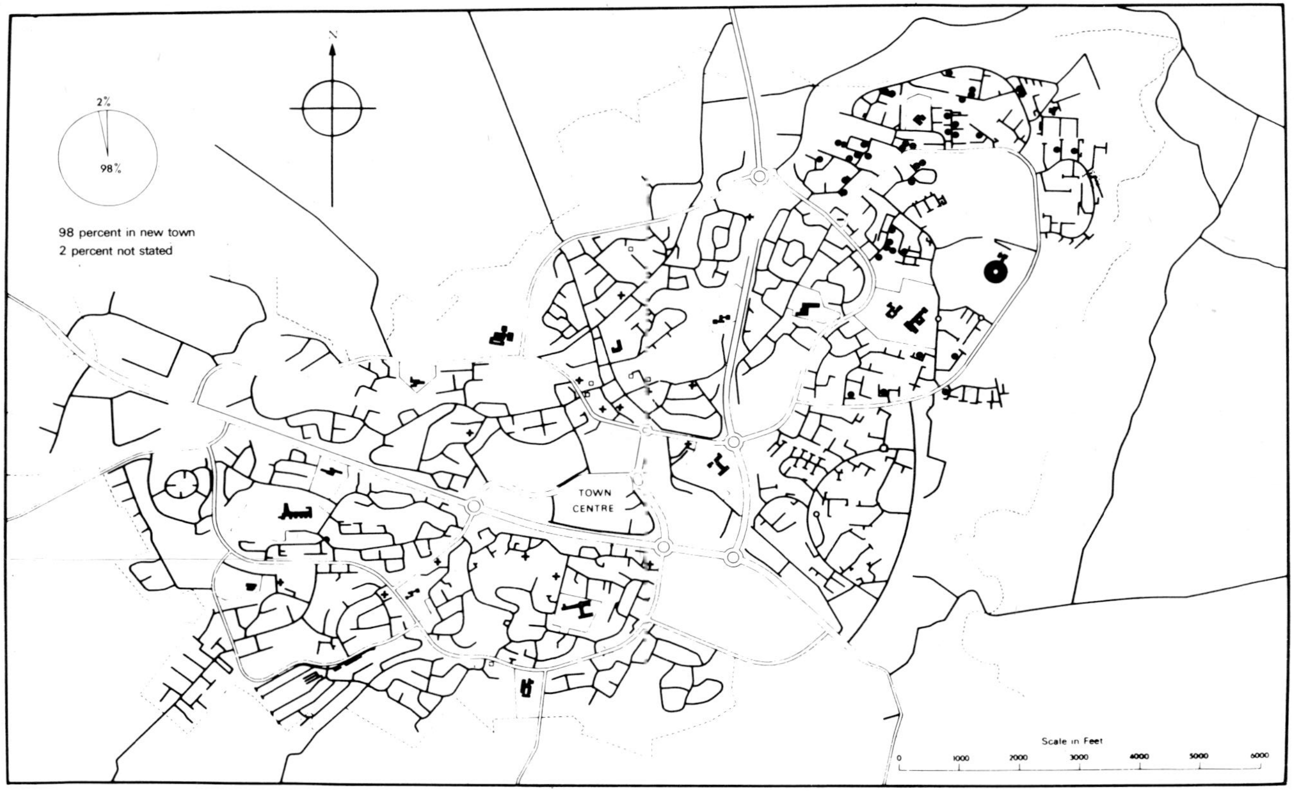
N
2%
98%
98 percent in new town
2 percent not stated
TOWN
CENTRE
Scale in Feet
0
1000
2000
3000
4000
5000
6000

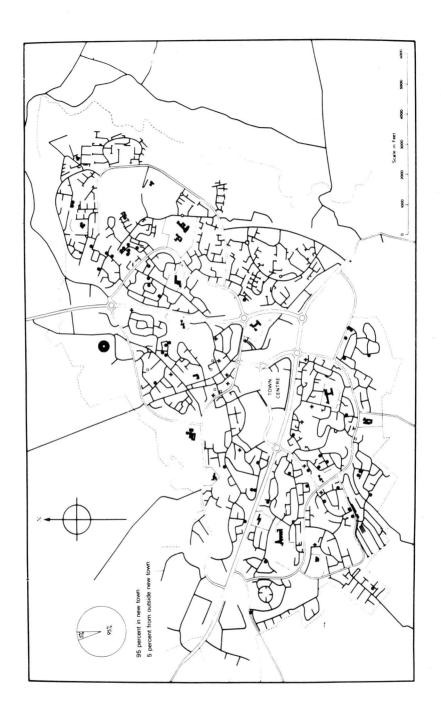

Fig. 6.15 Air Training Corps: location of members/premises

161

Fig. 6.16 Heathery Knowe Co-operative Youth Club: location of members/premises

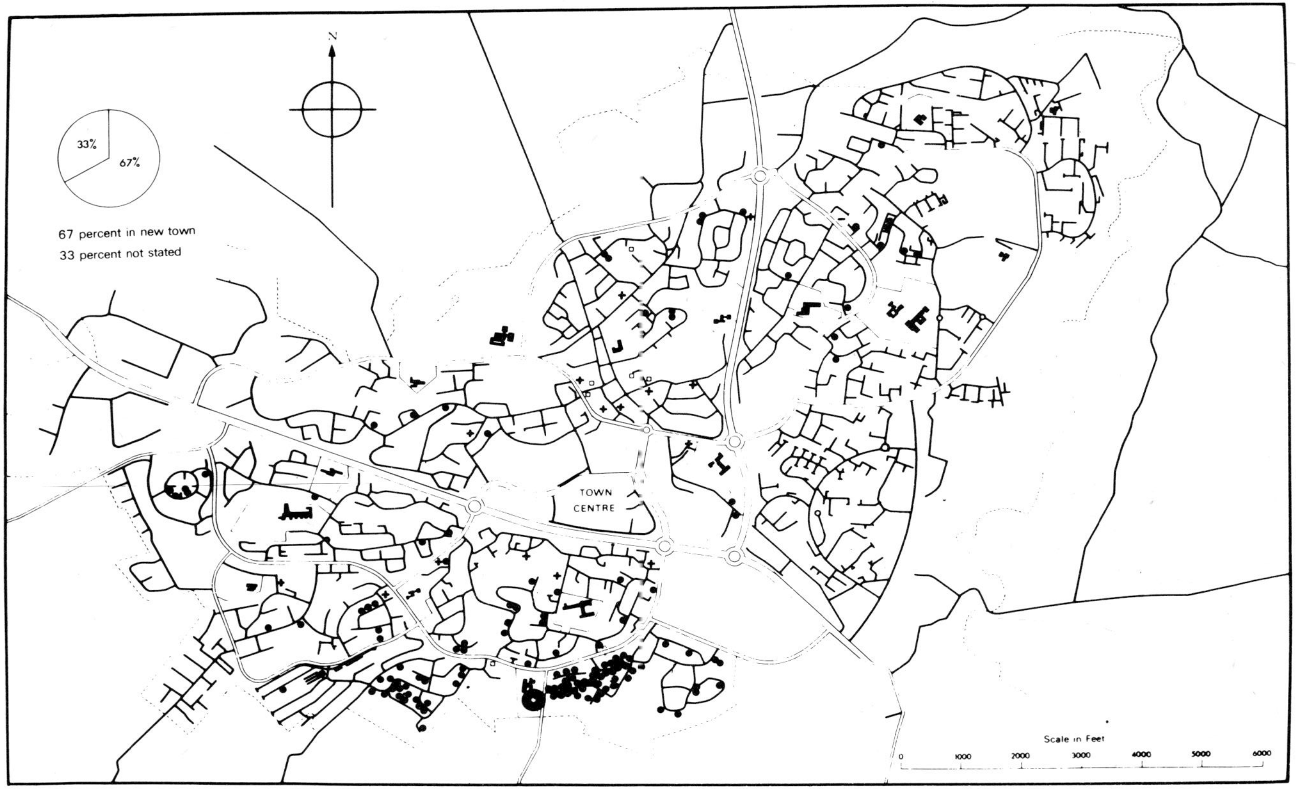
N
33%
67%
67 percent in new town
33 percent not stated
TOWN
CENTRE
Scale in Feet
0
1000
2000
3000
4000
5000
6000

programme and activities this was a youth club which did not pursue a rather more specialised activity (such as ATC). The only condition of membership would appear to be that the parents of the children concerned should be members of the Co-operative Movement but, according to the leader, this was never checked. This is, therefore, a typical neighbourhood youth club, the appeal of which is fairly localised, although there are a few members who are attracted from other parts of the town. The proximity of the majority of members to the meeting place would, therefore, suggest that in this case, along with other youth groups offering a similar programme, the location of the premises used has a bearing on recruitment. (Compare also with fig. 6.3, which represents a similar organisation in Glenrothes.)

Again, as was the case in Glenrothes in the category arts and cultural organisations, a higher proportion of groups also had members from outside the new town, albeit to a differing degree than, for instance, the youth and women's organisations.

1 MUSIC CLUB
   Founded 1968
   Membership: 65
   Proportion in new town: 63 per cent
   Meeting place: The Stuart Hotel

The following points of interest emerge from the distribution of membership on this map, see fig. 6.17. First of all, almost a third of the membership consisted of husband and wife teams (as indicated by the symbol **⚭**). Secondly, a comparison with fig. 6.12 shows that a considerable number of members lived in the owner-occupied area of the old village. Since the breakdown of membership into occupational groups was not available, it was not possible to link this directly to a status factor and claim that this was a 'highbrow' activity. However, it is known that 60 per cent of the members were between 30 and 60, and 35 per cent over 65 years of age. If this map is compared with fig. 6.13, it will become evident that, with the exception of the cluster of members in Calderwood, the bulk of members live in the parts of the town which were completed by 1959. It can, therefore, be said that although the society was only in its infancy at the time of this study, its main appeal extended to the middle-aged and elderly. The distribution of the membership in the town would tend to bear this out. Furthermore, the map serves to illustrate that this is the kind of organisation where the recruitment of membership in East Kilbride too is not confined to the immediate vicinity of the meeting place.

164

Fig. 6.17 Music Club: location of members/premises

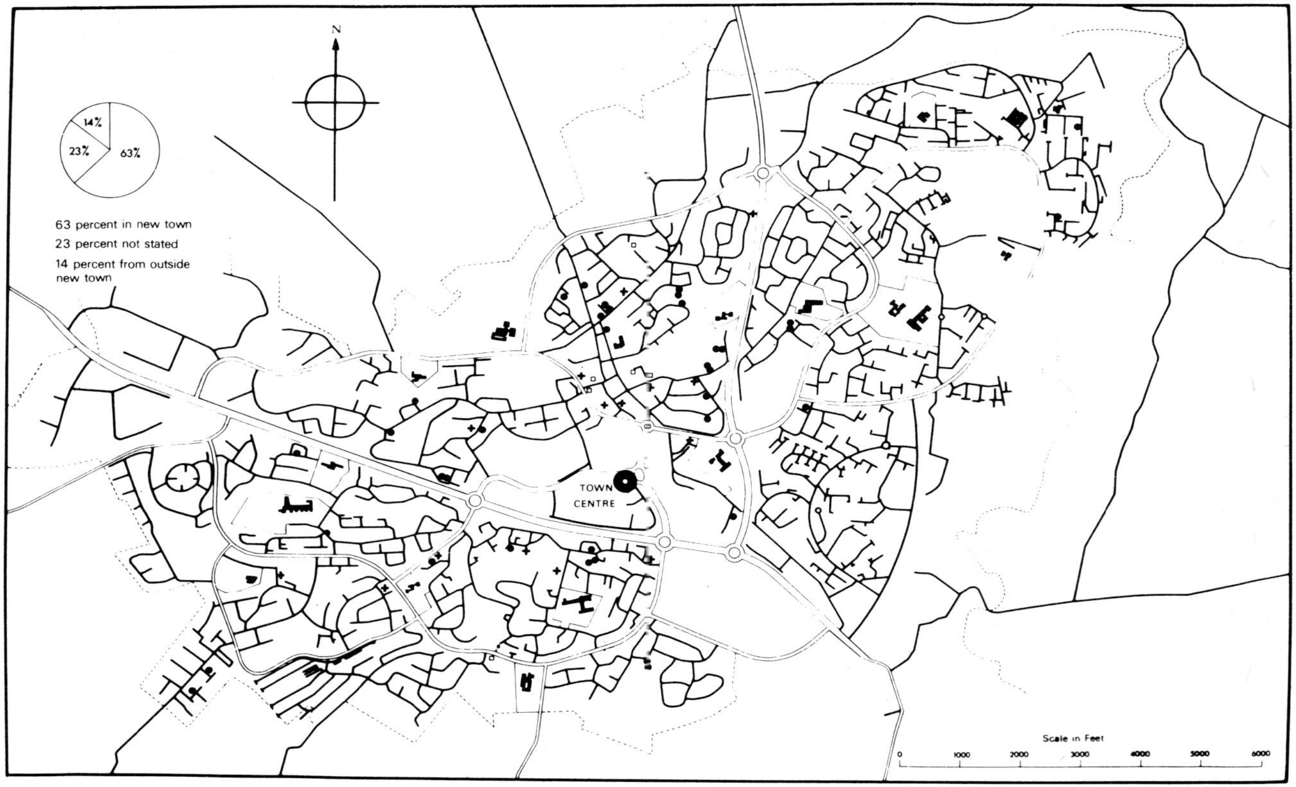

63 percent in new town
23 percent not stated
14 percent from outside
new town

63%
23%
14%

TOWN
CENTRE

Scale in Feet
0   1000   2000   3000   4000   5000   6000

N

In Glenrothes it was found that typically the women's organisations were very localised as far as their membership intake was concerned. This was also true of the organisations in the same category in East Kilbride, of which the following is a good example, although it also displayed some of the characteristics in its membership distribution (see fig. 6.18), of an organisation which was the only one of its kind in town.

1   TOWNSWOMEN'S GUILD
     Founded 1956
     Membership: 71
     Proportion in new town: 93 per cent
     Meeting place: Torrance Hotel

This group was reformed in 1956, after an earlier Townswomen's Guild which was started in 1950 had ceased to function due to lack of leadership. The pattern which emerged from this map would suggest that this organisation, to some extent, has the character of a neighbourhood women's group. A great many of the members lived in the immediate vicinity of the meeting place; no specific qualifications were required for membership; and the programme was sufficiently general to have a wide appeal. These characteristics however, are combined with those of the kind of organisation of which there is only one in town. In other words, if a woman in Westwood or Calderwood wanted to join a Townswomen's Guild, she had to join this one, although it meets in the centre of the old village. And lastly, the recruitment policy of this group also would appear to be reflected in the distribution of membership, as evident from this map. The Towns Women's Guild did not, in any way, advertise its activities, but relied solely on members introducing their friends. It was for this reason that those members who did not live in the immediate vicinity of the meeting place by and large were found in clusters of varying sizes throughout the town. As can be seen, very few of the members lived any distance away from the next member. The system of recruitment whereby friends and neighbours bring friends and neighbours was, therefore, apparent on this map, perhaps most markedly in East Mains and parts of West Mains.

Once again, as was the case with Glenrothes, in the category hobby/special interest groups the actual location of the meeting place was less important, as the club described below illustrates.

1   PHOTOGRAPHIC CLUB
     Founded 1959
     Membership: 59

Fig. 6.18 Townswomen's Guild: location of members/premises

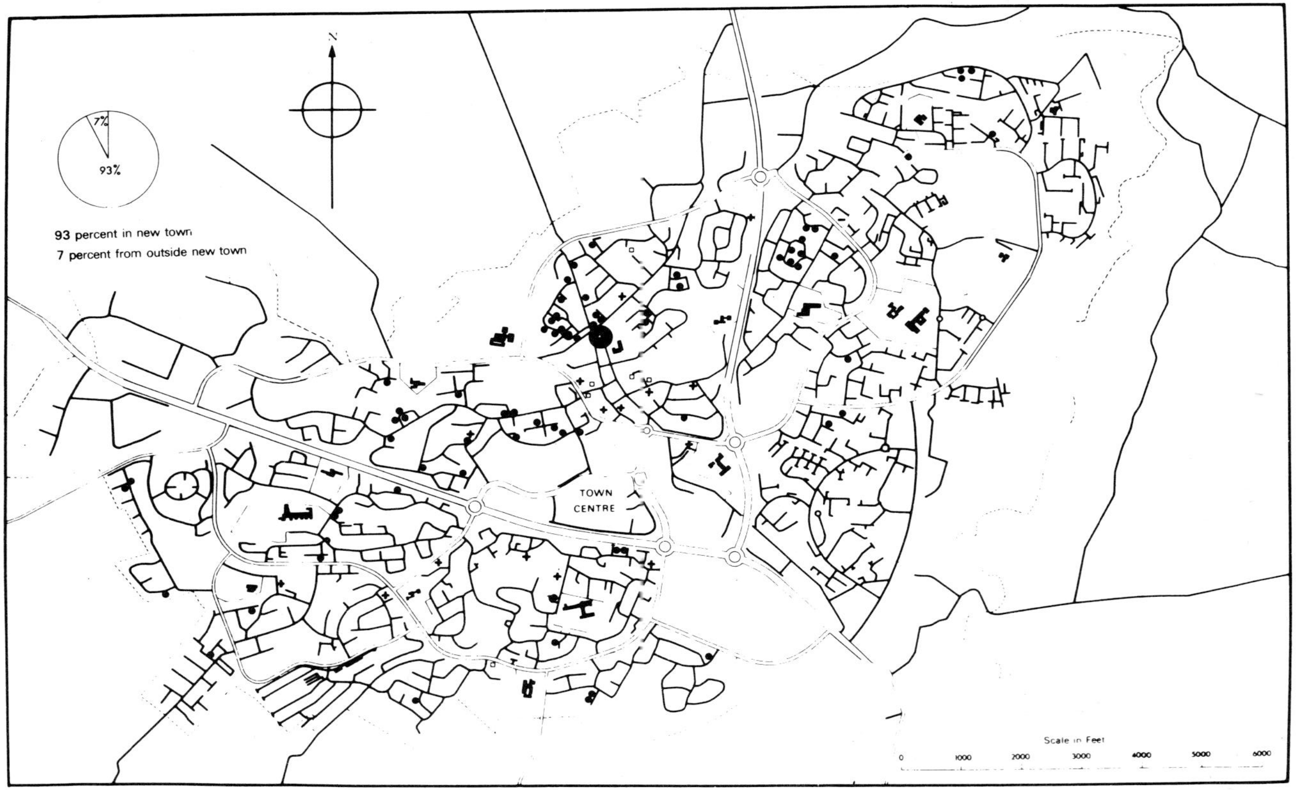
N
7%
93%
93 percent in new town
7 percent from outside new town
TOWN
CENTRE
Scale in Feet
0
1000
2000
3000
4000
5000
6000

Proportion in new town: 92 per cent
Meeting place: Hunter High School

This club was started by a school teacher. As can be seen from fig. 6.19, a certain amount of 'neighbourhood recruitment' would appear to have taken place, but the bulk of the membership was distributed throughout the town. Since this was the only club of its kind in town, relative remoteness of the meeting place, say from Westwood, did not appear to deter members from joining, although the secretary claimed that a more central location would increase membership. However, this statement may or may not be correct and could only be tested if it were possible for this club to move to a central location for a given period, and then see whether such a move had resulted in an increase in membership. Since however the pattern of membership distribution which emerged on this map had many similarities with that of the Camera Club in Glenrothes (see fig. 6.10) it is reasonable to suggest that the suitability of the equipment and the premises were more crucial than their actual location.

The requirements of various sports organisations differ very widely, according to their particular pursuit. In this category it was therefore particularly difficult to establish a common denominator on the basis of which it would be possible to generalise about the needs of sports organisations, both in terms of premises and indeed location. A curling club or a gun club may, for instance, be more concerned with finding a suitable ice rink or a rifle range, almost regardless of its location in the new town itself or the wider district, whereas a bowling club frequently also has some of the features of a 'neighbourhood club', as the example below illustrates.

2   BOWLING CLUB
     Founded 1872
     Membership: 160
     Proportion in new town: 98 per cent
     Meeting place: Own clubhouse and bowling green

The Bowling Club was, after the Curling Club, the second oldest club in East Kilbride. It had its own facilities in the old village part of East Kilbride, which included a clubhouse and bowling greens (see fig. 6.20). A comparison with figs. 6.12 and 6.13 illustrates that the majority of members lived either in the former village itself, or in the longer-established parts of the town. It was also particularly noticeable that there did not appear to be another club with as big a number of members resident in the houses owned by East Kilbride Burgh Council. Although

Fig. 6.19   Photographic Club: location of members/premises

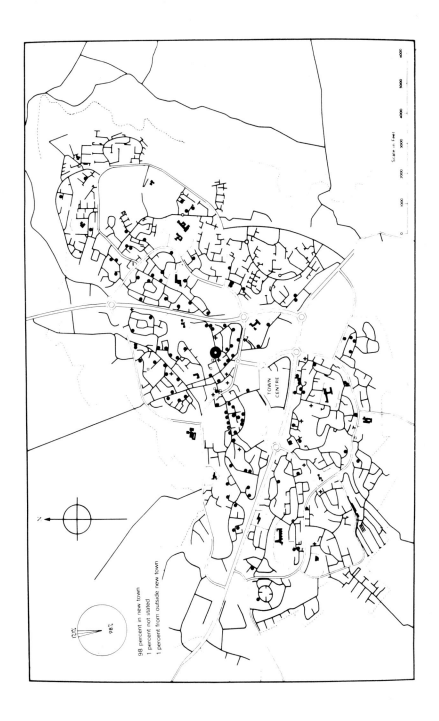

Fig. 6.20   Bowling Club: location of members/premises

98 percent in new town
1 percent not stated
1 percent from outside new town

Scale in Feet

TOWN CENTRE

169

the club secretary was not able to give a breakdown of the age structure, it can reasonably be assumed that the majority of members will be middle-aged to elderly. The pattern of membership distribution would appear to support this, since hardly any of the members lived in the more recently developed parts of the town. As far as occupational class structure was concerned, the secretary indicated that about half the members were in class 1, and the remainder in the other four. This too was apparently supported by the pattern shown on this map, since members were found in council housing as well as in owner-occupier areas, at least in the more centrally located ones. The fact that this club was established in pre-new town days determined to some extent its present location, and the cluster of members found in the vicinity suggests that it also acted as a kind of 'neighbourhood club' for the old village, membership of which was not easily obtainable for newcomers now since the club had closed the membership roll and established a waiting list.

6.4   Livingston

Livingston New Town was started almost twenty years after Glenrothes and East Kilbride — and at the time of this study the town was still in its early stages. Similarly to Glenrothes however, the development of the town was planned to take place along an east—west axis, with Craigshill the first new district to be finished, followed by Howden. By building the town in this way, it was felt that the disruption which would be caused by later 'filling in' of a given area could be avoided. From the social point of view, this policy would also mean that once a group of newcomers had settled in, no more newcomers would move to a completed area, subject to the normal movements of population. Just as the physical development of the town was in its early stages at the time of this study, so were practically all of the social organisations represented in this sample. Figure 6.21 indicates the completion dates of the various parts of the respective districts, which in turn had a bearing on the dates of foundation of the various organisations. Only about a third of the organisations (i.e. 35 per cent) in the sample from which these illustrations were picked were able to supply lists of members' addresses. This was due partly to the fact that some of these groups had only just started and had not, at that stage compiled membership registers. The list of organisations, which was published by the 'welcoming committee' and from which the original sample was chosen, contained mostly organisations which met in Craigshill and Howden, since these were the only districts then fully or partially

170

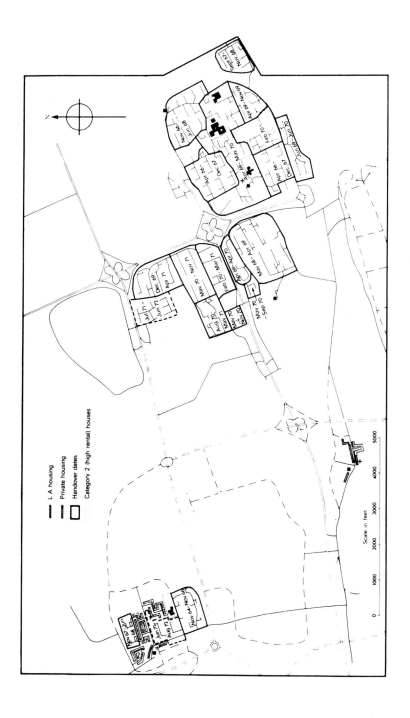

Fig. 6.21   Housing completion dates and forms of tenure: Livingston

completed, with the exception of some parts of the Deans district and parts of the old village of Livingston. Figure 6.21 also illustrates that these two last-mentioned areas contained some private and some local authority housing. The following table shows the forms of tenure and the proportions in which they occurred in Livingston at the time of this study.

Table 6.6

Forms of tenure − Livingston

Forms of tenure	No. of houses	Percentage of total
LDC (Craigshill)	1,561	55·6
LDC (rest of Livingston)	899	32·0
Owner-occupied houses	114	4·1
County Council and SSHA	236	8·3
Total	2,810	100·0

Again, as was the case in the other two new towns, the development corporation, as the housing authority for the new town, not only built, but owned, let and factored by far the greatest number of houses available.

In Craigshill itself, there were no owner-occupier areas − but there existed a more 'select area' in the district just the same, in the south-east corner (Almond South) and Almond Park, which overlook the River Almond. If, therefore, in the other two towns members with a high occupational status were found frequently to be living in owner-occupier areas, in Craigshill they would be found in these two areas, where housing was set aside for 'executives' and the rent was accordingly higher.

The maps also illustrate that the social interchange between Deans district and the Craigshill/Howden districts at that particular stage of the town's development was still negligible, but no doubt as the town expands westwards the contact between the different parts of the town will increase.

Among the most flourishing organisations in Livingston were the youth organisations. In the words of one of the cub scout leaders it was 'difficult to keep numbers down' and, as will be seen from the membership patterns on the maps described below, the younger the members the more 'localised' the group became. With over 30 per cent of the population

172

being under nine years of age at the time, there was obviously a great demand for such groups.

1 CUB SCOUTS
    Founded March 1968
    Membership: 38
    Proportion in new town: 97 per cent
    Meeting place: Letham Primary School

This group already had a waiting list due to lack of suitable leaders. The distribution of members (see fig. 6.22) was a clear indication of the extent to which groups catering for young children (8–11 years) are usually 'localised'. The leader himself lived in the recruitment area and was therefore very likely known to the parents. This pattern was also an indication in a sense as to how far parents are prepared to let their children walk in the absence of a bus service (frequently combined, at the early stages, with inadequate street lighting and lack of pavements). The previously made observation about the relevance of premises being available in the immediate neighbourhood for young children would seem to be well supported by the distribution pattern on this map.

2 LETHAM JUNIOR YOUTH CENTRE
    Founded October 1968
    Membership: 60
    Proportion in new town: 85 per cent
    Meeting place: Youth wing, Letham Primary School

This club catered for the 12–15 age group. It met once a week in the youth wing attached to the Letham Primary School. There were approximately sixty 'members', though this club did not run on a membership basis and offered an 'open door' to any youngster in this age range who wished to come along. The members represented on this map (fig. 6.23) were a 100 per cent sample of children attending the centre on a given Sunday evening, which according to the leader was a 'normal club night'. Again, as in the case of fig. 6.22, the distribution of the membership was very localised, within immediate walking distance of Letham Primary School. Again, it was the leader's impression that parents were not too willing to let their children walk too far to a youth club of this sort. This related particularly to the younger children in this age range. However, the older ones, i.e. the fifteen-year-olds in this case, were usually those who came to the club night not only from areas of Craigshill outside the immediate vicinity of the meeting place, but also the Howden district, and indeed some came from East and Mid Calder, and others

Fig. 6.22 Cub Scouts: location of members/premises

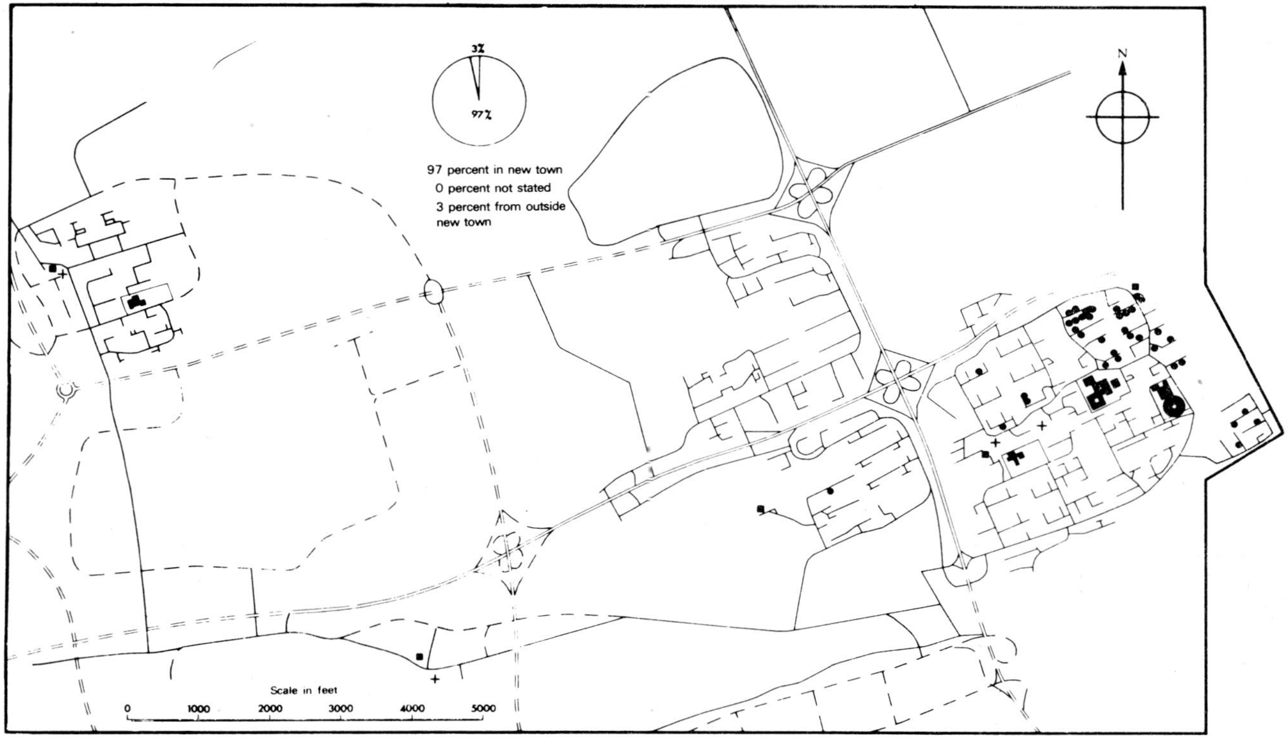

174

Fig. 6.23   Letham Junior Youth Centre: location of members/premises

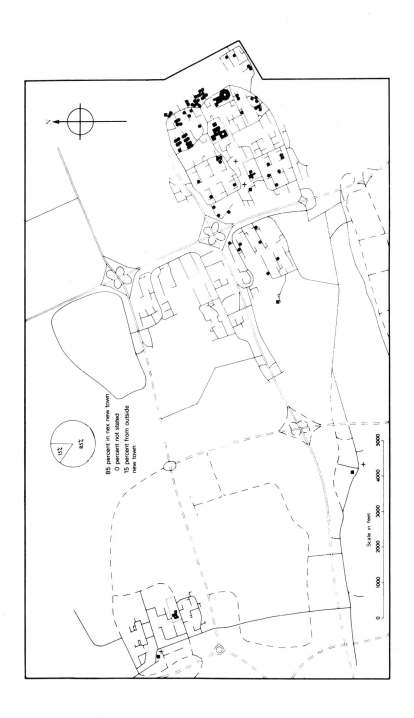

85 percent in nex new town
0 percent not stated
15 percent from outside
new town

Scale in feet

'walked across the fields' from Pumpherston, which is the nearest village to the east of the new town boundary. In a sense therefore, at least for the older and more mobile teenagers in the areas surrounding Craigshill, this club offered a facility which was new and modern and of a kind which was not readily found in these villages.

3   1ST LETHAM BROWNIE PACK
     Founded end of 1967
     Membership: 36
     Proportion in new town: 100 per cent
     Meeting place: Letham Primary School

Most of the comments made under fig. 6.22 applied to fig. 6.24 in the same way. This was a group catering for young children, the membership of which was drawn again from a very limited area within easy walking distance of the meeting place. Again, it was only the lack of leadership which prevented more of these groups from being established. These were children of newcomers who had all only just arrived (see completion dates on fig. 6.21) and who by and large had parents under forty years of age.

4   1ST RIVERSIDE BROWNIE PACK
     Founded August 1967
     Membership: 30
     Proportion in new town: 100 per cent
     Meeting place: Riverside Primary School

This pack was the first to be started in the new town in August 1967, by a young teacher at Riverside School, after the headmaster intimated that several of his pupils would be interested. A comparison of fig. 6.25 with fig. 6.21 illustrates that the children were drawn mainly from the two areas north and south of the school which were completed by December 1967 and which, again, were in the immediate vicinity of Riverside School: and also from Howden, immediately to the west of the meeting place. A comparison with fig. 6.24 shows how the two Brownie Packs divided their respective 'territories' – in fact the only member living in the northeast corner of Craigshill was the leader who incidentally also started the Letham Pack. It can thus be seen that the respective recruitment areas of the Brownie Packs were based on these two schools.

5   RIVERSIDE YOUTH WING OVER 15's CLUB
     Founded end of 1966
     Membership: approximately 140
     Proportion in new town: 60 per cent
     Meeting place: Riverside Youth Wing

Fig. 6.24 1st Letham Brownie Pack: location of members/premises

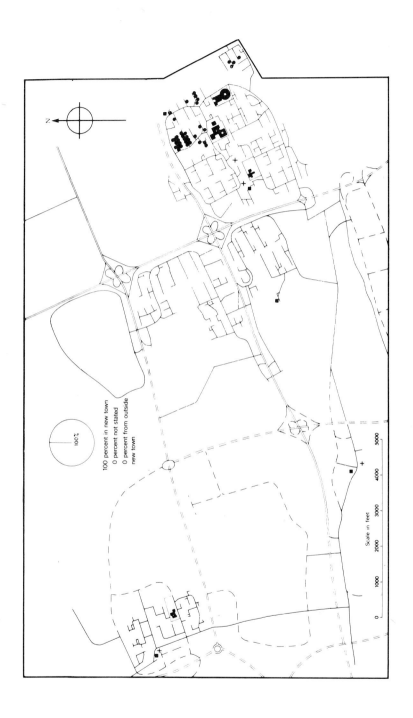

100 percent in new town
0 percent not stated
0 percent from outside
new town

Scale in feet

0   1000   2000   3000   4000   5000

Fig. 6.25   1st Riverside Brownie Pack: location of members/premises

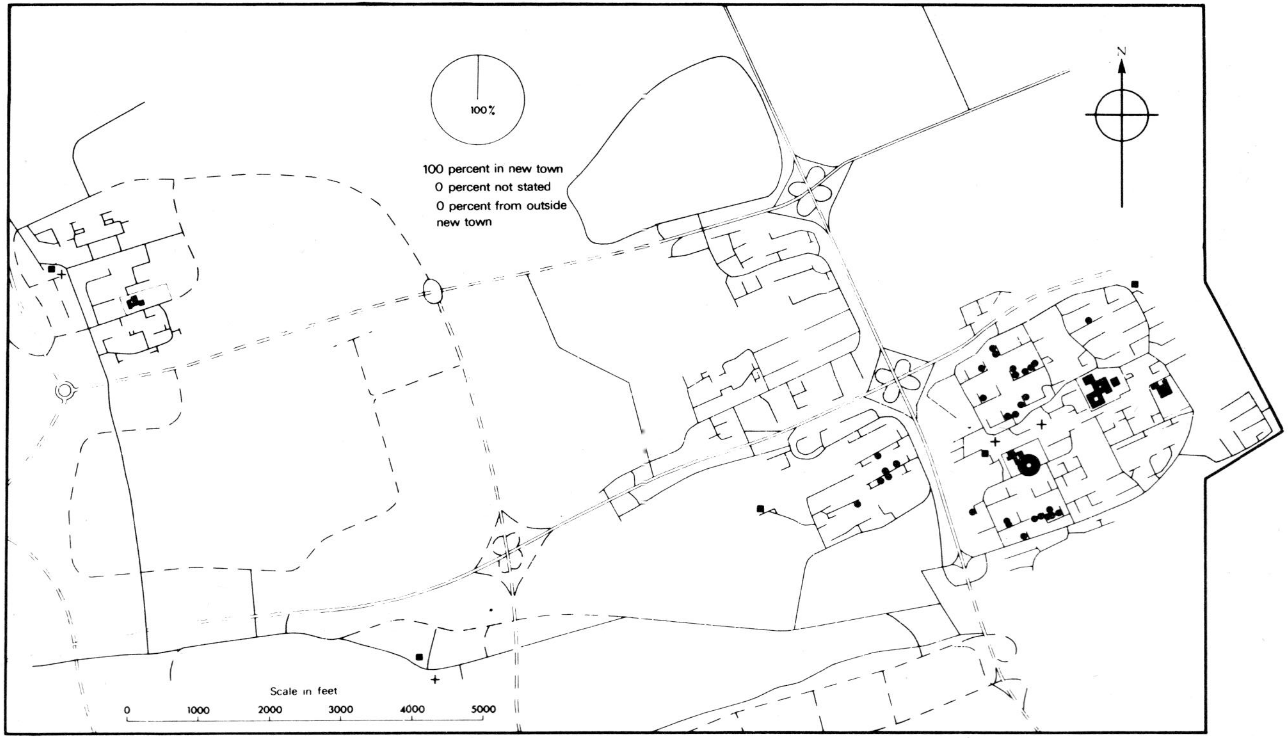

This club was started by a youth leader employed by the Midlothian Education Committee. Again, this was the kind of club which operated on an open door principle and therefore did not keep a comprehensive membership list. The twelve members represented on fig. 6.26 therefore only represented a one-in-four sample of members taken on an ordinary club night. Throughout the winter session some seventy 'members' attended a club night. However, this sample illustrates the point regarding the increased mobility which exists among the older teenagers. Only about 60 per cent of the members actually are known to live in the new town, the others came from villages surrounding the town. Again, the new facilities offered at Craigshill exerted an attraction which covered a wider area than the new town. It is also of interest to note that in this sample three members were found to travel across the new town from the Deans district. This map, in spite of the limited sample it covers, is therefore a useful illustration, particularly when compared with figs. 6.24 and 6.25, of how with increase in age of the children and young people catered for the actual location of the meeting place appears to become less vital.

Next in importance to the organisations catering for young people and children in this 'young' new town were those for their mothers and other women, which, as the maps show, were, like their equivalents in the other two new towns, fairly 'localised' in their membership intake.

1   CRAIGSHILL CO-OPERATIVE WOMEN'S GUILD
    Founded September 1968
    Membership: 26
    Proportion in new town: 100 per cent
    Meeting place: Riverside School

This was the kind of group where recruitment was confined largely to the particular neighbourhood in which the guild was operating. Their method of recruitment was described as 'members bringing along friends and neighbours'. The clusters of members which are shown in fig. 6.27 would suggest that this was in fact what happened in practice. Furthermore, the secretary herself lived in Doon Walk, in the south-west corner of Craigshill, where most of the members also happened to come from.

2   HOWDEN LADIES SOCIAL CLUB
    Founded February 1969
    Membership: 85
    Proportion in new town: 100 per cent
    Meeting place: Howden House

This group was started by the district midwife, who canvassed the idea

Fig. 6.26   Riverside Youth Wing Over 15's Club: location of members/premises

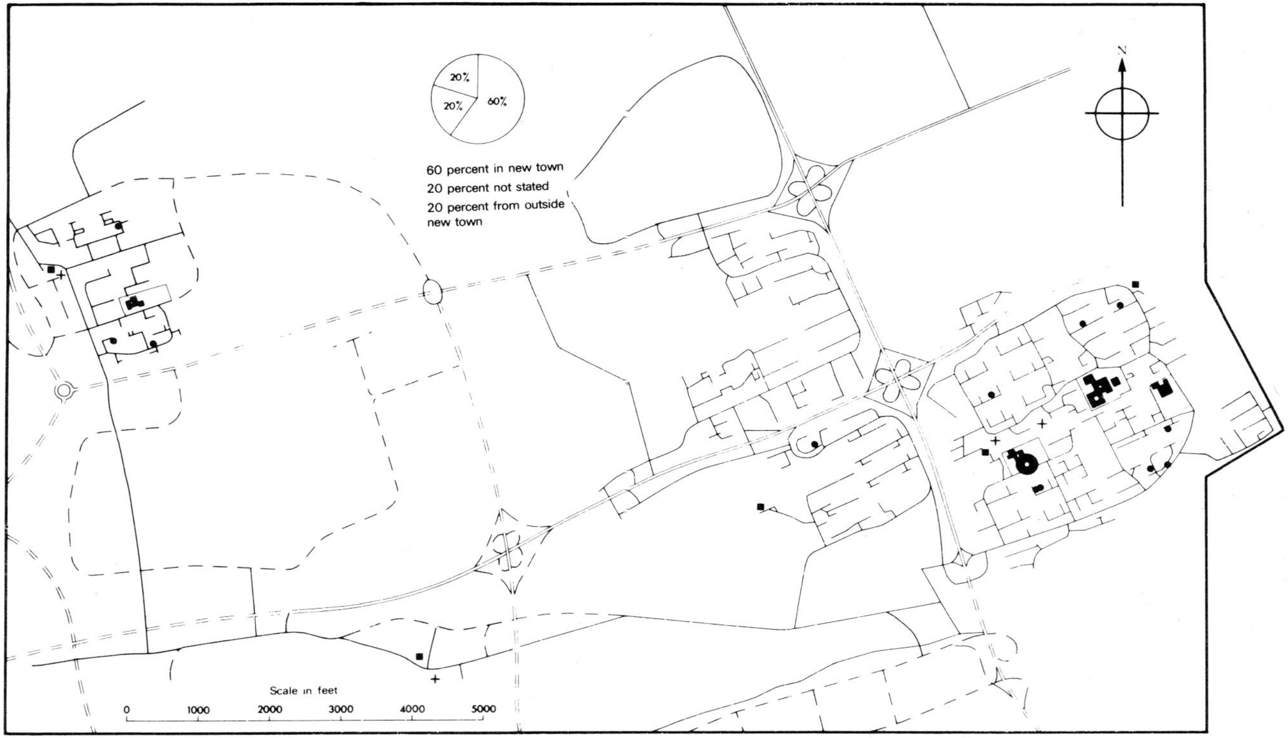

60 percent in new town
20 percent not stated
20 percent from outside
new town

60%
20%
20%

Scale in feet

0   1000   2000   3000   4000   5000

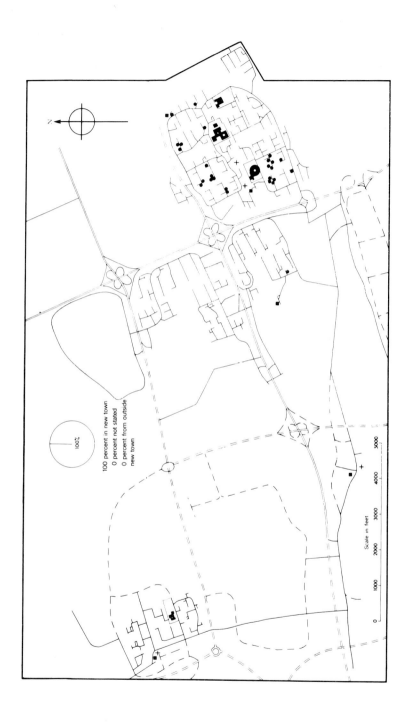

Fig. 6.27 Craigshill Co-operative Women's Guild: location of members/premises

100 percent in new town
0 percent not stated
0 percent from outside new town

100%

Scale in feet

0   1000   2000   3000   4000   5000

among the young mothers she was visiting in the course of her duties (over 80 per cent of members were under 30 years of age). She herself was resident in Toronto Avenue, in the Howden district, where virtually every housewife living in this street became a member. They used as their meeting place Howden House, which is within easy walking distance of the Howden district. This is another good example as to how receptive new arrivals are to the idea of forming a club in which they can meet their new neighbours on 'neutral territory'. The particular area of Howden in which most members were found (see fig. 6.28) was completed between May 1968 and April 1969. By the time this group was started even those who had been there longest had been in residence only about eight or nine months. The reason for starting this group was given by its founder as follows: 'to get all the new arrivals as speedily socialising as possible', and it looks as if this objective had been achieved, since every woman within that specific neighbourhood would appear to have joined. This example also illustrates that sometimes although 'the time is ripe' for a given group to be started, it still needs someone with sufficient drive and time to actually make the first move − the district midwife in this case. It is only fair to say that because of her special relationship with these young wives, who looked for a great deal of advice from her, particularly in a situation where their own mothers were likely to be living in another town, she was very likely to have met with a more enthusiastic response than perhaps anyone else.

Finally, the organisation described below may be taken as representative of the category sports organisations.

1 LIVINGSTON AND DISTRICT RUGBY FOOTBALL CLUB
    Founded 1968
    Membership: 70
    Proportion in new town: 43 per cent
    Meeting place: Whitburn Academy (plus own cottage)

As the name suggests, the membership of this club was drawn from a wider area than the town itself. The members living outside Livingston were mainly drawn from Armadale, Bathgate and Whitburn in West Lothian, but some were also found further afield, in Edinburgh to the east and Airdrie to the west. The club held its winter training sessions at Whitburn Academy (previously it had used Letham School at Craigshill). Furthermore, for social purposes the club also had a cottage at Bankton Mains which is within the designated area of Livingston, but was undeveloped at the time. As fig. 6.29 illustrates, the members who lived in Livingston were found in all parts of the town which had been developed

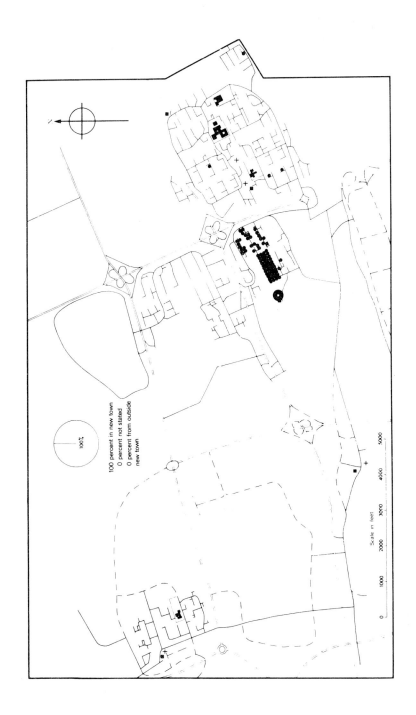

Fig. 6.28 Howden Ladies' Social Club: location of members/premises

100 percent in new town
0 percent not stated
0 percent from outside new town

100%

Scale in feet

0   1000   2000   3000   4000   5000

183

Fig. 6.29 Livingston and District Rugby Football Club: location of members/premises

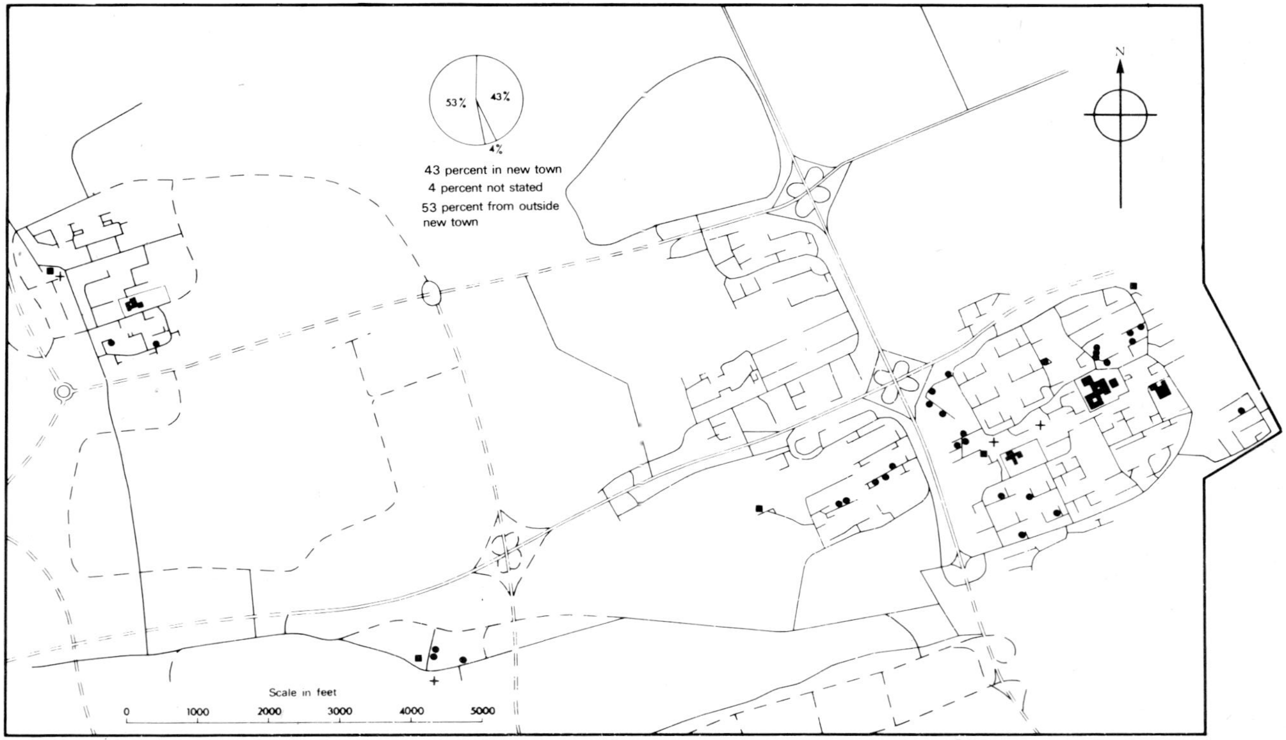

43 percent in new town
4 percent not stated
53 percent from outside new town

53%
43%
4%

N

Scale in feet

0   1000   2000   3000   4000   5000

by then, i.e. Craigshill, parts of Howden, Deans and the old village of Livingston itself. Again, as has been found to be the case with other more specialised interests, the siting of the actual meeting place is not as important as the enthusiasm of the 'aficionados' of a particular sport or hobby — who were willing and able to travel, at times a considerable distance, in pursuit of their interest.

Notes

[1] See Osborn and Whittick, *The New Towns,* Leonard Hill, London 1969, p. 366.

[2] When these maps were completed they, and the writer's comments upon them, were discussed with the planners in each of the three new towns. Their comments were then incorporated in the discussion of the maps which follows.

[3] Cadham is a separate village, to the north of Glenrothes, within the designated area, but not included in the maps which follow.

[4] Glenrothes Development Corporation, 18th Annual Report, 1966—67, p. 116, para. 24.

[5] Regrettably, the East Kilbride Development Corporation did not have data which could substantiate this notion, although verbally the planners agreed with it.

7 Social Development in New Towns: The Role of The Social Development Officer

Social organisations in new towns have an important part to play as a means by which residents are able to put down roots in a place in which most of them are relatively recent arrivals.

To enable them to perform this useful and desirable function, it was argued above, they require certain social facilities in which to meet and pursue their activities. A development corporation has an important role to play in the provision of these facilities. But should their contributions end there? As important, in many ways, as the provision of buildings, is the provision of staff who can actively foster the process of social development. In most new towns in England and Wales this has in fact happened and the purpose of the social development officer can be summed up in the words of an SDO who described his function as follows:

> In a new town everyone is now insecure, taking this plunge – often for the first time . . . I often say that part of my job is to help put down foundations, roots and traditions far earlier than would happen of their own accord. This is a great deal what we are all about – settling down an area as quickly as possible by whatever means come to hand.[1]

However, as we shall see in this chapter, the situation in Scotland was somewhat different and, in letter anyway if not in spirit, more akin to the original assumptions of the Reith committee in this matter.

The Reith committee, as noted in chapter 1, had very definite ideas relating to the 'social development' of new towns. However, in its final report, it did not include the position of the social development officer among the list of recommended personnel. It may be that the evidence it had gathered from Letchworth and Welwyn Garden City suggested that the social life in these two towns prospered so successfully,[2] without any assistance from specialists such as social development officers, that it was assumed that this pattern would be repeated in the other new towns. The

Reith committee was in no doubt that the existence of all kinds of social organisations and facilities for new residents was vital to the life of a new community. But it may have assumed that opportunities to participate in a variety of activities would arise automatically, without any special assistance and leadership being provided. Within the context of its own time this assumption is understandable, particularly since in the only two new towns from which it could draw any previous experience, a lively and varied programme of social activities had developed.

After the new town legislation was passed, no instructions relating to the appointment of social development officers were sent out from the ministry to the newly appointed development corporations. However, the first appointment of a social development officer in an English new town was made in Hemel Hempstead in 1949, by Lord Reith himself, who was then the chairman of the development corporation. He appointed Gerald Brooke-Taylor, who has become probably the most distinguished social development officer in the country and is now Director of Social Development in Telford New Town. Other appointments followed sporadically in other new towns, but no record was kept at the ministry. However, although it is true that the ministry did not issue specific instructions on this matter, a circular[3] was sent to all new town development corporations in August 1963, setting out the role of a social development officer in new towns. There were no direct recommendations made to the effect that every corporation should now appoint one, but the circular stressed the importance of the social development officer's work and described his functions as follows:

1 *Social Planning*

It is desirable that a Social Development Officer should be appointed early in the Development Corporation's life. During the planning stage of the town, he must be available — and indeed encouraged — to assist in policy decisions on size and type of dwellings related to the structure and changes of the population, types of employment, standards for recreation and community activities, social effects of proposed lay-out, and so on. He must be of sufficient calibre to join on equal terms in discussions [presumably with the other chief officers, such as architects, planners, engineers, finance officers etc.].[4]

2 *Relationships with other organisations*

Much of the success of a town which is rapidly and newly-built rests on the activities of organisations and groups both statutory, voluntary and commercial, outside the Development Corporation. A Social Development Officer must have knowledge of the structure and finance of these organisations, encourage and use of their powers and resources, have the imagination to foresee new possibilities and stimulate these, and to be tactful so as to achieve the best relationships with them. His job is to see that there are a variety of community facilities, that social provision in its widest sense is achieved by the use of both public and private enterprise, and that as full a range as possible of statutory and voluntary welfare services are available.

3   Community Development

The Social Development Officer should attempt to encourage the growth of voluntary organisations and civic and cultural activities, and to establish lines of communication between the residents and the Development Corporation and district and county councils. He must be actively aware of the needs of the residents in the town and the provision to be made for them.

4   Public relations and information

The Social Development Officer should see that facilities are available to give a service of information and advice to any resident who may need it on any problem that may arise, e.g. a tenant's handbook. Public relations may also be part of his work and, if so, he should be knowledgeable on press and publicity, handouts, exhibitions, etc. These activities would normally be closely linked with the General Manager's office.

5   Research

Comprehensive records of both incoming and outgoing tenants should be kept by the Housing Management Department and demographic information compiled and kept up to date. Statistical information of this sort becomes increasingly important as the town develops, since it influences day-to-day decisions on the quantity rate and type of further development both by the Corporation and other bodies, e.g. the education authority.

The circular then went on to emphasise that any person appointed to such a post should be of sufficient calibre to join on equal terms in discussions with professional colleagues and, if need be, to put his point of view direct to the general manager. It was also made quite clear that no one person would necessarily be expected to incorporate all four functions mentioned above, but that staff should be appointed to 'complement' the social development officer's own specialism.

Although this circular was not issued till 1963, i.e. seventeen years after the publication of the Reith report, it would appear to have filled a gap in the recommendations of that report. This was the first official indication that the ministry, which was concerned with the building and developing of new towns, began to show an interest in aspects of social development. It is, of course, not possible to try and determine what exactly caused this circular to be published, but it is reasonable to assumes that, by now, more was known about the work of people like Brooke-Taylor. He incidentally described his task as 'lubricator of the body politic'.[5] Furthermore, although it is not possible to establish a direct link, it is interesting to note that by the time this circular was published the report of the Bristol social project had been submitted,[6] describing the role of the community organiser in relation to social problems of newly developed areas.

In a pamphlet published in 1963 which arose out of the work of the Bristol social project,[7] Professor Roger Wilson made a strong plea for the employment of community organisers. As he saw it, the work of such a community organiser would take three forms all of which, in terms of the above definitions of the functions of the social development officer, could be subsumed under 'community development'. These three forms of work would be:

(a) to act as a link between authority and people — explaining and representing both ways, and in the process affecting the attitudes of both parties.
(b) to help people to bring to fruition constructive group intentions; that is to say, where people want to get something done or get a new social activity underway, the community organiser should be available to give them advice and support.
(c) to try to generate social groups of one sort or another where he sees promise which does not look as if it would mature of its own accord.

It is, of course, true to say that Professor Wilson was thinking mainly of housing estates, such as those which were the subject of the Bristol social project investigation, but nevertheless it is readily apparent that these recommendations apply equally well to new towns. Indeed, it could be said that in practice some of the early new towns, such as Hemel Hempstead, led the way in this field.

Whether or not there was any direct connection between the

recommendations published by Wilson and the appearance of the above-quoted ministry circular would be difficult to establish, and the fact that both were published in 1963 may be mere coincidence. It is, however, interesting to note that ideas about social development in new towns and new urban estates had now matured, as a result of the work of people like Brooke-Taylor in the new towns, and the research undertaken by the Bristol social project. Taking a different route, their recommendations pointed in the same direction, as a comparison between the functions of a social development officer and a community organiser (as defined above) illustrates. Circular XT/290/5/2 was sent only to the new town development corporations and was never made public. However, in a further ministry publication four years later,[8] the 'social relations officer', as the committee writing this report preferred to call him, was given the same four functions, i.e. social planning and advice; public relations; community development; and research and information. Again they saw the social relations officer as a senior officer in the general manager's department. The report also stated that such officers had, by then, been appointed in most of the older new towns, and significantly in all more recent new towns. They then went on to recommend that every expanding town should appoint similar officers.

Lastly, the Gulbenkian Foundation published a report in 1968[9] in which, once again, the functions of a new town social relations officer were described. In terms of social policy implications, this particular statement went further than any of the above-mentioned. Not only was the function of the new town social relations officer seen as including research, public relations and community development, but the officer was also thought to be the 'primary Corporation contact with the County Medical Officer of Health, the County Education Officer, and County Welfare Officer, the County Librarian, the Corporation's representative on the Council of Social Service; the County Playing Fields Association; the regional Sports Council; the local Arts Council and the Town and Country Planning Association'. Clearly this has to be taken as a statement of an ideal – a set of desiderata rather than an account of what is practicable in each situation.

As will be shown, the situation in the Scottish new towns differed significantly from that described in the above reports, since no appointments along the suggested lines have so far been made.

Of course this does not mean that none of the three new towns in this study had any policy regarding the social development of its town, but what policy it had did not express itself in the appointment of a social development officer and the establishing of a separate department to discharge the above-mentioned functions.

In *East Kilbride*, in the course of our research, the following picture emerged relating to the question of social development. During the early years of the corporation's existence there was no public relations department, nor was there a regular collection of demographic data. Functions (4) and (5), as defined in the ministry circular, were therefore not being fulfilled. (One must remember that East Kilbride Development Corporation was appointed in 1948 – whereas this comprehensive definition of the function of a social development officer was not circulated until 1963.) However, there were already in existence a number of groups in the old village, and the county council (i.e. the education authority) ran a programme of evening hobby classes. Requests for help and advice were received by the general manager, who in turn asked the legal adviser to help in drawing up constitutions for newly formed groups. Once groups of residents had taken the initiative, the corporation was willing to help in a practical way – but not by way of finance. This was a different approach from the one envisaged and recommended by all three of the above statements relating to social development (and social development officers). They called for a much more active approach towards the formation and fostering of social organisations in the community.

It appears that although the subject of social development had been discussed frequently the corporation had decided to leave this largely to the education authorities. A corporation official in an interview also mentioned 'that there was no need for the corporation to do anything in the sphere of social development – since the churches did it all'. Whilst this statement illustrates the important role played by the various churches in new towns, it was perhaps somewhat unfair on the corporation, since they had held regular meetings with residents' associations from each neighbourhood. Until a few years ago they also invited every new group of residents to a 'Talk and Tea'. It would appear that discussions on the subject of social development by the development corporation centred round the question: What was more important, staff or premises?

Since there were severe restrictions placed on the corporation regarding the provision of premises, it was left mainly to the county council, and later to the town council, to provide these. It was also felt that existing staff, working in the field of housing management, legal advice and, later, public relations, could perform the remaining social development functions. What effect, if any, the absence of trained staff, who could have concerned themselves more actively with the growth of voluntary associations and the development of cultural and other activities, has had on the development of social organisations, is almost impossible to assess from today's perspective. One can only speculate on this, but the fact remains that today there exists in East Kilbride an impressive variety of organisations which have been founded and grown up with a minimum of help from outside. Perhaps the help the corporation, and the churches etc., were able to give was 'sufficient'. Whether there would be more of them today if there had been a social development officer (or a community organiser) would be difficult to establish, particularly in the absence of firm criteria as to what, for instance, would constitute an 'optimum number of organisations'. But it seems clear that, particularly in the light of the evidence presented in the 'Needs of new communities' report, such an officer would have been able, given the right qualities and imagination, 'to foresee new possibilities and to stimulate them'. Co-ordinating bodies, such as the East Kilbride Sports Council, might have been created sooner given the drive and the leadership of a full-time official who could have taken a more positive lead in fostering relationships between different organisations. The same could be said relating to an arts council in the town which would co-ordinate more effectively the different cultural activities. A social relations officer whose main function is 'to liaise with other bodies' might also have been able to bring about a council of social service, which, in turn, could act as a vehicle to co-ordinate the efforts of the various groups concerned in the field of voluntary social service. These are just some of the gaps which exist today, or have existed until very recently (in the case of the sports council) which it would seem a social development officer, given the right imaginative approach, could have helped to bridge. This co-ordinating function, therefore, can transcend the remit of any one single function, such as public relations, or research, which are carried out by specialist officers working in a different department. Similarly, specific groups relating to all kinds of social activities can be started by individuals in their spare time, helped by churches and be given advice on the drawing up of their constitutions. When, however, the need arises for co-ordination of these individual activities, perhaps in pursuit of a more comprehensive policy, the positive role of a social development officer becomes most apparent. It can therefore be claimed that although East Kilbride is now a fully developed town, the need for an officer with such a function has not been superseded by time. Whether he should more appropriately be placed within the social work department, which was formed in 1968 after the burgh had achieved large burgh status, is a matter for debate. In this respect, East Kilbride is unique among the Scottish new towns, in as much as it became the only one with large burgh status and has, therefore, its own social work department. Indeed the 'Town Council's desire to obtain Large Burgh status was strongly motivated by their concern to improve the Health, Welfare and Children's Services in the Burgh'. [10] This would, in many ways be an appropriate move since the social welfare function which the Gulbenkian report definition ascribed to 'their' new town social relations officer has been taken over by the above department.

In *Glenrothes* too, the development corporation was asked to give the reasons they may have had for not setting up a social development department, or appointing a social development officer. From the answer received and from discussions with members of the staff of the development corporation the following emerged. In the early days, the need for a social development officer did not occur to the corporation and the question was not considered. It was felt that the separate functions which have been ascribed to the social development officer were taken care of by the demographic research section of the planning department, by the housing officer and his department (part of his remit is, in fact, concerned with 'social relations', inasmuch as he acts as a 'broker' between the newcomers and the existing organisations), and by individual members of the staff on a voluntary basis.

It is now the opinion of the corporation that the town has reached a stage of development where the need for such an officer 'is to a great extent diminished in that the social facilities and clubs are in the main, now self-generating'.

It is also interesting to note that it was felt that circular XT/290/5/2 was applicable to England and Wales only. In a strict legalistic sense this is, of course, true, since documents relating to Scottish new towns would have to come through the Scottish Development Department. However, since this circular was in no way prescriptive, but was merely pointing out the importance and the functions of a social development officer, the Scottish new towns would in no way have been prevented from making use of the information it contained and putting it into practice by appointing such officers. It is true to say that the demographic research unit are supplying the planners with all the data they require. Indeed, in the case of Glenrothes, the staff of that unit had interpreted their remit much more widely, and were instrumental in bringing about, for instance, an information kiosk in the town centre which provides residents with readily accessible information about the town and the services available to them. But when the same staff wanted to promote an adventure playground during the summer school holidays, their efforts were thwarted by their superior officers on the grounds that this was not an appropriate activity for such a unit. This is a useful illustration of the point, which both circular XT/290/5/2 and the report on 'Needs of new communities' state unequivocally, when they suggest that a social development officer should have chief officer status, which would allow him to 'join on equal terms in discussions with professional colleagues and, if need be, to put his point of view direct to the General Manager'. In the above case, the demographic research section forms part of the planning department, at the head of which is the chief architect and planner. In this instance he had asked his researchers to undertake a survey of children's play needs in the new town. [11] The findings of this report led the researchers to believe that the operation of an adventure playground would make a major contribution to the play needs of the town's children during the summer vacation. They were prepared to 'mount the exercise' with the help of students, who would have been paid by the corporation. In the event, however, their chief officer did not see this as part of the function of the planning research unit and the scheme did not materialise. In a strict sense he was right — runnning (or starting up) an adventure playground is not part of the remit of a planning research unit — but, in the absence of any other existing channels within the development corporation, there was no officer specifically responsible for such an enterprise. Had there been a social development officer whose views carried sufficient weight with his fellow chief officers, events might have taken a different turn. Once the researchers showed that a real need existed, he could have acted upon these findings.

Moreover, there is no specific public relations department within the development corporation. Public relations, with a view to attracting industry to the town, are handled by a London consultant. Visitors to the town are ably received by the assistant to the general manager, and in this respect 'these activities are closely linked with the General Manager's Office', as the circular suggests. But his portfolio involves so many other duties that his time does not allow him to give a widely available service of information and advice to the residents of the town. Again the initiative for such a service, which resulted in the provision of an 'information kiosk', came from the planning research unit, who had discovered the need for it through their close contact with the population. In this instance their recommendations had been eventually accepted by their superiors — but if they had not been well received, the researchers would have had no power to implement the results of their findings, which a social development officer might well have had.

Of course, it is also true that the idea of combining the housing officer's duties with those of a social relations officer (and incorporate this in his designation) has certain attractions. Indeed, this is how Cumbernauld,

Livingston and Glenrothes have decided to solve this particular problem. Since, as shown in chapter 6, at the time of this study the development corporations in the new towns in this sample own and let approximately 90 per cent of all houses, the housing manager comes in contact with most residents in one way or another. He has an opportunity to find out about people's hobbies and interests and directs them to existing clubs which cater for these interests. He may also have a housing visitor (welfare officer) on his staff, who will act as a kind of 'arrivals officer', [12] and who will help to smooth over problems relating to settling in a new house. Similarly, if people are in difficulty regarding their rent, they may get a sympathetic hearing from the housing officer.

On the other hand, he is also the officer who has to procure references about prospective residents, and has to enforce certain rules and regulations regarding tenancy of corporation houses, and ultimately he may also be the officer responsible for arranging an eviction for an 'unsatisfactory tenant'. Thus it can be seen that he has a number of functions, some of which may be conflicting and create tension, such as combining a welfare function with that of a factor doing his duty *vis-à-vis* the landlord over the question of rent arrears. The 'Needs of new communities' report [13] was aware of this problem. Paragraph 219 states:

> We draw attention to a major problem which must be guarded against. One of the main functions of a Social Relations Officer is to liaise with other bodies. He will thus have close contact with voluntary bodies, the local statutory services and other departments of the local authority. *By the nature of his work, he will be concerned to see that gaps in provision are filled.* But he must take care not to fill them himself; he must not become a social worker as well as a Social Relations Officer. We see this as a very real danger, particularly in areas where the social services are understaffed. It is, of course, an even greater danger if the Social Relations Officer combined some or all the functions of an Arrivals Officer. [14]

Undoubtedly, the writers of this report would agree that the same could be said about a combination of the role of a housing officer with that of the social relations officer. Then there is the more immediate practical problem as to how much time the housing officer will have left, after he has done all that is required of him *qua* housing officer, to 'liaise with other bodies' and promote and encourage the growth and development of social organisations in his town.

But of course members of the corporation staff, particularly in Glenrothes, have played an important part in the life of a great many social and cultural activities. It would seem that all the fragmented contributions to the 'area of social development' which have been forthcoming — through the planning research unit, the housing department, from individual members of the staff on a voluntary basis, and by the efforts of the general manager and board members — valuable as they are, did not add up to a comprehensive policy. The argument is that, as in the case of East Kilbride, a social development officer, even after more than twenty-five years of the town's existence, would still have a vital role to play in co-ordinating statutory and voluntary efforts and in marshalling the resources of the local authority, the development corporation and the community, as well as in helping to initiate new activities.

Whereas both East Kilbride and Glenrothes were started more than twenty-five years ago, and therefore before the time when ideas relating to social development in new towns were more widely canvassed, *Livingston New Town* is a relatively recent creation. It is reasonable to assume that the collective experience of other new communities might have been of some use to the development corporation charged with making Livingston a 'good place' to live in. Even if one agreed, as Glenrothes Development Corporation claimed, that the ministry circular only applied to England, Livingston had the opportunity of learning from the experience of other new towns, and especially from the mark 1 towns. If one used as a model, however, the definition of a social development officer as given in the ministry circular or in the 'Needs of new communities' report, then the arrangement which Livingston Development Corporation chose to make regarding such an appointment still falls short of the ideal. The Livingston situation represents a kind of 'middle position' between the practice in Glenrothes and East Kilbride and the ideal set out in the above papers, an ideal which incidentally is also found to be operating in some of the English new towns.

In Livingston too, as in Glenrothes, the office of housing manager incorporates some of the social development functions. The officer is termed 'property manager and social relations officer'. He is not a chief officer, but attends the chief officers' conferences. He in turn has on his staff a community development and an assistant community development officer. It was pointed out to us that to combine the position of property manager with that of social relations officer was thought to be 'logical', since it is the property manager who has the first contact with newcomers to the town. Like his opposite number in Glenrothes, he enquires about the various activities in which a family might be interested, and then arranges a meeting between members of a club pursuing a particular activity, or, through his staff, tries to bring about the formation of such a club, if it does not already exist. Considerable help has already been given by his department, particularly through the social development officer, which resulted, directly or indirectly, in a remarkable growth of new organisations. [15] The aspect of the social development function relating to fostering and nurturing new groups seems to be taken care of, and the corporation now plays an active part in this. However, initially, as was said to have been the case in East Kilbride, 'the churches did it all'. Or, if not all, then at least they, through their team ministry and the Church of Scotland youth workers, also produced a house-to-house news sheet *Newsflash*; similarly, the Craigs Farm Centre created the initial impetus leading to the formation of several groups. This was then gradually followed up by the development corporation which now plays an active part in the social development of this new community.

The research function, as was the case in Glenrothes, is being carried out within the planning department itself. The social development officer is, therefore, not part of the planning team. It appears that the social development officer in this case is not involved in advising the planners on the social implications of their physical plan.

The property manager, by training and experience, is a 'housing administrator', on to whose remit the function of social relations officer was grafted. The social development officer, on the other hand, whom the property manager considers to be his 'grass-roots worker', has a responsibility which is confined primarily to the development of contacts with the residents and to helping them in the initiation and support of organisations. But there is a difficult problem in the conflict of roles. He is seen as an extension of the housing manager's office, and in this role he is required to help in the resolution of difficulties which arise between landlord and tenant. At the same time he wishes to enjoy the confidence and trust of the residents in order to be able to work with them in his role as social development officer. There exists, therefore, a role conflict which is built into an appointment which combines the functions of housing management and social development. Although the logic regarding the first point of contact looks at first deceptively attractive, discussions and observations confirm the view of the 'Needs of new communities' report, that such a combination of functions is not helpful, and that the resulting role conflicts are likely to create more problems than they solve.

Furthermore, since the terms social relations officer and social development officer are used synonymously in relation to new towns, [16] confusion was often caused when the social development officer, who was junior to the Property Manager, was thought to be a social development officer in the 'received sense'. (For instance, by English social development officers.) This situation has since been rationalised inasmuch as the term 'community development officer' is now being used. Apart from avoiding the above kind of confusion, it also more accurately describes the function of this officer. Therefore, it can be said that although the development corporation through its property manager/social relations officer, and community development officer plays an active part in the promotion of 'social relations' in the town, the different function of planning advice, public relations, community development and research are again fragmented, and any advantages which might derive from a closer co-ordination between these four functions under one department are therefore forfeited.

However, if increased co-ordination between different organisations is ever required — and it is reasonable to assume that when the present spurt of new formations slows down this will be necessary — then the corporation will be able to take an active part, even through its present 'imperfect' system. The fact that the corporation employs specific staff to do this work, represents a considerable advance over the position of the other two new towns.

The presence or absence of a social development officer, although of interest and importance, is not in itself sufficiently accurate an indication of the corporation's attitudes and policy *vis-à-vis* social organisations. In order to establish more accurately whether there is a marked difference between a new town which has had the benefit of a social development department and one which has not, it would be necessary to match certain new towns very carefully, and establish a set of criteria by which this could be judged. Although such criteria are not available at present, it would nevertheless seem that the balance of the evidence collected by the 'Needs of new communities' report, and indeed the findings of this research, suggest that all three new towns, whether substantially complete or still in the early stages of development, could benefit from the appointment of social development officers with a comprehensive remit such as outlined in that report.

A further criterion of the 'social policy' of a new town development corporation might be reflected in the use it has chosen to make of its powers to provide social amenities. Here also there are marked differences in practice between Scotland and England. What has really been lacking, perhaps above all, is a more coherent policy based on a real understanding of the needs of these new communities at the various stages of their development. All three development corporations took the social aspects of their work seriously: none appointed experts to advise them. Indeed, in fairness, one must add that few experts were available for them to appoint, at least initially. One also gets the impression that perhaps to some degree they still share the feelings which Stevenage Corporation expressed, when they disbanded their social development department in its third year:[17] 'Social Development is not a thing apart, and must be the direct concern of every one of the Corporation's officers'. While nobody would want to dispute the sentiment contained in the latter part of this statement it is also significant that a few years later Stevenage Corporation set up a new social relations department.

Notes

[1] M. Horrocks, 'Social development work in the new communities', occasional paper no. 27, University of Birmingham Centre for Urban and Regional Studies, 1974 p. 50.

[2] See also Osborn and Whittick, *The New Towns*, Leonard Hill, London 1969, ch. 4, p. 59.

[3] Ministry of Housing and Local Government, circular XT/290/5/2, 1963.

[4] Author's comments in brackets

[5] G. Brooke-Taylor, 'Community life in new towns', *Social Service Quarterly*, vol. 32, 1959, p. 148.

[6] Spencer, Tuxford and Dennis, *Stress and Release in an Urban Estate*, Tavistock Publication, 1964.

[7] R. Wilson, 'Difficult housing estates', Tavistock pamphlet no. 5, 1963, p. 23.

[8] Cullingworth et al., 'The needs of new communities', HMSO, 1967, ch. 5.

[9] 'Community work and social change', Gulbenkian Foundation 1968, p. 165.

[10] See also 'Consultative document on social work policy, issued by East Kilbride Town Council, January 1972.

[11] 'Children's play survey', unpublished report, Glenrothes Development Corporation, Planning Research, March 1970.

[12] For further details of the function of this officer, see 'Needs of new communities', op.cit., p. 55.

[13] Ibid., p. 60.

[14] Author's italics.

[15] At the time of the study there were just over forty organisations. There are now three times as many.

[16] Circular XT/290/5/2 uses one, 'Needs of new communities' the other — both describe the same office.

[17] Third Annual Report of Stevenage Development Corporation 1949/1950, PP 1950/51 (7)XVII, HMSO 1950, p. 185.

8 Conclusion and Summary

The new towns were seen by the Reith committee, and by the first postwar government which implemented its recommendations, as an instrument not only of economic policy, but also as one of social policy. In fact, it could be argued that by incorporating and stressing 'social development' as an inherent activity of the respective development corporations, the Reith committee added a new dimension to the goals of social policy. This final chapter will draw together some of the findings, relate them to, and compare them with the assumptions of the Reith report regarding social development in new towns. These have already been outlined in chapter 1 and will, therefore, only be reproduced here in summary form, but in the order in which they appeared in the text of the Reith report.

Assumption 1: 'People need a sense of belonging and an opportunity for participation.'

The Reith report[1] expected the various social organisations to provide the opportunity for a sense of belonging and for participation. Judging by the number of organisations which exist in the three new towns investigated, and the great variety of activities which can be pursued through them, it would appear that this opportunity to participate is indeed available. Furthermore, it would seem that the number of people who actively participate is high. Tables 3.1, 3.2 and 3.3 give an indication of the rate of participation among residents, according to age groups. From these tables it also becomes evident that the life cycle of the members of the population has an influence on the degree of participation in each age group.[2] For instance, it was found that the 10–19 age range had higher overall membership figures than any other age group. (In Livingston, for instance, the number of memberships held by this age group accounted for 80·2 per cent of the population in that age range.) By and large, there were slightly more women members than men in almost all age groups. But, as the tables show, there were different patterns of participation emerging from the different towns. For instance, in Livingston a higher proportion of male teenagers and young women in the 20–29 age group were in membership than in either of the other two new towns. This, it has been claimed, is to some extent due to the full-time leadership which was available in Livingston almost from the beginning, and which helped to promote participation, particularly in these two groups, which were singled out by these leaders as their special remit.

On the other hand, in Glenrothes there was a higher proportion of the over–60 age groups, male and female, in membership of organisations catering for old people. It also happens that Glenrothes would appear to have more facilities (and perhaps better leadership through its two committees which concern themselves exclusively with the welfare of old people) than the other two new towns. One would have to qualify this statement by adding that of course the proportion of over 60's in the Livingston population is very much smaller than that of the other two towns. But in East Kilbride and Glenrothes the proportions in the population were similar, or certainly not dissimilar, enough to account for the difference in the levels of participation. It would therefore seem that where facilities and leadership are available, the level of participation is higher.

Therefore, it can be said that the opportunity to 'acquire a sense of belonging' through participation in the activities of a multitude of organisations exists in each of the three new towns. The level of participation, however, differs from town to town. An attempt to identify some of the factors which account for these differences has been made in chapter 3. Availability of facilities and leadership would appear to be among the most important of these.

Assumption 2a: Social cohesion is a desirable goal of social policy;
and 2b: Voluntary organisations have a role to play in bringing
about opportunities for participation, and through it, social cohesion.

The concept of social balance which is inherent in the above two assumptions has undergone considerable changes since the time the Reith report was written. As seen in chapter 4.1, a number of writers on the subject, such as Mann and Heraud, would prefer the idea of social balance to be 'quietly buried'. The objective of achieving social balance at the level of the neighbourhood has indeed been recognised as being too idealistic and impracticable – but it has not been given up as an ideal worth striving for at the level of the whole town, not least for reasons of economic policy. The maps, particularly figs. 6.1, 6.12 and 6.21, illustrate that in each of these towns there are areas which are almost exclusively inhabited by owner-occupiers, or at least reserved for executives who pay a higher rent.

The reservation of whole areas where houses are for sale, rather than 'sprinkling' individual owner-occupier houses among council houses, or houses let by the respective development corporation, has been found to be the only practicable way for the development corporation to avoid what Glenrothes called the 'five o'clock executive exit'. In other words, the objective of achieving a heterogeneous community at town level is being pursued by the development corporations, although it meant sacrificing the achievement of social balance at neighbourhood level as, for instance, Lewis Silkin envisaged it, when he steered the New Towns Bill through Parliament. However, the development corporations would appear to agree with the assumptions of the Reith report which looked towards the various social organisations for providing a platform on which the different sections of the community could meet. The objective of bringing about a measure of social cohesion remains, therefore, in operation. For instance, East Kilbride Town Council were reported to have decided 'to give priority in their support to those clubs which already served the widest cross-section of the community'. If this is taken to mean[3] 'cross-section' in terms of occupational groups, then the findings of chapter 4.2 are particularly relevant, since they might provide tentative guidelines to policy makers in these new towns and elsewhere to decide which type of organisation should be given priority. This is on the assumption that their policy was one in which those organisations which are seen to reflect most closely in their membership the social structure of the population at large, are given support. Tables 4.4, 4.5 and 4.6, which contain the chi-squared comparisons between the occupational status of the population of each of the three towns with the membership of respective organisations, show the level of 'representativeness' of each organisation. In Glenrothes (table 4.4) it was found that a youth organisation (Exit Club, no. 22) registered the lowest chi-square value, followed by the Horticultural Society (no. 20). In East Kilbride (table 4.5) the two organisations which would appear to reflect the composition of the population most closely were the Curling Club (no. 140) and the Calderwood Ladies' Club (no. 98). In Livingston (table 4.6) the two organisations in the sample which scored the lowest chi-square value were the Craigshill WRI (no. 169) and the Scottish National Party (no. 176).

Interesting though these individual scores are, it is perhaps more relevant to try and perceive trends not in terms of individual organisations, but in the categories by which they were grouped. Table 4.8 provides a summary for all three towns, from which it can be noted that in all three towns it was the youth organisations which provided the kind of platform referred to above. On the other hand, the 'social service' organisations, as was the case in Bottomore's Squirebridge,[4] are by and large made up of those who can 'afford to dispense charity' and may be motivated by the *noblesse oblige* syndrome. Women's organisations, as also becomes apparent from the bar-charts on figs. 4.5, 4.15 and 4.22 in all three towns tend to cater for specific, and sometimes limited, status groups only, often leaving out group 5 altogether. Table 4.8 also illustrates that in this case, as in many others, there exist similarities between Glenrothes and East Kilbride which do not apply to Livingston, as the most recent of the three towns.

For instance, in the case of the hobby/special interest groups in both Glenrothes and East Kilbride, it can be said that they do provide a meeting place for the various sections of the community, where they were third and fourth in rank order, whereas in Livingston they were last (largely due to the 'exclusiveness' of the Bridge Club). It would, however, appear that over time organisations in all categories become more representative of the town's population. This was borne out by the fact that East Kilbride, which is nearly completed, had the lowest chi-square value overall, and Livingston the highest, with Glenrothes figuring in between the two, but displaying characteristics closer to East Kilbride (see table 4.8).

Chapter 4.2 not only showed who the 'joiners' are, in terms of occupational groups, but also who provides the leadership. Figures 4.2 – 4.25, wherever possible, show the occupational status of the leaders in separate bar-charts. Tables 4.1, 4.2 and 4.3 show the chi-square comparison between the occupational status of the membership and that of the leadership. These tables show the chi-square value for each organisation which could give this information. Table 4.9 gives a summary and rank order for the different categories in each new town. It is striking to note from this table that in Glenrothes and East Kilbride the lowest chi-square value was recorded by the women's organisations, and in Livingston too they ranked among the first three. The youth organisations too, by and large, had a leadership which was representative of the membership in terms of occupational status. On the other hand, it was also remarkable to note that the political organisations ranked last in East Kilbride and Livingston, and second last in Glenrothes. In other words, taken as a category, they would appear to be least representative of their membership in their leadership.

Overall, with only a few exceptions which have been referred to in chapter 4.2, the differences which were noted between the occupational status distribution of the membership and the leadership can be accounted for by a 'shift of dominance' towards the higher status groups. It can be shown that they tend to be represented in the leadership to a greater extent, proportionately, than in membership. In this respect, the findings of this study concur with a number of other studies in this field, such as Bottomore, Reissmann, Bell and Force, Vereker and Mays, Willmott and Young, Cauter and Downham, and J. Klein, which have already been referred to in chapter 4.2. It can therefore be said that organisations in these three towns do indeed cater for a wide cross-section of these communities, but to different degrees. The extent to which they differ can be seen from the figures which illustrate chapter 4 and the tables, where comparisons have been made between the occupational status composition of all the organisations, with that of the population of the town in which they operate.

Assumption 3a: Certain minimum facilities are to be regarded as essential in a new town from the very outset; and 3b: A diversity of buildings is desirable.

In theory, the Scottish new towns appear to have accepted the need for minimum facilities in the early stages, and a diversification of facilities at a later stage. In practice, as the early history particularly of East Kilbride shows, there have been special difficulties due to the climate of economic stringency which prevailed throughout the country at the time. As was noted above, in the mid-fifties the East Kilbride Development Corporation[5] expressed the view to the Secretary of State that: 'new towns ought to have more power to provide community service halls, and the impression is that English new towns are better served in this respect'. Seven years later[6] the corporation made the same point again, but perhaps even more forcibly when they stated:

> Every year that passes, there are more young people in the town seeking outlets for their energies and aspirations. Equally, there are more adults freed from the obligations of looking after young children, and, therefore, are able to participate in community activities beyond the family circle. Plans must be made immediately to provide meeting places which will be in increasing demand. Some help from outside is to be expected in a town lacking the social equipment which established places enjoy as a result of past patronage and capital investment.

207

These last comments were made just a year prior to the introduction of the Major Amenity Fund, which allowed development corporations to spend £4 per head of target population on 'social equipment'.

The remarks in the Seventh Annual Report of East Kilbride Development Corporation, relating to English new towns being better served, refers to a handicap which particularly affected the Scottish new towns. Since the rents in Scottish new towns were considerably lower than those charged in the English new towns, the Scottish new towns accumulated a deficit on the housing revenue account and were therefore not allowed, as housing authorities, to reserve an element in the rents for the purpose of financing community facilities.

From the annual reports it would appear that East Kilbride was very much more acutely affected by the lack of community buildings in those early days than Glenrothes, simply because the East Kilbride population grew so much more rapidly. Furthermore, in Glenrothes, which was largely geared to the needs of the coal industry up to the beginning of the sixties, the coal industry social welfare organisation made a substantial contribution to the provision of community facilities. However, apart from that, the same restrictions applied to Glenrothes, although they would appear to have been less acutely felt.

The case of Livingston differs from that of the two other earlier new towns in some respects, although they too were subject to the same restriction regarding the size of community buildings which the Secretary of State would allow them to build.[7] However, by the time Livingston began to be built, the Major Amenity Fund provision had come into operation, which would have allowed the development corporation to spend capital on community buildings. As a matter of policy, however, they decided to accumulate this fund and spend it at a later date. Livingston, in this respect, had an advantage over the other two new towns, but one of which the development corporation did not appear to wish to make early use. Ironically, however, the main intention behind the introduction of the Major Amenity Fund provision was to allow the development corporations to promote the building of community provisions at an early stage in the development of the town, before such time that the income from rates would make it possible for the local authority to spend substantial sums on community facilities in the new town within its sphere of influence.

In theory, however, the importance of community facilities was recognised, since the report of the Lothian Regional Survey and Plan[8] has been accepted, which stated: '... the recreational and community facilities must be provided, but provided in an accessible and inviting way, to serve as social stabilisers in an area which will be characterised by accelerated immigration'. Tables 5.1, 5.2 and 5.3 illustrate what kind of accommodation was available to social organisations in Glenrothes, East Kilbride and Livingston. From these can be seen that in Livingston, at least, there is very little diversity of accommodation available. This was reflected in tables 5.4, 5.5 and 5.6, which indicate how far the organisations considered their accommodation to be suitable. In Glenrothes 71·2 per cent and East Kilbride 69·5 per cent thought their accommodation was suitable, whereas in Livingston only 53·3 per cent were satisfied with their accommodation.

Naturally, it can be said that the increased level of satisfaction in the older new towns is largely a function of time and maturity of the town. To some extent this has to be accepted, but, as seen above, the early years of these two towns were fraught with frustrations due to the inability of the development corporations to provide the facilities they felt they wanted to provide. With the introduction of the Major Amenity Fund provision it had, therefore, become possible for more recent towns like Livingston to avoid some of these frustrations and build facilities at an earlier stage, if they so choose to do. However, until June 1970 the Major Amenity Fund had not been touched and, apart from Howden House which the corporation bought but adapted with Carnegie Trust funds, all the other facilities, such as they were, had been provided by the education authorities (youth wings), Church of Scotland Home Board (Craigshill Farm community development project) and a firm of brewers (Craigshill Social Club).

The example of Livingston has been dealt with at some length, not so much in order to criticise the policy and practice of Livingston Development Corporation which, as seen in chapter 7, has proved to be perhaps more enlightened regarding the appointment of social development officers than the other two towns, but to illustrate the fact that the introduction (and existence) of permissive social legislation (as contained in the New Towns Act, 1965, ss. 3 and 3(3) (b), relating to the powers of corporations to contribute to the cost of amenities in new towns) does not automatically ensure that such powers will be used in the way they may have been intended.

Nevertheless it can be said that by and large, in spite of initial difficulties, as the towns 'matured' and are still maturing, facilities have been provided. As pointed out in chapter 5, there are still certain gaps, but the relatively high levels of satisfaction, particularly in Glenrothes and East Kilbride, would indicate that in spite of set-backs in the early days a good deal of progress has been made, and no doubt given time the same will be true of Livingston.

Assumption 4a: New town residents will come from diverse cultural backgrounds; and 4b: Facilities and activities should take account of the culture that people brought with them.

In Glenrothes it was found that some 55 per cent of all the residents of the new town came originally from the County of Fife, whereas only some 16 per cent came from Glasgow and the West of Scotland; 7·7 per cent came from England and Wales, and only 0·6 per cent from abroad.

This particular mixture of inhabitants would not appear to correspond very closely to the kind of population the Reith committee assumed would predominantly move into new towns. It foresaw the bulk of them to be coming from inner parts of large cities. Glenrothes would appear to be something of an exception to this pattern, since more than half its residents moved in to the town from the surrounding area of Fife. To some extent this illustrates the (new although not the original) function of that particular new town in that area. As more and more coal mines in Fife closed, Glenrothes was there to take up 'the slack', by offering alternative employment; but only 4·3 per cent of the population came as a result of the 'overspill agreement' with Glasgow. The main reason for this, apparently, was the fact that Glenrothes is considered by potential applicants from Glasgow to be too far away, which would make visiting of relatives and friends too difficult.

East Kilbride, on the other hand, would appear to conform much more to the pattern foreseen in the Reith report. Some 54 per cent of the residents came from Glasgow, and a further 26 per cent from the surrounding County of Lanarkshire. Whether or not this factor has affected the social and cultural activities in East Kilbride in any way would be difficult to assess within the frame of reference of this particular study. Glasgow is only six miles away, and at least initially, if it is so desired, it is perfectly possible to continue the pursuit of activities which take place in the big city. In order to assess how much of the informal social life of the East Kilbride residents takes place in Glasgow, a different kind of study would be required, although the levels of participation detailed in chapter 3 would suggest that commuting for social purposes, if it takes place, would not seem to be detrimental to the level of participation in activities in East Kilbride.

In Livingston some 42 per cent of the residents came from within the designated area, and from the two counties in which Livingston New Town is being built. As was the case in Glenrothes, only a relatively small proportion, i.e. 12 per cent, came from Glasgow, in spite of the existence of 'over-spill' agreements between these towns. Again, according to

210

officials of the development corporation, this was mainly due to the distance (or at least as it is being perceived by potential applicants) between the two towns. On the other hand, an increasing number of residents appear to be moving to Livingston from Edinburgh. This may result in a certain amount of 'social commuting', particularly among the more mobile sections of the community, but this would not appear to affect adversely the level of participation in activities in the new town itself. It would be an interesting study to try and assess in what way different cultural backgrounds affect people's views and attitudes towards the new town into which they have moved, but within the context of this particular study this was not possible.

However, it would appear that many organisations were started by people who moved into the new town, had a specific interest which was not catered for, looked for a group of like-minded people and got together to meet this particular need. The range of organisations available and the bodies they were affiliated to (see chapter 2) would suggest that new town residents, coming from diverse cultural backgrounds as they do, bring their 'culture' with them, as was in a sense assumed by the Reith report. In other words, if there is such a phenomenon as a 'new town culture', then at least as far as it is reflected in the existence of organisations in these three new towns, there does not appear to be any evidence for it. Very few, if any, organisations were not also found in other established towns. It is true that in some instances new ground was being broken, as in the case of the youth organisations in Livingston, some of which have moved away from the traditional membership-based pattern, and have become 'open-door type clubs' – open to anyone who cared to come along any given evening. In this they reflected not a specific 'new town pattern', but a trend which has also been apparent in the youth service in established communities.

Assumption 5a: Characteristics of buildings required at an early stage: the need to be both multi-purpose in nature and to contain a number of smaller rooms; and 5b: The location of buildings is important.

These two assumptions were contained in para. 189 of the Reith report summary,[9] and specifically refer to the type of building required at the very beginning of the building of the new town. The same paragraph then went on to recommend that permanent buildings should be provided in advance of full demand. It would seem, for reasons described above, that the East Kilbride and Glenrothes Development Corporations were not able to provide facilities in the early days to meet existing demand, let alone in 'advance of full demand'.

The contribution of the churches, which made available their halls as meeting places, was therefore particularly important. However, in Livingston the pattern was, once again, different — the first meeting places available were the school halls and the youth wings attached to the two primary schools in Craigshill. Since some of the churches, which formed themselves into a team ministry, did not see the provision of a separate church building as a first priority, they, in fact, made use of the school halls for their services and meetings. The youth wings at Riverside and Letham were the first facilities available for young people, but, as a paper on the subject [10] by one of the youth leaders illustrates, there were a number of problems related to the use of these. These problems partly arose out of their siting, partly their design, and partly the way they were administered.

The problems relating to design particularly illustrate the 'wisdom' of the Reith report recommendation that premises should contain a number of rooms. Letham youth wing was designed on an L-shaped open-plan basis, which means that frequently only one activity can take place at a time. What might, therefore be thought of as flexibility in design, in fact creates inflexibility in the use to which the building can be put at any one time. A more general problem, which is related to design but was found in all three towns, relates to the problem of storage of which there never seemed to be enough, particularly when facilities were being used by different groups at different times. The problem of administration mainly revolved round the fact that although the education authority provided the building, they did not provide the personnel to administer it in order to ensure maximum use. These youth wings were only open for very limited times, since the janitor and the headmaster who were responsible for the running of the adjacent school, had neither the time nor the inclination to promote the use of a community facility which was tagged on to their building, and the administration of which was tagged on to their job. In order to ensure therefore that these youth wings can make a valuable contribution to the life of the community, separate staff ought to be appointed to run them.

In the same paragraph, the Reith report stressed the importance of the location of premises. Tables 5.7, 5.8 and 5.9 show what the various categories considered to be their ideal location. In Glenrothes nearly half of the organisations (i.e. 45·8 per cent) considered the centre of the town to be the ideal location for their meeting place. However, although in half

212

the categories the majority of groups looked upon the town centre as an ideal location, there were other groups for whom a central location was not important, or for whom location as such did not matter at all. For instance, the majority of youth organisations and sports clubs expressed a preference for a location 'on the edge of town'. The youth organisations which indicated this were usually those which had the occasional beat bands as part of their programme, the noise of which frequently brought complaints from neighbours if their premises were within a residential area.

To most of the hobby groups, location of the meeting place did not matter as much as the suitability of the premises available to them, almost regardless of their position. On the other hand, groups such as the Musical and Operatic Society and the Theatre Club, which from time to time put on productions for the whole town, wish to be in the centre. Those groups which did prefer a location in the residential areas (neighbourhoods) were usually those catering for the needs of young children, housewives, and old people, who all seemed to prefer their meeting place to be within 'toddling', pram-pushing and 'hobbling' distance of their homes.

In East Kilbride the proportion of organisations which expressed preference for a central location was very similar to that in Glenrothes (i.e. 42·7 per cent). Old people's groups were the strongest supporters of the local centre as the ideal location. Attachment to a school was again not considered to be ideal. As seen above, of 141 organisations which made up the Glenrothes and East Kilbride sample, only 2 looked upon a school as their ideal location. In East Kilbride the proportion of those who indicated that location did not matter to them was lower (4·9 per cent as compared to 13·6 per cent). This difference may be a function of the different sizes of the two towns.

In Livingston the pattern of preferences differed markedly from that of the other two towns. Nevertheless, the town centre emerged again as the location which was preferred by most organisations, but the proportion was smaller (21·9 per cent) than in the other two towns. It was suggested that this might be due to the fact that the town centre does not as yet exist, other than on the master plan. The organisations were, therefore, dealing with an abstract alternative, whereas in Glenrothes and East Kilbride, since the towns were substantially completed, a town centre had emerged.

It would, therefore, appear from the findings of this part of the study, that a great many organisations wish to have meeting places and premises in central locations. This confirms Brook-Taylor's claim that 'in future, the emphasis must be on more central facilities'. [11] However, it also shows that there are some distinct sections of the population, chiefly the very young, the housewives and the old, for whom it is important to have a meeting place within easy walking distance of the home, as was envisaged in the concept of the neighbourhood unit, on the basis of which the early new towns were built. Yet as Hume has shown in her study of Neighbourhoods in Scottish New Towns, [12] the neighbourhoods, largely due to increased mobility, have ceased to be of any relevance as a social entity to the majority of the population. The findings of the present study tend to support this claim on the basis of the small proportion who looked upon the centre of the neighbourhood as their ideal location. This does not suggest, however, that only central facilities should now be provided, but it does support the suggestion by Cullingworth [13] that an attempt should be made to establish a 'hierarchy of social facilities', which takes account of the different needs of different sections of the population when decisions regarding location of premises have to be made. The maps described in chapter 6 also illustrate, in individual cases, how far the location of a particular meeting place, in effect, influences the recruitment of members from different parts of the town, and indeed from outside it.

One further point needs to be made when the importance of more central facilities is being stressed. The new town development corporations are required, over a period of time, to balance their books. In order to be able to do this they feel they must maximise their assets — and central sites, in the town centre, which can be let to commercial enterprises are such assets. It requires, therefore, a deliberate policy decision on their part to be able to reserve a commercially valuable site, say for an arts cum cultural centre, which will not be able to pay the same rent as a commercial enterprise; although in order for it to make maximum impact on the town, it might well be desirable that it should be on such a central site. This is, therefore, a case where it might well be that purely commercial considerations should be overruled by considerations of social development, if the preferences of the users of such facilities are to be given any weight at all in the planning of future facilities.

**Assumption 6: 'Young people have special needs,
which need special consideration'.**

The Reith report, in making the above assumption, [14] accepted that schools' playing facilities were the concern of the local education authority. It also anticipated that the provision of playgrounds and premises for youth clubs 'may be largely a matter for the agency [i.e. Development Corporation] itself'. In the event, however, it would seem that the three development corporations did not respond in the way the Reith report assumed they would, but largely were content to leave the provision of facilities and leadership to the education authorities. Yet there can be no doubt that the report was right in stressing the special needs of the young. It is generally accepted that new towns have a youthful population, but just how youthful becomes apparent from tables 3.1, 3.2 and 3.3, relating to Glenrothes, East Kilbride and Livingston. These tables show that about a quarter of the population of Glenrothes was under 10 years old, in East Kilbride the proportion in this age group was slightly less but still more than a fifth, and in Livingston it was almost a third. (East Kilbride, once again, displayed signs of being a more mature new town.) The age group 10—19 in Glenrothes accounted for approximately 16 per cent of the population, in East Kilbride for about 18 per cent, but in Livingston, largely due to a 'lack' of teenagers, which is typical of a young new town, this age group accounted for approximately 11 per cent of the total population.

If the percentages in each of the three towns are added for the young people (males) under 20, three sets of remarkably similar figures are arrived at. The proportions of the population which they account for are: Glenrothes 43·4 per cent, East Kilbride 41·1 per cent and Livingston 43·3 per cent. These figures emphasise that the young people in new towns require special consideration. However, it would seem that until very recently, [15] provision, particularly for children under the age of fourteen lagged behind, due to a curious dilemma they found themselves in. As pointed out, the development corporations were looking to the local education authorities to provide for the recreational needs of these children. The local education authorities would do so directly through their own youth service, or give grant-aid support to voluntary organisations who would work with young people. In either case, however, the youth service age range, which was stipulated by the Albermarle report, covered only the 14—20 age range. The youth service itself therefore offered very few activities in which the under 14-year olds could join, and the voluntary organisations, if they chose to work with the younger age range, could not get grant-aid for the purpose.

However, as the above tables show in each of the towns there are a large number of children below the age of 14. The only youth organisations available to them were the Cub Scouts, the Brownies and the Lifeboys, which would take children from the age of 8 onwards. These are also the organisations which require skilled leadership and which impose a strict upper limit on the number of members. This dilemma was particularly highlighted in Livingston, where the leader of the cub scouts stated that only the lack of suitable leaders was preventing them from multiplying at a much faster rate. This was also illustrated by the Brownies in Livingston, where a young teacher started a pack then left it to start a second one, and in the meantime the first one collapsed due to lack of suitable leadership. The problem of finding suitable leadership in a young new town is so much more difficult, for a number of reasons, than even in a more established new town. In spite of these difficulties which particularly affected the younger children, as tables 3.1, 3.2 and 3.3 illustrate, the opportunities for participation were there for young people.[16] The fact that the special needs of young people were recognised, in spite of the drawbacks mentioned above, is also illustrated by the fact that by and large the first organisations to be started in a new town (apart from a few which have existed before the start of the new town) were the youth organisations.

The example of Livingston also illustrates the impact the provision of full-time leadership can have on the level of participation among young people. In chapter 5 it was also found that young people have special needs regarding meeting places, and these will be dealt with under assumption 7 below.

Assumption 7: There is a need for a diversity of buildings in relation to the diversity of activities

The suitability of buildings used has already been referred to briefly — this particular part is, therefore, only dealing with some of the categories in each town, for whom the above assumption would appear to be particularly appropriate. For instance, in Glenrothes three organisations in the arts and cultural category could not find any suitable accommodation in town, since none of the halls available had either a raked auditorium or adequate stage facilities. They were the Film Society, the Little Theatre and the Musical & Operatic Society. It would seem that lack of diversity in the equipment of the halls available failed to satisfy the requirements of specialised activities like those which could be met with the building of a multi-purpose theatre cum arts centre, in a similar way in which the needs of most of the sports organisations have now been met in Glenrothes with the provision of a multi-purpose swimming pool and sports complex.

In East Kilbride, on the other hand, it was the lack of diversity of accommodation available to sports organisations which proved to be the largest single gap which could be filled with the provision of a multi-purpose sports building similar to the one in Glenrothes. It could, therefore, be said that standard halls and meeting places are able to cope with the needs of the organisations which commonly started operating first. However, as the town grows, the pursuits available to the population become more sophisticated and hence the need for more diversified accommodation increases.

In the case of Livingston it was more difficult to identify the area where 'diversification of accommodation' should have taken place, particularly since the sample of cultural organisations was still very small, and 80 per cent of the sports organisations were satisfied with the accommodation available to them.

However, the Reith report also recommended that facilities should sometimes be provided in advance of full demand. A case can therefore be made for anticipating the demand which has been shown to arise over a period of time in the other two towns, by providing an arts and cultural centre and a multi-purpose sports centre, and at least the basis for these to which, if the design is flexible enough, can be added later. This would also make it possible for those engaged in the promotion of leisure pursuits, such as the social development officer, or for staff employed to run these centres, to stimulate a demand which may be latent but which has not yet manifested itself.

Therefore, it would seem, perhaps contrary to the practice of new towns, but in the spirit of the assumptions of the Reith report, that it is not always appropriate for development corporations to delay the provision of a community facility such as a sports hall, until such time as they have irrevocably established that the demand has now reached a level at which the building of such premises can be fully justified. After all, the infra-structure, such as roads, electricity supply and sewers, are being built in advance of full demand, and advance factories are being provided before a customer is found for them. Why should different criteria be applied to the provision of social facilities? In fact, it could be argued that the provision of some major facilities as described above, in advance of full demand, might not only hasten the arrival of that demand, but also help to act as an incentive for employers and employees to move to that particular town. Far from being a waste of capital, such early provision could make sound economic sense.

When the Rouse brothers started to build Columbia, a private enterprise new town in Maryland, USA, they built first of all the swimming pools, a golf course, lakes and community buildings and other amenities. Only then did they start building houses to sell, and the town became an immediate success. Naturally, the circumstances which prevail in America are different from those under which the British and (when it comes to amenities) particularly the Scottish new towns are being built. But even a 'new town's expert' of the calibre of Frank Schaffer [17] suggests that 'we could well take at least half a leaf out of their book'.

In fairness, it must be added that this is not a decision which development corporations can take on their own, since their spending is subject to central government approval. A change of policy at that level is also required, if these priorities are to be changed

Assumption 8: Certain groups will only flourish if they are able to have accommodation of their own.

With this assumption, the authors of the Reith report mainly had the youth organisations in mind, which they felt, in order to be effective, should be able to run a programme every night of the week, and should not have to share premises with other kinds of organisations. It has been found that the uniformed organisations also preferred premises of their own, even if it was only a modest Scout Hut, in which they could keep permanent fixtures such as patrol corners, charts and other items of equipment. However, apart from certain youth organisations, there were others such as art clubs, camera clubs and political parties which felt that it was essential for their purposes to have premises of their own. In Glenrothes and East Kilbride exactly the same proportion, i.e. 47·5 per cent, of all organisations preferred to own their premises, whereas in Livingston the figure was 65·6 per cent.

Assumption 9: Social activities in which all members of a family can share, help to strengthen the unity of family life, by giving it a common loyalty.

Having stated that certain groups will only flourish if they do not have to share accommodation with other organisations, the Reith committee was now anxious to avoid the impression that it might have thought no facilities of which 'all social groups, adults as well as juvenile' made common use should be provided. In fact it felt that additional provision of such facilities was invaluable, particularly when they made it possible for the whole family to join in. As noted in chapter 3, the new towns are towns for young families. However, from the sample of social organisations which have been investigated in Glenrothes, there is little evidence that any organisations have developed which cater for the whole family. It has also been stated that there was no evidence of new towns having produced their particular brand of culture, or perhaps a new form of organisation. Most organisations found in these new towns were also found in established communities. Similarly, in established communities few social organisations, if any, cater for the whole family. Therefore, it would seem that if a certain type of organisation does not already exist in an established town, it is unlikely to be started up in a new town. Of course, it is true that a few organisations have members of the same household, but not one organisation was found to cater for the whole family. It may be that this indicates that there was simply no need for such an organisation, particularly since it has been found that a 'new culture of the home' has developed in the new towns as elsewhere. Ferdynand Zweig, in his study of Cumbernauld, [18] chose to call this 'homecentredness' an 'excessive psychological investment in the family'. Others, such as Nicholson, [19] saw the retreat to the home as an expression of the satisfaction the home gave, and Cullingworth's social survey of Swindon [20] found that the TV set (and possibly the car and garden) absorbed the interests of at least the adult members of the family. In the 1967 survey of Cumbernauld undertaken by Strathclyde University, [21] it was found that for 80 per cent of respondents 'staying at home' or 'watching TV' was the standard reply to a question of how they spent their previous evening. Zweig [22] claims, however, that although 'both TV and the car erode the texture of urban life — in the case of new towns, they help enormously to develop the new town in its initial stages when no amenities were available. People would not have withstood the complete lack of amenities, if the TV was not providing the main entertainment'.

Once again it seems that the leisure habits of the people in new towns do not differ so markedly from the people in the rest of the country, as might have been suggested above. Sillitoe's national survey [23] is only one of a number of studies which shows that watching television has become the nation's number one leisure pursuit. Any organisation therefore wishing to attract the whole family (including the adult members) to its activities has to overcome formidable competition. However, as previously noted, it is difficult to conclude whether so far families have not been joining organisations because there was no demand for them. It may well be that formal organisations, of the traditional kind and which have been the subject of this study, are not the appropriate medium to provide activities for families to share. For instance, in Livingston one of the community workers commented on the fact that he could not get any of the parents to join in regular activities, but when an occasional bonfire cum barbecue was organised, to which all the families were invited, often they were unable to cope with the numbers who wanted to participate. In other words, special occasions of this kind brought a very favourable response. The question then arises as to who should organise these 'occasional activities', since most 'leaders' are attached to membership-based organisations – and yet it would seem that part of the success of such occasional ventures lies in the fact that they do not bring with them a membership commitment.

The answer could well be that it is a proper function of the social development officer to organise a series of such ventures, where the whole family will be able to participate. Traditional organisations, as they tend to categorise themselves at present into youth organisations, women's organisations, sports clubs etc., do not appear to lend themselves as suitable vehicles to promote family participation. (Always assuming, of course, that family cohesion is accepted as a suitable goal of social policy.)

Furthermore, experience at other centres, such as the Billingham multi-purpose sports complex, has shown that if amenities are made available, such as swimming pools and other sports facilities with suitable crèche arrangements and a café families will turn out and participate in an imaginative programme of activities. This may be included among the other reasons why such facilities should be provided, possibly even in 'advance of demand', as pointed out under assumption 7.

These then are some of the findings, as they specifically relate to Reith report assumptions. Taken as a whole they would support Sir William Hart's claim [24] that the Reith report would 'repay reading again'.

The new towns legislation was part of an impressive list of legislative measures relating specifically to social policy, which were passed in the closing years of the Second World War, and in the immediate postwar years, and which included the Education Act 1944, the Family Allowances Act 1945, the Housing and New Town Acts 1946, the Town and Country Planning Act 1946, the National Health Service Act 1946, the National Assistance Act 1948, the Children Act 1948, the Criminal Justice Act 1948, and the Legal Aid and Advice Act 1949. The student of social administration will know that most of these Acts have since been amended or superseded by new legislation, which was considered to be necessary due partly to the appearance of new areas of need, and partly to the 'non-implementation' of parts of these Acts, which still left gaps in the field of social policy requiring to be filled.

The same was true of the original new towns legislation, which followed the recommendations of the Reith report. Subsequent legislation relating to the provision of amenities in new towns has enabled development corporations to pursue a more active policy of 'social development', if they wished to do so. Due to economic crises, and to a certain lack of awareness of this area of need among those who determined priorities of capital spending, for some years it looked as if the new towns would be unable to fulfil their promise (see also Lloyd Rodwin). [25] However, as shown above, significant progress in the direction of social development has been made in these three Scottish new towns, thus perhaps taking them nearer to becoming 'essays in civilization' as the founders of the modern new town idea envisaged them. Dumazedier [26] underlined the 'capital importance of leisure in the humanization of our technical civilization'. From the very beginning new towns were meant to help to provide more leisure, by making it feasible to cut down the long journey to work, and providing an environment in which it was possible to make use of it. Social organisations are expected to make a significant contribution to preventing leisure from becoming 'the great emptiness – a gift many are not prepared to use'. [27] This study has shown that these organisations are making their contribution. According to Chembart de Louwe [28] such organisations 'are playing a key role in the individual's satisfactory integration into his society – attention must therefore increasingly be directed towards them'.

This study has aimed at a critical analysis of some aspects of the policy and major assumptions of an important Government report and of the legislation which followed it. The method has been through an empirical analysis of organisations in three Scottish new towns. The conclusions reached suggest that, by and large, these assumptions have stood the test of time.

Notes

[1] Final Report of the New Towns Committee, 1946, HMSO, Cmnd 687b, para. 186.

[2] This has also been borne out by the findings of K.K. Sillitoe, 'Planning for leisure', HMSO, London 1969, p. 40.

[3] According to information received from the then Provost of East Kilbride, this was what they meant.

[4] T.B. Bottomore, in D.V. Glass (ed.), *Social Mobility in Britain*, Routledge and Kegan Paul, 1954, p. 360.

[5] Seventh Annual Report of the East Kilbride Development Corporation, year ended 31 March 1955.

[6] Fourteenth Annual Report of the East Kilbride Development Corporation, year ended 31 March 1962.

[7] Seventh Annual Report of the Livingston Development Corporation, year ended 31 March 1969.

[8] Lothian Regional Survey and Plan: Scottish Development Department HMSO 1966 p. 183.

[9] Final Report of the New Towns Committee, op. cit.

[10] Max Cruickshank, 'Youth wings', January 1970, unpublished.

[11] G. Brooke-Taylor 'Crawley – a study of amenities in a New Town', Commission for the New Towns London 1966.

[12] Valerie Hume, 'Neighbourhoods in Scottish New Towns', Edinburgh University Ph.D. Thesis, 1969.

[13] J.B. Cullingworth et al., 'The needs of new communities' HMSO 1967.

[14] Para. 219, op. cit.

[15] See also note [7] chapter 3.

[16] See, for instance, membership percentage as a proportion of total population in tables 3.1, 3.2 and 3.3.

[17] Frank Schaffer, *The New Town Story,* MacGibbon and Kee, London 1970, p. 209.

[18] F. Zweig, 'The Cumbernauld Study', Urban Research Bureau, London 1970.

[19] J.H. Nicholson, 'New communities in Britain', NCSS, London 1961.

[20] J.B. Cullingworth, 'Swindon social survey' *Sociological Review,* vol. 9/19.

[21] A. Sykes et al., 'Cumbernauld household survey and report', University of Strathclyde Occasional Paper no. 1, 1967.

[22] F. Zweig, op. cit., p. 51.

[23] K.K. Sillitoe, op. cit., table 8, p. 41.

[24] Sir William Hart, 'Administration and new towns' *Town and Country Planning,* vol. 36, nos. 1–2, 1968.

[25] Lloyd Rodwin, *The British New Towns Policy,* Harvard University Press, 1956, p. 54.

[26] Joffre Dumazedier, 'Travail et loisir', traite de sociologie, Paris 1964.

[27] Nils Andersen, *Work and Leisure,* Routledge and Kegan Paul, London 1961.

[28] Chombart de Louwe, 'Handbook for social research in urban areas', UNESCO, Paris 1965.

Appendix

Sample

The sample used in this study consists of social organisations in the new towns of East Kilbride, Glenrothes and Livingston, which are generally open to membership for any newcomer to the town. The names and addresses of the secretaries of these organisations were taken from the tenants' handbook in the case of East Kilbride, from the list of organisations maintained by the housing officer in Glenrothes, which is distributed to every newcomer, and the list published by the welcoming committee in Livingston. In each case the most up-to-date list available was used. It was assumed that an organisation featuring in any of these three documents would generally be open to any resident or newcomer to the town, and on these grounds they were included in this sample. Social clubs which are attached to specific firms were not included, and neither were organisations attached to specific churches, unless they were open to wider recruitment. Similarly, trade unions were not included, since membership is restricted to clearly specified occupational groups. On the other hand, political parties were asked to participate, since they seek to recruit members from a wide cross-section of the public. A list of the organisations which made up this sample follows.

Glenrothes

1. Alburne Knowe Scottish Country Dance Club
2. Festival Society
3. Amateur Boxing Club
4. Townswomen's Guild
5. Art Club
6. Conservative Association
7. Round Table
8. Aeromodelling Club
9. Scottish National Party
10. Gaelic Club
11. Rotary Club

12   Archery Club
13   Musical and Operatic Society
14   Chess Club
15   Red Cross
16   Film Society
17   Co-operative Guild (Woodside Branch)
18   Old People's Welfare Committee (Wayside Cottage Club)
19   Social Amenities Council
20   Glenrothes & District Horticultural Society
21   Glenrothes Recreation Centre and Social Club
22   Exit Club
23   Bridge Club
24   St Pauls & St Mary's Catholic Women's Guild (Leslie)
25   Camera Club
26   Preston Youth Club
27   Sunshine Club
28   Glenrothes (CISWO) Bowling Club
29   South Parks Farmhouse Ladies' Social Club
30   Rothes Invitation Club (Racing Pigeons)
31   Old People's Welfare Committee
32   British Legion
33   Glenrothes Little Theatre
34   St Andrews Ambulance Association
35   YM/YWCA
36   Golf Club
37   Old Folks' Treat Committee
38   Glenrothes Community Association
39   Rothes WRI
40   234 Leslie/Glenrothes Squadron Air Training Corps
41   WRVS
42 . Institute of Advanced Motorists
43   Communist Party (Women's Section)
44   Mustard Seed Woodside Women's Fellowship
45   Glenrothes Toastmasters' Club
46   Mountaineering Club
47   Young Wives' Group (YWCA)
48   Greenhouse Club
49   Boys' Brigade
50   Young Conservatives
51   Glenrothes and District Floral Art Club
52   Boy Scouts Association

53   Glenrothes Angling Club
54   Glenrothes Junior Football Club
55   Communist Party
56   Glenrothes Women's Club
57   Auchmuty Co-operative Guild
58   Girl Guides Association
59   Glenrothes Local Labour Party

East Kilbride

60   1st East Kilbride Scout Group
61   3rd East Kilbride Scout Group
62   4th East Kilbride Scout Group
63   5th East Kilbride Scout Group
64   6th East Kilbride Scout Group
65   East Kilbride Scout Association
66   8th East Kilbride Scout Group
67   9th East Kilbride Scout Group
68   10th East Kilbride Scout Group
69   East Kilbride E. District Venture Scouts
70   East Kilbride Angling Club
71   East Kilbride Sports Club Men's Hockey Section
72   East Kilbride Conservative & Unionist Association
73   East Kilbride Boys' Football League
74   East Kilbride Rugby Club
75   East Kilbride Netball Club
76   East Kilbride Branch National Federation of OAPs.
77   East Kilbride Baptist Church Youth Club
78   East Kilbride and District Badminton Association
79   East Kilbride Catholic Youth Council
80   East Kilbride Light Opera Club
81   East Kilbride South Parish Youth Club
82   East Kilbride OAP Social Club
83   East Kilbride & District Young Farmers' Club
84   Rolls Royce Male Voice Choir
85   Calderwood: East Kilbride Rangers FC Supporters' Club
86   East Kilbride and District Horticultural Society
87   Trefoil Guild
88   East Kilbride Civic Association
89   Scottish Co-operative Women's Guild (Bosfield Branch)

90	East Kilbride Labour Party
91	East Kilbride Labour Party Westwood Ward
92	Westwood Parish Church Youth Fellowship
93	Glasgow: East Kilbride Railway Development Association
94	East Kilbride Burgh Pipe Band
95	Ladies' Loyal Orange Association
96	Girl Guides and Brownie Guides
97	East Kilbride Old Parish Youth Fellowship
98	Calderwood Ladies' Club
99	East Kilbride Amateur Boxing Club
100	East Kilbride Sports Club Tennis Section
101	Murray: East Kilbride Youth Club
102	The Whitehills Group
103	Duncanrig Youth Services Club
104	Scottish Society for Mentally Handicapped Children
105	Whitemoss Residents' Association
106	WRVS
107	United Nations Association
108	Lodge St Andrew East Kilbride No. 524 (Freemasons)
109	West Mains Labour Association
110	British Legion East Kilbride Parish Branch
111	St Leonards Women's Guild
112	South Park Youth Centre
113	East Kilbride Fabian Society
114	St Andrews Ambulance Association
115	East Kilbride & District Savings Committee
116	East Kilbride YMCA
117	East Kilbride Round Table
118	Auldhouse WRI
119	East Kilbride Cricket Club
120	East Kilbride Music Club
121	East Mains Residents' Association Committee
122	East Kilbride Choral Society
123	Inner Wheel
124	Business & Professional Women's Club
125	East Kilbride Ladies' Hockey Club
126	RSSPCC
127	East Kilbride Educational Association
128	British Red Cross Society
129	East Kilbride Photographic Club
130	Boys Brigade/Life Boys Battalion (7 companies)

131   East Kilbride Old Time and Modern Sequence Dancing Club
132   East Kilbride Townswomen's Guild
133   Royal National Life Boat Institution
134   East Kilbride Bridge Club
135   Torrance Rifle Club
136   Sub-Aqua Club
137   East Kilbride Girl Guides Association
138   East Kilbride Chess Club
139   East Kilbride Motor Club
140   East Kilbride and Hairmyres Curling Club
141   East Kilbridge ATC
142   East Kilbride Homing Club
143   Family Planning Association (Committee)
144   East Kilbride Rangers FC Supporters' Club
145   East Kilbride Sports Council
146   Heathery Knowe Co-operative Youth Club
147   East Kilbride Hamilton and District Gun Club
148   Bowling Club
149   East Kilbride Repertory Theatre Club

Livingston

150   Cub Scouts
151   Pre-School Playgroups Association
152   YMCA/YWCA
153   Letham Junior Youth Centre
154   Girls Brigade
155   1st Letham Brownie Pack
156   1st Riverside Brownie Pack
157   Girl Guide Association
158   1st Calders District Rangers Unit
159   Riverside Table Tennis Club
160   Letham Youth Wing (Under 15's Club)
161   Riverside Youth Wing (Over 15's Club)
162   Riverside Youth Wing (Football Section Under 15's)
164   Livingston and District Model Railway Club
165   Livingston Choir
166   Livingston Floral Art Club
167   Citizens' Advice Bureau
168   St Andrews Ambulance Association

169   Craigshill SWRI
170   Howden Ladies' Social Club
171   Church Women's Meeting
172   Craigshill Co-operative Women's Guild
173   Livingston Bridge Club
174   Livingston Knitmaster Club
175   Calders Amateur Camera Club
176   Scottish National Party (Craigshill Branch)
177   Grove Badminton Club
178   Riverside Badminton Club
179   Craigshill Social Club
180   1st (Craigshill) New Livingston Boys Brigade Company
181   St Andrews RC Church Guild
182   Livingston & District Rugby Football Club

In order to facilitate comparability with other studies as far as possible the organisations were grouped into the following ten categories, according to their purpose and primary activities: (1) youth organisations; (2) arts and cultural; (3) social services; (4) women's organisations; (5) hobby/special interest; (6) political; (7) sport; (8) social and dancing; (9) old people; and (10) other. At the time of the initial data collection (end of 1969) these organisations represented 96·7 per cent of all known organisations in Glenrothes, 65·9 per cent in East Kilbride and 78·6 per cent in Livingston. Such organisations are akin to 'live organisms' — they grow and contract, are born and sometimes die — any attempt to study them can therefore be no more than a still picture of an ever changing situation. This is particularly true of Livingston as the youngest of the three new towns, and whose growth has been more dynamic in recent years than perhaps was the case with the other two new towns.

Bibliography

Anderson, N., *Work and Leisure,* Routledge and Kegan Paul, London 1961.

Bell, W. and Force, M., 'Urban Neighbourhood Type and Participation in Formal Associations', *American Sociological Review,* vol. 21, no. 1, 1956.

Bottomore, T., 'Social Stratification in Voluntary Organisations', in *Social Mobility in Britain,* ed. D.V. Glass, Routledge and Kegan Paul, London 1954.

Broady, M., *Planning for people,* NCSS, London 1968.

Brooke-Taylor, G., 'Community Life in New Towns', *Social Service Quarterly,* 32, 148, 1959.

Brooke-Taylor, G., *Crawley: A study of amenities in a New Town,* Commission for the New Towns, London 1966.

Cauter, T. and Downham J.S., *The Communication of Ideas; a study of contemporary influences on urban life,* Chatto and Windus, London 1954.

Central Advisory Council for Education, Reports 15–18, vol. ii, HMSO 1960.

Chombart de Louwe, P., *UNESCO Handbook for Social Research in Urban Areas,* UNESCO, Paris 1965.

Collison, P., 'Neighbourhood and Class', *Town and Country Planning,* July 1955.

Cullingworth, J.B., 'Swindon Social Survey: A second report on the social implications of overspill', *Sociological Review,* vol. 9, 1961.

Cullingworth, J.B., *The needs of new communities,* Ministry of Housing and Local Government, HMSO 1967.

Department of Education and Science, *Youth and Community Work in the 70's* HMSO 1969.

Dumazedier, J., 'Travail et Loisir', *Traite de sociologie,* Paris 1964.

East Kilbride Town Council, *Consultative Document on Social Work Policy,* January 1972.

Gans, H.J., 'The Balanced Community — Homogeneity or Heterogeneity in Residential areas', *Journal of the American Institute of Planning,* vol. XXVII, no. 3, 1961.

Glenrothes Development Corporation, 18th Annual Report 1966–67, HMSO, 1967,

Glenrothes Development Corporation, Planning Research Unit, *Children's Play Survey,* unpublished report, March 1970.

Hart, Sir William, 'Administration and new towns', *Town and Country Planning,* vol. 36, no. 1–2, 1968.

Heraud, B.J., 'Social Balance in New Towns', *Urban Studies,* vol. 5, no. 1, 1968.

Horrocks, M., *Social Development Work in the New Communities,* Occasional Paper No 27, University of Birmingham Centre for Urban and Regional Studies, 1974.

House of Commons Debates, Sessions 1945/46, vol. 422, 8 May 1946.

Howard, E., *Garden Cities of Tomorrow,* Faber and Faber, London 1945.

Hume, V., 'Neighbourhoods in Scottish New Towns', Edinburgh University Ph.D. thesis, 1969.

Jephcott, P., *Time of one's own,* Oliver and Boyd, Edinburgh 1967.

Klein, J., *Samples from English Cultures,* vol.1, Routledge and Kegan Paul, London 1965.

Livingston Development Corporation, *Livingston New Town Master Plan,* 1963.

Mann, P., 'A socially balanced neighbourhood unit', *Town Planning Review,* no. 29, 1958/59.

Morley, K., *Social Activity and Social Enterprise – a study of voluntary social organisations in the New Town of Redditch,* Redditch College of Further Education, 1967.

Ministry of Education, *The Youth Service in England and Wales,* CMND 929, HMSO 1960.

Ministry of Health, *Design of Dwellings,* HMSO 1944.

National Council of Social Service, *Size and Social Structure of a Town,* London 1943.

Nicholson, J.H., *New Communities in Britain,* NCSS, London 1961.

Orlans, H., *Stevenage – a sociological study of a New Town,* Routledge and Kegan Paul, London 1952.

Osborn, F.J. and Whittick, A., *The New Towns,* Leonard Hill, London 1969.

Perry, C., *Housing for the Machine Age,* Russell Sage Foundation, New York 1939.

Reissmann, L., 'Class, Leisure and Social Participation', *American Sociological Review,* vol. 19, 1954.

Reith, Lord, 'An essay in civilization', *Town and Country Planning,* vol. 36, No. 1–2, 1968.

Reports of the Development Corporations for the years 1950, 1955, 1962, and 1969, HMSO.

Report of the New Towns Committee (First Interim), CMND 6759, HMSO 1946.

Report of the New Towns Committee (Final), CMND 6876, HMSO 1946.

Report of the New Towns Committee (Second Interim), CMND 6794, HMSO 1946.

Schaffer, F., *The New Town Story*, MacGibbon and Kee, London 1970.

Scheuch, E.K., 'Family Cohesion in Leisure-time', *Sociological Review*, vol. 8, 1960.

Scottish Development Department, *The Lothians Regional Survey and Plan*, HMSO 1966.

Scottish Education Department, *Community of Interests*, HMSO 1968.

Silkin, L., 'Housing Layout in Theory and Practice', *Journal of the National Institute of British Architects*, 1948.

Sillitoe, K.K., *Planning for Leisure*, HMSO 1969.

Smailes, J., 'Balanced Towns', *Journal of the Town Planning Institute*, vol. 32, 1945.

Spencer, J.S., *Stress and Release in an Urban Estate*, Tavistock Publications, London 1964.

Sykes, A.J.M. et al., *Cumbernauld Household Survey and Report*, Occasional Paper no. 1, University of Strathclyde, 1967.

Sykes, A.J.M. and Woldman, E., *Irvine New Town Area – a summary and report on leisure activities*, Occasional Paper no. 2, University of Strathclyde 1968.

Thomas, R., *London's New Towns*, PEP Pamphlet no. 510, London 1969, p. 4.

Thorpe, J., 'Political Leaders and the Act', *Town and Country Planning*, vol. 36, no. 1–2, 1968.

Vereker, C. and Mays, J.B., *Urban Redevelopment and Social Change: A study of social conditions in central Liverpool 1955–56*, Liverpool University Press, 1961.

Viet, J., *New Towns – a selected annotated bibliography*, UNESCO no. 12, 1960.

Willis, M., *Meeting places for Hire in New Towns – a social survey*, Ministry of Housing and Local Government, London 1966.

Willmott, P. and Young, M., *Family and Class in a London Suburb*, Routledge and Kegan Paul, 1960.

Willmott, P., 'Some social characteristics of a Scottish and English New Town', *Town Planning Review* XXIV, 1963–64.

Wilson, R., *Difficult Housing Estates*, Tavistock Pamphlet no. 5, 1963.

Wyndham, T., 'In praise of a New Town', *The Times*, 4 April 1959.

Zweig, F., *The Cumbernauld Study*, Urban Research Bureau, London 1970.

Index

The Author

Hans Wirz trained as a youth and community worker and worked for a number of years for the YMCA. In 1965 he graduated from the University of Edinburgh and in 1972 he was awarded a doctorate. Since 1966 he has lectured in the Department of Social Administration, his special interests being in those areas of social policy relating to housing, community work, planning and new towns.